Flutter for Beginners Second Edition

An introductory guide to building cross-platform mobile applications with Flutter 2.5 and Dart

Thomas Bailey

Alessandro Biessek

BIRMINGHAM—MUMBAI

Flutter for Beginners
Second Edition

Copyright © 2021 Packt Publishing

All rights reserved. No part of this book may be reproduced, stored in a retrieval system, or transmitted in any form or by any means, without the prior written permission of the publisher, except in the case of brief quotations embedded in critical articles or reviews.

Every effort has been made in the preparation of this book to ensure the accuracy of the information presented. However, the information contained in this book is sold without warranty, either express or implied. Neither the authors, nor Packt Publishing or its dealers and distributors, will be held liable for any damages caused or alleged to have been caused directly or indirectly by this book.

Packt Publishing has endeavored to provide trademark information about all of the companies and products mentioned in this book by the appropriate use of capitals. However, Packt Publishing cannot guarantee the accuracy of this information.

Associate Group Product Manager: Rohit Rajkumar

Publishing Product Manager: Rohit Rajkumar

Senior Editor: Sofi Rogers

Content Development Editor: Rakhi Patel

Technical Editor: Shubham Sharma

Copy Editor: Safis Editing

Project Coordinator: Manthan Patel

Proofreader: Safis Editing

Indexer: Pratik Shirodkar

Production Designer: Shyam Sundar Korumilli

First published: September 2019

Second edition: October 2021

Production reference: 3190122

Published by Packt Publishing Ltd.
Livery Place
35 Livery Street
Birmingham
B3 2PB, UK.

ISBN 978-1-80056-599-9

www.packt.com

To my long-suffering wife, Laura Bailey, who allows me to embark on all manner of crazy projects, and my two lovely (most of the time) children, Lottie and Bobby, who keep life exciting and fresh. Love you all so much!

– Tom Bailey

Foreword

I have known and worked with Tom for more than 10 years. We met at an antenatal class as we both embarked on our journey into parenthood and have been close friends ever since.

Together we founded our education apps company, and from the very start we decided to go all-in on Flutter for all our apps. At the time Flutter was in beta, and I must admit I questioned Tom's decision to put all our eggs into such a new and untested basket.

Three years later and we have created a suite of high-quality education apps across Android, iOS, and, to some extent, the web, allowing us to keep development costs incredibly low relative to our competitors while creating apps that are very high quality.

In *Flutter for Beginners Second Edition*, Tom shares his learning from those 3 years of development. This book is written from the point of view of someone who has been there, all the way from justifying the use of the framework to the wider business team and learning the basics of the framework, through implementing the user experience defined by our designers, to testing and ultimately releasing to the iOS App Store and Google Play Store.

Why not join Tom and build some epic Flutter apps using this awesome framework?

Trevor Wills

Managing Director, Life Ninja

Contributors

About the authors

Thomas Bailey has an extensive background in tech, working for companies and high-profile firms as a senior developer, solutions architect, and IT director. His education technology company uses Flutter as the sole technology powering their education apps, and he has enjoyed watching Flutter move from its initial beta release to the fully fledged and highly popular framework we see today. He loves to talk tech over a hot chocolate with anyone who will listen and is constantly exploring the cutting edge of tech and how it will shape our industry in the future.

> *I want to thank the people who have been close to me and supported me, especially my wife, Laura, and my colleagues, who have been happy to allow me time to focus on the book when I should have been cutting code.*

Alessandro Biessek was born in the beautiful city of Chapecó, in the state of Santa Catarina, southern Brazil, in 1993. He is currently working on mobile application development for Android and iOS in his hometown. He has more than 9 years of experience in development, from desktop development with Delphi to backend development with PHP, Node.js, and Golang; mobile development with Apache Flex; and Java/Kotlin. Most of his time is devoted to the development of Android apps. Always interested in new technologies, he has been following the Flutter framework for a long time, watching with interest its growth and adoption in recent months.

About the reviewer

Adby Santos has a degree in IT from UFERSA; he is a co-organizer of and contributor to Flutterando, one of the world biggest communities about Flutter; he works at FTeam, a mobile apps specialist organization, as a Flutter development specialist. He is also a speaker and consultant; he has spoken and moderated at events like the Flutter Global Summit by Geekle. He also writes weekly about his professional and personal experiences on his LinkedIn.

I would like to thank Packt Publishing for the opportunity to review.
My special regards to Mr. Manthan Patel for the invite. I hope we could
contribute together in later opportunities.

Table of Contents

3

Flutter versus Other Frameworks

4

Dart Classes and Constructs

Section 2: The Flutter User Interface – Everything Is a Widget

5

Widgets – Building Layouts in Flutter

6

Handling User Input and Gestures

7

Routing – Navigating between Screens

Section 3: Developing Fully Featured Apps

8

Plugins – What Are They and How Do I Use Them?

9

Popular Third-Party Plugins

10

Using Widget Manipulations and Animations

Section 4: Testing and App Release

11
Testing and Debugging

12
Releasing Your App to the World

Preface

Flutter for Beginners helps you to enter the Flutter framework world and build awesome mobile applications. It'll take you from an introduction to the Dart language to an in-depth exploration of all the Flutter blocks needed to make a high-level app. Together, we will explore the whole Flutter life cycle, from project creation to app release. With clear code examples, you will learn how to start a small Flutter project, add some widgets, apply styles and themes, connect with remote services such as Firebase, get user input, add some animations to improve the user experience, and more. In addition, you will learn about why you should choose Flutter, how to test your app, how to monitor your app, and some common gotchas you may experience in the release process. In short, this book will prepare you for the future of mobile development with the amazing Flutter framework.

Who this book is for

This book is for developers looking to learn about Google's revolutionary framework, Flutter, from scratch. No knowledge of Flutter or Dart is required. However, basic programming language knowledge will be helpful.

What this book covers

Chapter 1, An Introduction to Flutter, introduces you to the world of Flutter.

Chapter 2, An Introduction to Dart, introduces the basics of the Dart language.

Chapter 3, Flutter versus Other Frameworks, explores the comparisons and similarities of other programming languages and frameworks, sharing the pros and cons and giving tips on how to transition to Flutter.

Chapter 4, Dart Classes and Constructs, provides solid foundational knowledge of Dart, which will set you in good stead as we move to a deeper exploration of Flutter.

Chapter 5, Widgets – Building Layouts in Flutter, looks at how to build layouts in Flutter.

Chapter 6, Handling User Input and Gestures, shows you how to handle user input with Flutter widgets.

Chapter 7, Routing – Navigating between Screens, explores how to add navigation to app screens.

Chapter 8, Plugins – What Are They and How Do I Use Them?, explores how to use plugins in Flutter apps.

Chapter 9, Popular Third-Party Plugins, teaches you about various third-party plugins and how to use them in Flutter apps.

Chapter 10, Using Widget Manipulations and Animations, gets into how to create unique visuals with graphic manipulations, giving you an insight into how to add animations to Flutter widgets.

Chapter 11, Testing and Debugging, delves into Flutter tools for improving productivity.

Chapter 12, Releasing Your App to the World, teaches you how to deploy your app to the world.

To get the most out of this book

You will be introduced to the requirements as we move through the chapters. To get started, you need to have access to a browser so you can access the DartPad website and play with Dart code.

To professionally develop and publish iOS apps, you need a developer license (paid annually), a Mac, and at least one device to test the applications. All this is not strictly necessary for the purpose of learning Flutter, but it might be useful to you.

The entire installation process and the requirements of the Flutter environment are available on the official website (`https://flutter.dev/docs/get-started/install`), but do not worry: you can start with the bare minimum and install any extras only when necessary.

Setup requirement	Options
Operating system	Windows or Linux for Android and web apps
	macOS for Android, iOS, and web apps
Integrated Development Environment (IDE)	Android Studio or Visual Studio Code
SDK	Flutter

If you are using the digital version of this book, we advise you to type the code yourself or access the code from the book's GitHub repository (a link is available in the next section). Doing so will help you avoid any potential errors related to the copying and pasting of code.

Download the example code files

You can download the example code files for this book from GitHub at `https://github.com/PacktPublishing/Flutter-for-Beginners-Second-Edition`. If there's an update to the code, it will be updated in the GitHub repository.

We also have other code bundles from our rich catalog of books and videos available at `https://github.com/PacktPublishing/`. Check them out!

Download the color images

We also provide a PDF file that has color images of the screenshots and diagrams used in this book. You can download it here: `https://static.packt-cdn.com/downloads/9781800565999_ColorImages.pdf`.

Conventions used

There are a number of text conventions used throughout this book.

`Code in text`: Indicates code words in text, database table names, folder names, filenames, file extensions, pathnames, dummy URLs, user input, and Twitter handles. Here is an example: "The `onTap` parameter takes a function as the argument, and we have placed an inline function that increments the `_counter` variable within the `setState` method."

A block of code is set as follows:

```
GestureDetector(
  onDoubleTap: () {
    setState(() {
      _counter++;
    });
  },
...
```

Any command-line input or output is written as follows:

```
C:\src\flutter>flutter doctor
```

Bold: Indicates a new term, an important word, or words that you see onscreen. For instance, words in menus or dialog boxes appear in **bold**. Here is an example: "Click the **Press this** button and you should navigate to a new screen with the **Go back** button showing."

> **Tips or Important Notes**
> Appear like this.

Get in touch

Feedback from our readers is always welcome.

General feedback: If you have questions about any aspect of this book, email us at `customercare@packtpub.com` and mention the book title in the subject of your message.

Errata: Although we have taken every care to ensure the accuracy of our content, mistakes do happen. If you have found a mistake in this book, we would be grateful if you would report this to us. Please visit `www.packtpub.com/support/errata` and fill in the form.

Piracy: If you come across any illegal copies of our works in any form on the internet, we would be grateful if you would provide us with the location address or website name. Please contact us at `copyright@packt.com` with a link to the material.

If you are interested in becoming an author: If there is a topic that you have expertise in and you are interested in either writing or contributing to a book, please visit `authors.packtpub.com`.

Share Your Thoughts

Once you've read Flutter for Beginners – Second Edition, we'd love to hear your thoughts! Scan the QR code below to go straight to the Amazon review page for this book and share your feedback.

https://packt.link/r/1800565992

Your review is important to us and the tech community and will help us make sure we're delivering excellent quality content.

Section 1: Introduction to Flutter and Dart

In this section, you will gain an understanding of the core Flutter framework, explore the basics of the Dart language, learn how to set up your own environment, and finally learn how to get started with it.

This section comprises the following chapters:

- *Chapter 1, An Introduction to Flutter*
- *Chapter 2, An Introduction to Dart*
- *Chapter 3, Flutter versus Other Frameworks*
- *Chapter 4, Dart Classes and Constructs*

1
An Introduction to Flutter

In this chapter, you will learn the basics of the Flutter framework, the reasons for its creation, and what the future of Flutter may hold. You will learn about the thriving Flutter community, how it is contributing to the continued evolution of Flutter, and how and why Flutter has grown so quickly in the last couple of years. Along the way, you will see how to make (and run!) your first Flutter project, experience the excellent Flutter documentation, and see how Flutter is designed to work across a range of platforms including iOS, Android, Web, Windows, and Mac.

The following topics will be covered in this chapter:

- What is Flutter?
- Hello Flutter – a first glimpse of Flutter
- Widgets, widgets, everywhere
- Building and running Flutter

Technical requirements

In this chapter, we will create, build, and run a Flutter application. To do this, you will need to set up your system so that it is capable of doing this.

Specifically, you will need to set up your system to have the following:

- A Flutter **software development kit (SDK)** installed and added to your PATH
- An **integrated development environment (IDE)** where you can view and edit Flutter code
- Android Studio and/or Xcode so that you can use the Android and iOS development tools and iOS simulators/Android emulators

The chapter will give you some guidance on how to set up your system, but as you will discover, the Flutter documentation is excellent and includes very accurate and up-to-date getting started guides: https://flutter.dev/docs/get-started/install.

Feel free to set up your system now or at the specific points required during the chapter.

You can find the source code for this chapter on GitHub at https://github.com/PacktPublishing/Flutter-for-Beginners-Second-Edition/tree/main/hello_world/lib/chapter_01.

What is Flutter?

Since the advent of the Apple App Store (and subsequently the Google Play Store), there has been a way for organizations to share programs with mobile users in a very controlled and managed way. Much like web pages on the internet, mobile apps have proliferated to encompass all aspects of our life. And much like web pages, over the years, developers have iteratively discovered and learned the best ways to create reliable, scalable, and intuitive mobile apps.

As developers have learned to work within the mobile ecosystem, they have followed similar design patterns and framework ideas as were created to deal with the web ecosystem. Much like the complications of developing code for multiple browsers, in the mobile ecosystem, there has been the challenge of developing code that can work on both iOS and Android devices, with the dream always being to have one code base that works on all devices and even the web.

Flutter is a framework that is the culmination of this learning. Like most other frameworks, developers use a programming language specified by the framework, and structure their code in a way that aligns with the needs of the framework so that ultimately, the developer creates the least amount of "boilerplate" code and can focus on their business needs. Examples of "boilerplate" code would be how to manage touch input, how to connect to the internet, and how to package the app code to work with the App Store, Play Store, or web hosting service.

Flutter is a very new framework, and this means that it does not have a big section of the mobile development market yet, but this is changing, and the outlook for the next few years is highly positive.

When choosing a new programming language or framework, it is hugely important to developers and software companies that what they have chosen has certain key aspects that will ensure it is easy to pick up and that it has a bright future. Investing time and money into learning a new solution, and then developing a code base and development processes around that language and framework, is incredibly expensive. If that solution becomes outdated after a short period of time, there is poor support and documentation, there are a lack of new developers available to take your product forward, or the solution has scaling issues or usability problems, then that investment is wasted. Let's look at some of the aspects that suggest Flutter may be a good long-term investment.

Backed by Google

Flutter, and the **Dart** programming language it depends on, were created by Google, and although they are open source, they continue to be backed by Google. This ensures the framework has all the tools it needs to succeed in the community, with support from the Google team, presence at big events such as *Google I/O*, and investment in continuous improvements in the code base.

From the launch of the first stable release during the *Flutter Live Event* at the end of 2018, the growth of Flutter is evident:

- More than 200 million users of Flutter apps
- More than 50,000 Flutter apps on the Play Store
- Nearly 500,000 developers
- The 18th most popular software repository on GitHub

Let's look at some of the reasons why Flutter has become so popular.

Fuchsia OS and Flutter

It's not a secret anymore that Google has been working on a new operating system called Fuchsia OS, which has been rumored to be a potential future replacement for the Android OS. One thing to pay attention to is that Fuchsia OS may be a universal Google operating system that runs on more than just mobile phones, and this would directly affect Flutter adoption. This is because Flutter will be the first method of developing mobile apps for the new Fuchsia OS, and, not only this, Fuchsia uses Flutter as its UI rendering engine. With the system targeting more devices than just smartphones, as seems to be the case, Flutter will certainly have a lot of improvements.

The growth of the framework's adoption is directly related to the new Fuchsia OS. As it gets closer to launch, it is important for Google to have mobile apps targeting the new system. For example, Google has announced that Android apps will be compatible with the new OS, making the transition to, and adoption of, Flutter significantly easier.

Dart

The Dart programming language was first unveiled by Google at the *GOTO* conference in 2011, and Dart 1.0 was released at the end of 2013. Initially viewed as a replacement for JavaScript (the main web programming language), the uptake of Dart by developers was relatively low. However, thanks to the emergence of Flutter and its reliance on Dart, the Dart programming language has seen a huge rise in usage.

So why did the Flutter project choose the Dart programming language? Since its inception, one of Flutter's main goals was to be a high-performance alternative to existing cross-platform frameworks. But not only that; to significantly improve the mobile developer's experience was one of the crucial points of the project.

With this in mind, Flutter needed a programming language that allowed it to accomplish these goals, and Dart seemed to be the perfect match for the following reasons:

- **Dart compilation**: Dart is flexible enough to provide different ways of running the code, so Flutter uses Dart **ahead of time** (**AOT**) compilation with performance in mind when compiling a *release* version of the application, and it uses **just in time** (**JIT**) compilation with sub-second compilation of code in development time, aiming for fast feedback for code changes. Dart JIT and AOT refer to when the compilation phase takes place. In AOT, code is compiled during the build process and before running the code; in JIT, code is compiled while running (check out the *Dart introduction* section in the next chapter).

- **High performance**: Due to Dart's support for AOT compilation, Flutter does not require a slow bridge between realms (for example, non-native Flutter code to native device code), which makes Flutter apps responsive and allows a fast startup.

- **Garbage collection**: Flutter uses a functional-style flow with short-lived objects, and this means a lot of short-lived allocations. Dart garbage collection works without locks, helping with fast allocation.

- **Easy to learn**: Dart is a flexible, robust, modern, and advanced language. The language has been adapted as Flutter has become more popular, with lots of syntactic sugar, and fundamental design changes, that really help with Flutter app creation. Although it is still evolving, the language has a well-defined object-oriented framework with familiar functionalities to dynamic and static languages, an active community, and very well-structured documentation.

- **Declarative UI**: In Flutter, you use a declarative style to lay out widgets, which means that widgets are immutable and are only lightweight "blueprints." To change the UI, a widget triggers a rebuild on itself and its subtree. In the opposite imperative style (the most common), we can change specific component properties after they are created.

> **Declarative UI**
>
> We will explore this a lot more throughout the book, but if you want to understand the concept of the Flutter declarative UI at this point, then take a look at the official introduction to declarative UI from Flutter: `https://flutter.dev/docs/get-started/flutter-for/declarative`.

- **Dart syntax for layout**: Different from many frameworks that have a separate syntax for layout, in Flutter, the layout is specified inline within the Dart code. This gives greater flexibility and reduces the developer's cognitive load. Flutter has great tools for debugging layout as well as rendering performance.

These are great reasons why Dart fits perfectly with Flutter. However, there is a key area of Flutter that is probably why you are learning and using it, and why it is a game-changer in the app development world, and that is a single code base for multiple platforms. Let's take a look at that now.

One code base to rule them all

The primary goal of the Flutter framework is to be a toolkit for building apps that are equivalent in performance, usability, and features to native apps (apps created directly for iOS or Android) while using only a single code base. You may have heard it stated often that there are big advantages to having a single code base. Let's see why that is the case:

- **Multiple languages to learn**: If a developer wants to develop for multiple platforms, they must learn how to do something in one OS and programming language, and later, the same thing in another OS and programming language. The developer then needs to decide whether to focus on one platform for a period of time, causing a mismatch of features/bug fixes between the apps, or constantly switch between platforms, impacting productivity and potentially introducing bugs.

- **Long/more expensive development cycles**: If you decide to create multiple development teams to avoid the previous issues, there are consequences in terms of cost, multiple deadlines, different capabilities of native frameworks, and disparate sets of bug reports.

- **Inconsistency**: Different native capabilities, or different development teams developing features in slightly different ways, may lead to inconsistencies between apps, annoying users and making bug reporting more complicated to diagnose.

Flutter is not the first attempt to create a single code base and there are existing frameworks available that have similar promises. However, they can suffer from some serious drawbacks:

- **Performance**: Some frameworks use workarounds to allow consistency of user experience across platforms. One of these is to effectively have a web page running inside a native app using a **webview** (a built-in web browser). This tends to have much worse performance than native apps, leading to a poor user experience.

- **Design constraints**: Some frameworks are based on languages that were designed before the mobile experience was created. This can mean they are not designed well for certain user interactions or certain device capabilities, leading to complicated or obscure code, and the inherent maintenance issues this can cause.

- **Not quite one code base**: Although some frameworks suggest a single code base approach to app development, once you get into the details, you find that you still need to write some platform-specific code, which causes code duplication and allows single platform bugs to creep in.

Now let's see how Flutter counters these problems.

High performance

Right now, it is hard to say that Flutter's performance is always better in practice than other frameworks, but it's safe to say that its aim is to be. For example, its rendering layer was developed with a high frame rate in mind. As we will see in the *Flutter rendering* section, some of the existing frameworks rely on JavaScript and HTML rendering, which might cause overheads in performance because everything is drawn in a webview (a visual component like a web browser).

Some use **original equipment manufacturer (OEM)** widgets but rely on a bridge to request the OS API to render the components, which creates a bottleneck in the application because it needs an extra step to render the **user interface (UI)**. See the *Flutter rendering* section for more details of the Flutter rendering approach compared to others.

Some points that make Flutter's performance great are the following:

- **Flutter owns the pixels**: Flutter renders the application pixel by pixel (see the next section), interacting directly with the Skia graphics engine.

- **No extra layers or additional OS API calls**: As Flutter owns the app rendering, it does not need additional calls to use the OEM widgets, so no bottleneck.

- **Flutter is compiled to native code**: Flutter uses the Dart AOT compiler to produce native code. That means there's no overhead in setting up an environment to interpret Dart code on the fly, and it runs just like a native app, starting more quickly than frameworks that need some kind of interpreter.

Full control of the UI

The Flutter framework chooses to do all the UI by itself, rendering the visual components directly to the canvas, as we have seen previously, requiring nothing more than the canvas from the platform so it's not limited by rules and conventions. Most of the time, frameworks just reproduce what the platform offers in another way. For example, other webview-based cross-platform frameworks reproduce visual components using HTML elements with CSS styling. Other frameworks emulate the creation of the visual components and pass them to the device platform, which will render the OEM widgets like a natively developed app. We are not talking about performance here, so what else does Flutter offer by not using the OEM widgets and doing the job all by itself?

Let's see:

- **Ruling all the pixels on the device**: Frameworks limited by OEM widgets will reproduce at most what a native developed app would, as they use only the platform's available components. On the other hand, frameworks based on web technologies may reproduce more than platform-specific components, but may also be limited by the mobile web engine available on the device. By getting control of the UI rendering, Flutter allows the developer to create the UI in their own way by exposing an extensible and rich Widgets API, which provides tools that can be used to create a unique UI with no drawbacks in performance and no limits in design.

- **Platform UI kits**: By not using OEM widgets, Flutter can break the platform design, but it does not. Flutter is equipped with packages that provide platform design widgets, the Material set in Android, and Cupertino in iOS. We will see more on platform UI kits in *Chapter 5, Widgets – Building Layouts in Flutter.*

- **Achievable UI design requirements**: Flutter provides a clean and robust API with the ability to reproduce layouts that are faithful to the design requirements. Unlike web-based frameworks that rely on CSS layout rules that can be large and complicated and even conflicting, Flutter simplifies this by adding semantic rules that can be used to make complex but efficient and beautiful layouts.

- **Smoother look and feel**: In addition to native widget kits, Flutter seeks to provide a native platform experience where the application is running, so fonts, gestures, and interactions are implemented in a platform-specific way, bringing a natural feel to the user, like a native application.

We refer to visual components as widgets, which we will go into more detail on that in the *Widgets, widgets, everywhere* section in this chapter.

Open source framework

Having a big company such as Google behind it is fundamental to a framework such as Flutter (see React, for example, which is maintained by Facebook). In addition, community support becomes even more important as it becomes more popular.

By being open source, the community and Google can work together to do the following:

- Help with bug fixes and documentation through code collaboration
- Create new educational content about the framework
- Support documentation and usage
- Make improvement decisions based on real feedback

Improving the developer experience is one of the main goals of the framework. Therefore, in addition to being close to the community, the framework provides great tools and resources for developers. Let's see them.

Developer resources and tooling

The focus on developers in the Flutter framework goes from documentation and learning resources to providing tools to helping with productivity:

- **Documentation and learning resources**: Flutter websites are rich for developers coming from other platforms, including many examples and use cases, for example, the famous Google Codelabs (`https://codelabs.developers.google.com/?cat=Flutter`).

- **IDE integration**: Flutter, and Dart, have a completed, integrated IDE experience with Android Studio, IntelliJ, and Visual Studio Code. Within this book, we will show examples from Visual Studio Code, but these examples will work very similarly in Android Studio and IntelliJ.

- **Command-line tools**: Dart has tools that help with analyzing, running, and managing dependencies and these are also part of Flutter. In addition, Flutter has commands to help with debugging, deploying, inspecting layout rendering, and integration with IDEs through Dart plugins. Here's a list of the various commands:

Figure 1.1 – Available commands in Flutter

- **Quick setup**: Flutter has the `create` command shown in the preceding list that allows you to create a new and fully functional Flutter project with minimal input. IDEs also offer a Flutter project creation menu option, replicating the command-line functionality.

- **Environment issue diagnostics**: Flutter comes with the `flutter doctor` tool, which is a command-line tool that guides the developer through the system setup by indicating what is needed in order to be ready to set up a Flutter environment. We will see this tool in action when we set up your environment very soon. The `flutter doctor` command also identifies connected devices and whether there are any upgrades available.

- **Hot reload**: This is a huge benefit to developers and a feature that is getting a lot of attention. By combining the capabilities of the Dart language (such as JIT compilation) and the power of Flutter, it is possible for the developer to instantly see design changes made to code in the simulator or device. In Flutter, there is no specific tool for layout preview. Hot reload makes it unnecessary.

Now that we have learned about the benefits of Flutter, let's start looking at the software's compilation process.

Hello Flutter – a first glimpse of Flutter

OK, let's start getting our hands dirty with some code. Flutter comes with a simple Hello World app that we will get running and then look at in some detail. First of all though, we need to get your system ready for some Flutter action!

Installing Flutter

Flutter is very easy to install. Head over to the Flutter docs web pages to install Flutter and Dart for your operating system: `https://flutter.dev/docs/get-started/install`.

The installation documentation for Flutter is comprehensive, with explanations and potential issues all described there. Ensure that you read the installation documentation fully and complete all the steps so that your system is correctly prepared for our journey into Flutter.

You will download the SDK and place it somewhere on your filesystem. Note that downloading Flutter will also download a compatible version of Dart and the relevant `dart` command-line tool. You should not need to download Dart separately.

> **Updating your PATH**
>
> The installation documentation also explains how to update your PATH so that you can run Flutter commands from your command line. Please do follow these instructions because you will be using the command line regularly to interact with Flutter and Dart.

After installation and PATH setup, you should run the Flutter `doctor` command to see how ready your system is for Flutter. You will do this from your command line / terminal:

```
C:\src\flutter>flutter doctor
```

Here is an example of the output:

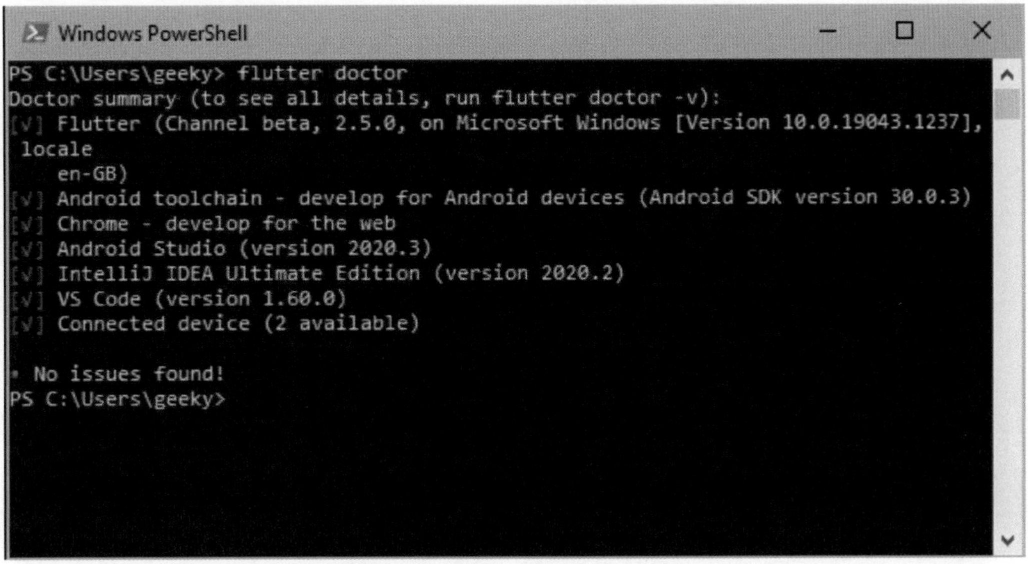

Figure 1.2 – Flutter doctor command-line output

You are likely to see errors in the `flutter doctor` report at this point because we haven't set up your development environment yet.

If you are unable to run the Flutter `doctor command`, then it is likely an issue with your PATH, as mentioned previously. Double-check that the path to your Flutter folder is correct and points to the `flutter/bin` subfolder. Also try closing your command line / terminal and opening it again because the PATH, in some situations, is only updated when the command line / terminal is opened.

Development environment

As mentioned previously, Flutter has excellent support in Android Studio, IntelliJ, and Visual Studio Code. This book will generally be agnostic of IDE, but, where required, will show examples from Visual Studio Code.

All three IDEs can be downloaded from the internet. Android Studio and Visual Studio Code are free, and IntelliJ has both a free **Community** edition and a paid-for **Ultimate** edition.

If you are planning to work with Android devices (and because Flutter is cross-platform I would expect you will), then you will need to download and install Android Studio regardless of the IDE you decide to develop code with. This is because installing Android Studio also installs the Android SDK, Android SDK command-line tools, and Android SDK build tools. These are required by Flutter when interacting with Android devices, running Android emulators, and building the app ready for use on the Android Play Store.

On macOS devices, you will also need to install and configure Xcode to allow you to build your app for iOS. Follow the instructions in the Flutter getting started documentation to ensure Xcode is configured correctly.

> **Important note**
>
> You can only build iOS apps on Macs. This is a restriction imposed by Apple and is imposed on all app development, not just Flutter. If this is an issue, then there are options such as cloud-based Mac instances you can use, or virtualization software to allow you to run a Mac virtual machine. An exploration of this is beyond the scope of this book. However, when developing Flutter apps, you can build and test quite happily on Android for the vast majority of the time, only switching to iOS for late-stage testing.

Once you have both your IDE installed and Android Studio (or just Android Studio if that is your IDE of choice), and Xcode installed and configured (if you are on a Mac), then rerun `flutter doctor` to check everything is ready to go.

Hello world!

With the Flutter development environment configured, we can start using Flutter commands. The typical way to start a Flutter project is to run the following command:

```
flutter create <output_directory>
```

Here, `output_directory` will also be the Flutter project name if you do not specify it as an argument. By running the preceding command, the folder with the provided name will be generated with a sample Flutter project in it. We will analyze the project in a few moments. First, it is good to know that there are some useful options to manipulate the resulting project from the `flutter create` command. The main ones are as follows:

- `--org`: This can be used to change the owner organization of the project. If you already know Android or iOS development, this is a reverse domain name, and is used to identify package names on Android and as a prefix in the iOS bundle identifier. The default value is `com.example`.

- `-s, --sample=<id>`: Most of the official examples for widget usage have a unique ID that you can use to quickly clone the example to your machine. Whenever you are exploring the Flutter docs website (`https://docs.flutter.dev`), you can take a sample ID from it and use it with this argument.

- `-i, --ios-language`, and `-a, --android-language`: These are used to specify the language for the native part code of the project, and are only used if you plan to write native platform code.

- `--project-name`: Use this to change the project's name. It must be a valid Dart package identifier. If you do not specify this parameter, it tries to use the same name as the output directory. Note that this argument must be the last in the list of arguments provided.

> **Valid Dart package identifiers**
>
> As specified in the Dart documentation: *"Package names should be all lowercase, with underscores to separate words, 'just_like_this'. Use only basic Latin letters and Arabic digits: [a-z0-9_]. Also, make sure the name is a valid Dart identifier – that it doesn't start with digits and isn't a reserved word."*

Let's see a typical Flutter project structure created with the `flutter create hello_world` command:

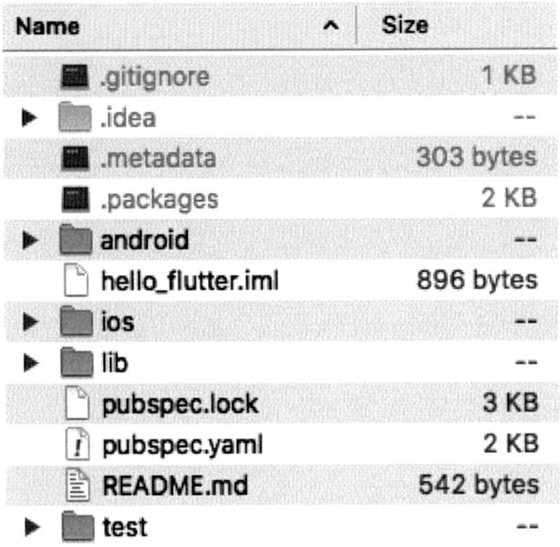

Name	^	Size
📁 .gitignore		1 KB
▶ 📁 .idea		--
📁 .metadata		303 bytes
📁 .packages		2 KB
▶ 📁 android		--
📄 hello_flutter.iml		896 bytes
▶ 📁 ios		--
▶ 📁 lib		--
📄 pubspec.lock		3 KB
📄 pubspec.yaml		2 KB
📄 README.md		542 bytes
▶ 📁 test		--

Figure 1.3 – Typical Flutter project structure

Listing the basic structure elements, we get the following:

- `android/ios`: This contains the platform-specific codes. If you already know the Android project structure from Android Studio, there is no surprise here. The same goes for Xcode iOS projects.

- `hello_flutter.iml`: This is a typical IntelliJ project file, which contains the `JAVA_MODULE` information used by the IDE.

- `lib` directory: This is the main folder of a Flutter application; the generated project will contain at least a `main.dart` file to start work on. We will be checking this file in detail soon.

- `pubspec.yaml` and `pubspec.lock`: This `pubspec.yaml` file is what defines a Dart package. This is one of the main files of the project and defines the app build number, lists dependencies on external plugins, images, and fonts and more. We will be looking at this in more detail in *Chapter 5, Widgets – Building Layouts in Flutter*.

- `README.md`: This is a standard README document that is very common in open source projects. It allows you to document how to set up and use your code so that other developers can easily get your code running.

- `test` directory: This contains all the test-related files of the project. Here, we can add unit tests and also widget tests to ensure we do not introduce bugs into our code as we develop it.

Most of the commands that we explore can be replicated in the IDE. It is worth noting that the IDEs use these command-line tools behind the scenes to interact with the project.

Now that you have created your first Flutter project (congratulations by the way!), you should open it up in your IDE so that you can start to explore it a lot more.

Widgets, widgets, everywhere

Flutter widgets are a core part of the framework and are used constantly throughout your code. You will hear the saying "Everything is a widget," and that is almost true in Flutter. In this section, we will see how Flutter renders the user interface and then how Flutter applies the widgets idea to app development to create awesome UIs.

Widgets can be understood as the visual (but not only that) representation of parts of the application. Many widgets are put together to compose the UI of an application. Imagine it as a puzzle in which you define the pieces.

The intention of widgets is to provide a way for your application to be modular, scalable, and expressive with less code and without imposing limitations. The main characteristics of the widgets UI in Flutter are composability and immutability.

Flutter rendering

One of the main aspects that makes Flutter unique is the way that it draws the visual components to the screen. A key differentiator to existing frameworks is how the application communicates with the platform's SDK, what it asks the SDK to do, and what it does by itself:

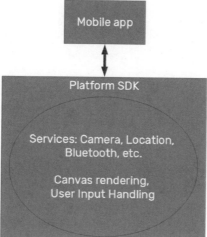

Figure 1.4 – Flutter communication with the platform SDK

The platform SDK can be seen as the interface between applications and the operating system and services. Each system provides its own SDK with its own capabilities and is based on a programming language (that is, Kotlin/Java for the Android SDK and Swift/Objective C for the iOS SDK).

Flutter – rendering by itself

Flutter chooses to do all the rendering work by itself. The only thing it needs from the platform's SDK is access to **Services** APIs and a canvas to draw the UI on:

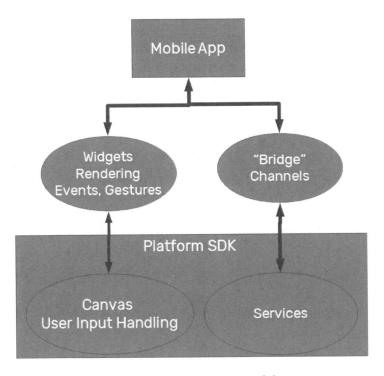

Figure 1.5 – Flutter access to services and the canvas

Flutter moves the widgets and rendering to the app, from where it gets the customization and extensibility. Through a canvas, it can draw anything and also access events to handle user inputs and gestures by itself. The bridge in Flutter is done by platform channels.

Composability

For the widget user interface structures, Flutter chooses composition over inheritance, with the goal of keeping each widget simple and with a well-defined purpose. Meeting one of the framework's goals, flexibility, Flutter allows the developer to make many combinations to achieve incredible results.

> **Composition versus inheritance**
>
> Inheritance derives one class from another. For example, you may have a class such as Vehicle and subclasses of Car and Motorbike. The Car and Motorbike classes would inherit the abilities of the Vehicle class and then add their own specializations. In this instance, Car **is a** Vehicle and Motorbike **is a** Vehicle.
>
> Composition defines a class as the sum of its parts. For example, you may have an Engine class and a Wheel class. In this model, a Car is composed of an Engine, four Wheels, and other specializations; a Car **has an** Engine and a Car **has** Wheels. Composability is less rigid than inheritance and allows for things such as dependency injection and modifications at runtime.

Immutability

Flutter is based on the reactive style of programming, where the widget instances are short-lived and change their descriptions (whether visually or not) based on configuration changes, so it reacts to changes and propagates these changes to its composing widgets, and so on.

A Flutter widget may have a state associated with it, and when the associated state changes, it can be rebuilt to match the representation.

The terms **state** and **reactive** are well known in the React style of programming, disseminated by Facebook's famous React library.

Everything is a widget

Flutter widgets are everywhere in an application. Maybe not everything is a widget, but almost everything is. Even the app is a widget in Flutter, and that's why this concept is so important. A widget represents a part of a UI, but it does not mean it's only something that is visible. It can be any of the following:

- A visual/structural element that is a basic structural element, such as the `Button` or `Text` widgets

- A layout-specific element that may define the position, margins, or padding, such as the `Padding` widget

- A style element that may help to colorize and theme a visual/structural element, such as the `Theme` widget

- An interaction element that helps to respond to user interactions in different ways, such as the `GestureDetector` widget

Let's have a quick look at a widget so you can get a feel for what we are referring to. Open your IDE and take a look at the `lib/main.dart` file. You will see a section like this:

```
class MyApp extends StatelessWidget {
  Widget build(BuildContext context) {
    return MaterialApp(
      title: 'Flutter Demo',
      theme: ThemeData(
        primarySwatch: Colors.blue,
      ),
      home: const MyHomePage(title: 'Flutter Demo Home Page'),
    );
  }
}
```

Not only is this your first example of a Flutter widget, it is also your first chance to see Dart. If you are from a Java, C++, Objective-C, and so on, background, then it should look relatively familiar to you. Components of code are held in Class definitions that describe fields and methods, with inheritance through the `extends` keyword.

This `MyApp` class runs the whole show and is itself a widget. In this instance, it is a `StatelessWidget`, as you can see from the `extends` section. We will explore `StatelessWidgets` (and their alter ego, the `StatefulWidget`) in a lot of detail later on, but for the moment, it's sufficient to know that a `StatelessWidget` holds no state, it exists to compose other widgets that may or may not hold their own state.

One key point to note is the `build` method. This method is used to update the display and is called when some external activity happens – for example, the user interacts with the device, some data is sent from a database, or a timer is triggered at a set time.

In this `build` method, the `MyApp` widget simply returns another widget, `MaterialApp`, which itself will have a `build` method that may also return widgets. Ultimately, you will reach leaf widgets that will render graphics to the display.

Widgets are the basic building blocks of an interface. To build a UI properly, Flutter organizes the widgets in a widget tree.

The widget tree

This is another important concept in Flutter layouts. It's where widgets come to life. The widget tree is the logical representation of all the UI's widgets. It is computed during **layout** (measurements and structural info) and used during **rendering** (frame to screen) and **hit testing** (touch interactions), and this is the thing Flutter does best. By using a lot of optimization algorithms, it tries to manipulate the tree as little as possible, reducing the total amount of work spent on rendering, aiming for greater efficiency:

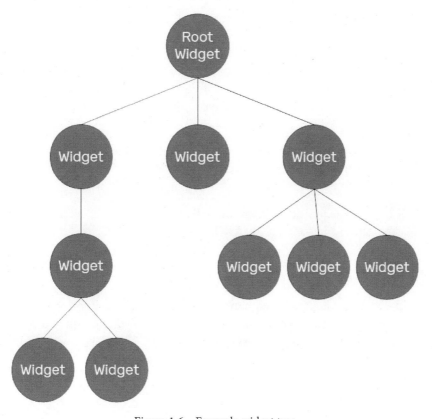

Figure 1.6 – Example widget tree

Widgets are represented in the tree as nodes. Each widget may have a state associated with it; every change to its state results in rebuilding the widget and the child involved.

As you can see, the tree's child structure is not static, and is defined by the widget's description. The children relations in widgets are what makes the UI tree; it exists by composition, so it's common to see Flutter's built-in widgets exposing `child` or `children` properties, depending on the purpose of the widget.

The widget tree does not work alone in the framework. It has the help of the element tree; a tree that relates to the widget tree by representing the built widget on the screen, so every widget will have a corresponding element in the element tree after it is built.

The element tree has an important task in Flutter. It helps to map onscreen elements to the widget tree. Also, it determines how widget rebuilding is done in update scenarios. When a widget changes and needs to be rebuilt, this will cause an update to the corresponding element. The element stores the type of the corresponding widget and a reference to its children elements. In the case of repositioning, for example, a widget, the element will check the type of the corresponding new widget, and if there is a match, it will update itself with the new widget description.

The element tree can be thought of as a pre-render auxiliary tree to the widget tree. If you need more information on that, you can check the official docs at `https://docs.flutter.io/flutter/widgets/Element-class.html`.

You have now learned the basics of how to put a Flutter app together, so let's look at the build process and options in some more detail.

Building and running Flutter

The way an application is built is fundamental to how it will perform on the target platform. This is an important step regarding performance. Even though you do not necessarily need to know this for every kind of application, knowing how the application is built helps you to understand and measure possible improvements.

As we have already pointed out, Flutter relies on the AOT compilation of Dart for release mode and the JIT compilation of Dart for development/debug mode. Dart is one of only a few languages that are capable of being compiled to both AOT and JIT, and Flutter makes the most of this advantage. Let's look at the different build options available, why you would use each one, and how the capabilities of Dart lead to an optimal developer and user experience.

Debug mode

During development, Flutter uses JIT compilation in debug mode. Debug mode compilation is optimized for fast feedback, and therefore sacrifices execution speed and binary size. However, due to the power of Dart's compiler, interactions between the code and the simulator/device are still fast, and debugging tools allow developers to step into the source code and analyze the widget layout.

Release mode

In release mode, debugging information is not necessary, and the focus is performance. Flutter uses a technique that is common to game engines. By using AOT mode, Dart code is compiled to native code, and the app loads the Flutter library and delegates rendering, input, and event handling to it through the Skia engine.

> **Skia graphics library**
>
> Skia is an open source library that provides APIs for 2D graphics. It is used in Flutter as well as Google Chrome, Android, Firefox, and many others. It is also backed by Google, like Dart and Flutter.

Profile mode

Sometimes you need to analyze the performance of your app. Profile mode retains just enough debugging ability to create a profile or your app's performance, while attempting to be a true reflection of your app's real-world performance. This mode is only available on physical devices because emulators will not have representative characteristics.

Supported platforms

Currently, Flutter supports ARM Android devices running at least on API 19 (Android 4.4 or KitKat) , and iOS devices on iOS 9 or later (which includes iPhone 4S and later). As you would expect, Flutter apps can be run on device emulators, and debugging works equally well on physical and emulated devices.

Additionally, Flutter Web is in the beta channel, and desktop support (Windows, macOS, and Linux) are available on the Alpha channel. As you can see, the vision for Flutter is to allow developers to have a single code base for mobile, web, and desktop!

We are not going to go into more detail on Flutter's compilation aspects as they are beyond the scope of this book. For more information, you can read `https://flutter.dev/docs/resources/faq#how-does-flutter-run-my-code-on-android` and `https://flutter.dev/docs/resources/faq#how-does-flutter-run-my-code-on-ios`.

The pubspec.yaml file

The `pubspec.yaml` file in Flutter is actually a file that is used to define Dart packages. Besides that, it contains an additional section for configurations specific to Flutter. Let's see the `pubspec.yaml` file's contents in details:

```
name: hello_flutter
description: A new Flutter project.
version: 1.0.0+1
```

The beginning of the file is simple. As we already know, the `name` property is defined when we execute the `pub create` command. Next is the default project `description`; feel free to change this to something more interesting. Note that if you do so, your IDE may suddenly run the `flutter pub get` command. We'll see why in a bit.

> **Description during create**
>
> Like many parts of the `pubspec.yaml` file, you can specify the description during the flutter `create` command by using the `-description` argument.

The `version` property follows the Dart package conventions: the version number, plus an optional build version number separated by +. In addition to that, Flutter allows you to override these values during the build. We will take a more detailed look at that in *Chapter 12, Releasing Your App to the World*.

Then we have the dependencies section of the `pubspec` file:

```
environment:
  sdk: ">=2.12.0 <3.0.0"


dependencies:
  flutter:
    sdk: flutter
  cupertino_icons: ^1.0.1
```

```
dev_dependencies:
  flutter_test:
    sdk: flutter
```

We start with the environment property. This specifies the version of Dart that your code will work with. This entry is specifying that your code will need version 2.12.0 of Dart or above, but will not run on Dart 3.0.0. As per standard versioning, you would expect that if Dart 3.0.0 is released, it will have some backward-incompatible changes that may stop your code from compiling. This happened when Dart was updated from 1.x.x to 2.x.x. By restricting your allowed Dart versions, this means your code will not need to support Dart 3.x.x until you are ready to do so. Note that Dart 2.12 is a significant milestone for Dart because it introduced the concept of null safety. We will explore null safety in *Chapter 2, An Introduction to Dart*.

Then we have the dependencies property. This starts with the main dependency of a Flutter application, the Flutter SDK itself, which contains many of Flutter's core packages.

As an additional dependency, the generator adds the cupertino_icons package, which contains icon assets used by the built-in Flutter Cupertino widgets (there's more on that in the next chapter).

As you add other dependencies (and I would bet my hat that you will add a lot of dependencies), they will also appear here.

The dev_dependencies property contains only the flutter_test package dependency provided by the Flutter SDK itself, which contains Flutter-specific extensions to the Dart test package. We will explore this in *Chapter 11, Testing and Debugging*

In the final block of the file, there's a dedicated flutter section:

```
flutter:
  uses-material-design: true

  # To add assets to your application, add an assets section,
  like this:
  # assets:
  #     - images/a_dot_burr.jpeg
  #     - images/a_dot_ham.jpeg
  # ...

  # To add custom fonts to your application, add a fonts section
  here,
```

```
# fonts:
#     - family: Schyler
#       fonts:
#         - asset: fonts/Schyler-Regular.ttf
#         - asset: fonts/Schyler-Italic.ttf
#           style: italic
```

This `flutter` section allows us to configure resources that are bundled in the application to be used during runtime, such as images, fonts, music, sound effects, and videos.

Let's have a closer look:

- `uses-material-design`: We will see the Material widgets provided by Flutter in the next chapter. In addition to them, we can use also Material Design icons (`https://material.io/tools/icons/?style=baseline`), which are in a custom font format. For this to work properly, we need to activate this property (set it to `true`) so the icons are included in the application.

- `assets`: This property is used to list the resource paths that will be bundled with the final application. The `assets` files and folders can be organized in any way; what matters for Flutter is the path to the files. You specify the path of the file relative to the project's root. This is used later in Dart code when you need to refer to an asset file. Here's an example of adding a single image:

  ```
  assets:
    images/home_background.jpeg
  ```

  Often you will want to add many images, and listing them individually would be onerous. An alternative is to include a whole folder:

  ```
  assets:
    images/
  ```

  You add the `/` character at the end of the path that is used to specify that you want to include all files in that folder. Note that this doesn't include subfolders; they would need to be listed as well:

  ```
  assets:
    images/
    images/icons/
  ```

- `fonts`: This property allows us to add custom fonts to the application.

We will be checking how to load different assets in the course of the book whenever we need to. Also, you can read more on asset specification details on the Flutter docs website: `https://flutter.io/docs/development/ui/assets-and-images`.

Running the generated project

The default application that we created earlier has a counter to demonstrate the React style of programming in Flutter. We will look in more detail at Dart code in the next chapter, but let's look at the `main.dart` file a little bit more before we try running the application.

The lib/main.dart file

We explored the `main.dart` file earlier to look at a widget. This file is also the entry point of the Flutter application:

```
void main() => runApp(MyApp());
```

The `main` function is the Dart entry point of an application; this is where the execution of your app will start. Flutter then takes over the execution in the `runApp` function, which is called by passing your top-level (or root) widget as a parameter. This is the widget we saw earlier, the `MyApp` widget.

Flutter run

To execute a Flutter application, we must have a connected device or simulator. The check is done by using the `flutter doctor` tool we have explored before, and the `flutter emulators` tool, which will run an emulator/simulator on your system. The following command lets you know the existing Android and iOS emulators that can be used to run the project:

```
flutter emulators
```

You will get something similar to the following screenshot:

```
● ○ ●                          hello_flutter — -bash — 80×24
[Alessandros-iMac:hello_flutter biessek$ flutter emulators
1 available emulator:

apple_ios_simulator • iOS Simulator • Apple

To run an emulator, run 'flutter emulators --launch <emulator id>'.
To create a new emulator, run 'flutter emulators --create [--name xyz]'.

You can find more information on managing emulators at the links below:
    https://developer.android.com/studio/run/managing-avds
    https://developer.android.com/studio/command-line/avdmanager
Alessandros-iMac:hello_flutter biessek$ ▌
```

Figure 1.7 – Output from the flutter emulators command

You can check how to manage your Android emulators on `https://developer.android.com/studio/run/managing-avds`. For iOS device simulators, you should use the Xcode Simulator developer tool.

> **Emulator versus simulator**
>
> You will notice that Android has emulators and iOS has simulators. The Android emulator mimics the software and hardware of an Android device. In contrast, the iOS simulator only mimics the software of an iOS device. It is therefore highly recommended that you test your app on a true iOS device before releasing it to the world to ensure there are no hardware issues such as excessive memory consumption.

Alternatively, you can choose to run the app on a physical device. You will need to set up your device for development, so for the moment it is probably easier to use an emulator or simulator.

After asserting that we have a device connected that can run the app, we can use the following command:

```
flutter run
```

You will see output similar to the following:

```
[Alessandros-iMac:hello_flutter biessek$ flutter run                    ]
Launching lib/main.dart on iPhone 6s in debug mode...
Starting Xcode build...
  ├─Assembling Flutter resources...              11.8s

  └─Compiling, linking and signing...            95.8s

Xcode build done.                                129.2s
112.0s
Syncing files to device iPhone 6s...             17.0s

🔥  To hot reload changes while running, press "r". To hot restart (and rebuild
state), press "R".
An Observatory debugger and profiler on iPhone 6s is available at:
http://127.0.0.1:50832/
For a more detailed help message, press "h". To detach, press "d"; to quit,
press "q".
```

Figure 1.8 – Output from the flutter run command

This command starts the debugger and makes the hot reload functionality available, as you can see. The first run of the application will generally take a little longer than subsequent executions.

The emulator or simulator should start up and, after a pause to load the operating system, it should run your Flutter application. If you see the following screen, then congratulations. You have just run your first ever Flutter application and should be proud of yourself!

Figure 1.9 – Emulator displaying the Flutter app

The application is up and running; you can see a debug mark in the top-right corner. That means it's not a release version running; the app is in debug mode, which means you have all the debug mode goodies available to you, such as hot reload and code debug facilities.

The preceding example was run on an iPhone 6s simulator. The same result would be achieved by using an Android emulator, or an **Android virtual device (AVD)**.

Summary

In this chapter, we started playing with the Flutter framework. First, we learned some important concepts about Flutter, mainly the concepts of widgets. We saw that widgets are the central part of the Flutter world, where the Flutter team continually works to improve existing widgets and add new ones. This is because the widget concept is everywhere, from rendering performance to the final result on screen.

We also saw how to start a Flutter application project with the framework tools, the basic project structure of files, and the peculiarities of the `pubspec.yaml` file. At the end, we saw how to run a project on an emulator or simulator.

In the next chapter, we will look deeper into Dart. You have had a sneak peek when we looked at widgets and you will have seen how similar it is to other common programming languages such as Java, C#, and Swift. Dart is a great language, and I must confess it is my favorite language to work with. Hopefully, you will share some of this love by the end of the next chapter.

2
An Introduction to Dart

The Dart language is at the core of the Flutter framework. A modern framework such as Flutter requires a high-level modern language so that it can provide the best experience to the developer, as well as make it possible to create awesome mobile applications. Understanding Dart is fundamental to working with Flutter; developers need to know the origins of the Dart language, how the community is working on it, its strengths, and why it is the chosen programming language for Flutter.

In this chapter, you will review the basics of the Dart language and identify resources that can help you on your Flutter journey. You will review Dart's built-in types and operators and how Dart works with **object-oriented programming** (**OOP**). By understanding what the Dart language has to offer, you will become comfortable experimenting with Dart yourself and expand your knowledge.

The following topics will be covered in this chapter:

- Getting started with Dart
- Variables and data types
- Control flows and looping
- Functions and methods

Technical requirements

In this chapter, we will explore the Dart language. You can do this via DartPad, which will be explained later in the chapter, or within your chosen **integrated development environment** (**IDE**), as discussed in *Chapter 1, An Introduction to Flutter*.

Either option will allow you to experiment with your code. If you choose to use your IDE, then you will need to ensure your system has been configured correctly to run Dart programs. Please refer to *Chapter 1, An Introduction to Flutter* for details on how to ensure your system is ready to do this.

You can find the source code for this chapter on GitHub at the following link: `https://github.com/PacktPublishing/Flutter-for-Beginners-Second-Edition/tree/main/hello_world/lib/chapter_02`.

Getting started with Dart

Dart aims to aggregate the benefits of most of the high-level languages with mature language features, including the following:

- **Productive tooling**: This includes tools to analyze code, IDE plugins, and big package ecosystems.
- **Garbage collection**: This manages or deals with memory deallocation (mainly memory occupied by objects that are no longer in use).
- **Type annotations (optional)**: This is for those who want security and consistency to control all of the data in an application.
- **Statically typed**: Although type annotations are optional, Dart is type-safe and uses type inference to analyze types at runtime. This feature is important for finding bugs during code compilation.
- **Portability**: This is not only for the web (transpiled to JavaScript) but it can also be natively compiled to **Advanced RISC Machines** (**ARM**) and x86 code.

All Flutter development involves having intimate knowledge of the Dart language; your application code, plugin code, and management of dependencies all use the Dart language and its features. Having a strong base understanding of Dart will allow you to be more productive with Flutter and will enable you to enjoy Flutter development more. Let's take a look at the Dart language in more detail, starting with where Dart came from.

The evolution of Dart

Unveiled in 2011, Dart has been evolving ever since. Dart saw its stable release in 2013, with major changes included in the release of Dart 2.0 toward the end of 2018, as outlined here:

- Initially focused on web development at its conception, with the main aim of replacing JavaScript, it is now focused on mobile development areas, as well as Flutter.

- **It tried solving JavaScript's problems**: JavaScript doesn't provide the robustness that many consolidated languages do, so Dart wanted to bring a mature successor to JavaScript.

- **It offers the best performance and better tools for large-scale projects**: Dart has modern and stable tooling provided by IDE plugins. It has been designed to get the best possible performance while keeping the feel of a dynamic language.

- **It is molded to be robust and flexible**: By keeping the type annotations optional and adding OOP features, Dart balances the two worlds of flexibility and robustness.

Dart is a great modern, cross-platform, general-purpose language that continually improves its features, making it more mature and flexible. That's why the Flutter framework team chose the Dart language to work with.

How Dart works

To understand where the language's flexibility came from, we need to know how we can run Dart code. This is done in two ways, as outlined here:

- Dart **virtual machines** (**VMs**)

- JavaScript compilations

Have a look at the following diagram:

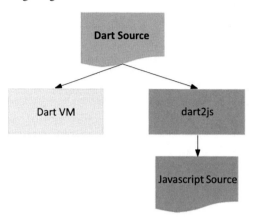

Figure 2.1 – Alternative ways to run Dart applications

As you can see, at the root of the diagram is your Dart code. It's worth noting that your code and dependency choices are agnostic to the way you run your application; there are no changes required to your code to make different options available to you.

Dart VM and JavaScript compilation

Dart code can be run in a Dart-capable environment. A Dart-capable environment provides essential features to an application, such as the following:

- Runtime systems
- Dart core libraries
- Garbage collectors

The execution of Dart code operates in two modes—**Just-In-Time** (**JIT**) compilation or **Ahead-Of-Time** (**AOT**) compilation. These are described in more detail here:

- A JIT compilation is where the source code is compiled as it is needed—just in time. The Dart VM loads and compiles the source code to native machine code on the fly. This approach is used to run code on the command line or during mobile application development to allow the use of features such as debugging and hot reload.

- An AOT compilation is where the Dart VM and your code are precompiled and the VM works more like a Dart runtime system, providing a garbage collector and various native methods from the Dart **software development kit** (**SDK**) to the application. This approach has huge performance benefits over JIT compilations, but other features such as debugging and hot reload are not available.

> **Hot reload**
>
> Dart contributes to Flutter's most famous feature, hot reload, which is based on the Dart JIT compiler. This allows developers to get very fast feedback on code changes, allowing them to iterate much quicker, leading to faster and higher-quality software development.

Before we start playing with Dart, let's understand a few fundamental aspects of the language.

Introducing the structure of the Dart language

If you already know some programming languages inspired by the old C language or have some experience with JavaScript, much of the Dart syntax will be easy for you to understand. Dart provides most of the standard operators for manipulating variables; the built-in types are the most common ones found in high-level programming languages, and the control flows and functions are very similar to what you will have experienced elsewhere.

Object orientation

As with most modern languages, Dart is designed to be **object-oriented** (**OO**). Briefly, OOP languages are based on the concept of **objects** that hold both data (called **fields**) and code (called **methods**). These objects are created from blueprints called **classes** that define the fields and methods an object will have.

Following OO principles ensures that Dart has the benefits of encapsulation, inheritance, composition, abstraction, and polymorphism. We will explore Dart classes in much more detail in *Chapter 4*, *Dart Classes and Constructs*, but suffice to say that if you have seen OO in other languages such as Java, then much of the Dart OO design will be very similar.

Dart operators

In Dart, operators are nothing more than methods defined in classes with a special syntax.

So, when you use operators such as x == y, it is as though you are invoking the x.==(y) method to compare equality.

As you might have noted, we are invoking a method on x. For all data types, unlike languages such as Java that have primitives, x is always an instance of a class that has methods. This means that operators can be overridden so that you can write your own logic for them.

Arithmetic operators

Dart comes with many typical operators that work like many languages; this includes the following:

- + for addition.

- - for subtraction.

- * for multiplication.

- / for division.

- ~/ for integer division. In Dart, any simple division with / results in a double value. To get only the integer part, you would need to make some kind of transformation (that is, typecast) in other programming languages; however, here, the integer division operator does this task.

- % for modulo operations (the remainder of integer division).

- -expression for negation (which reverses the sign of expression).

Some operators have different behavior depending on the left operand type; for example, the + operator can be used to sum variables of the num type, but also to concatenate strings. This is because the method they refer to is implemented differently in the different classes.

Dart also provides shortcut operators to combine an assignment to a variable after another operation. The arithmetic or assignment shortcut operators are +=, -=, *=, /=, and ~/=.

Increment and decrement operators

The increment and decrement operators are also common operators and are implemented on numbers, as follows:

- ++var or var++ to increment the value of the variable var by 1

- --var or var-- to decrement the value of the variable var by 1

The Dart increment and decrement operators behave similarly to other languages. A good application of increment and decrement operators is for count operations on loops.

Equality and relational operators

The equality Dart operators are described as follows:

- == checks whether operands are equal

- != checks whether operands are different

For relational tests, the following operators are used:

- `>` checks whether the left operand is greater than the right one
- `<` checks whether the left operand is less than the right one
- `>=` checks whether the left operand is greater than or equal to the right one
- `<=` checks whether the left operand is less than or equal to the right one

In Dart, unlike Java and many other languages, the `==` operator does not compare memory references but rather the content of the variable.

Also, unlike JavaScript, there is no `===` operator required because Dart type safety ensures that the `==` equality operator is only used on objects of the same type.

Logical operators

Logical operators in Dart are operators applied to `bool` operands; they can be variables, expressions, or conditions. Additionally, they can be combined with complex expressions by combining the evaluated value of the expression. The provided logical operators are described here:

- `!expression` negates the result of an expression—that is, true to false and false to true.
- `||` applies a logical `OR` operation between two expressions.
- `&&` applies a logical `AND` operation between two expressions.

Now we know the fundamentals of the Dart programming language, let's take a look at some real code!

Hands-on with Dart

The way Flutter is designed is heavily influenced by the Dart language, so knowing this language is crucial for success in the framework. Let's start by writing some code to understand the basics of the syntax and the available tools for Dart development.

DartPad

The easiest way to start coding is to use the DartPad tool, which you can access at the following link: `https://dartpad.dartlang.org/`.

This is a great online tool for learning and experimenting with Dart's language features. It supports Dart's core libraries, except for VM libraries such as dart:io.

This is what the tool looks like, although the code presented in the tool may be different:

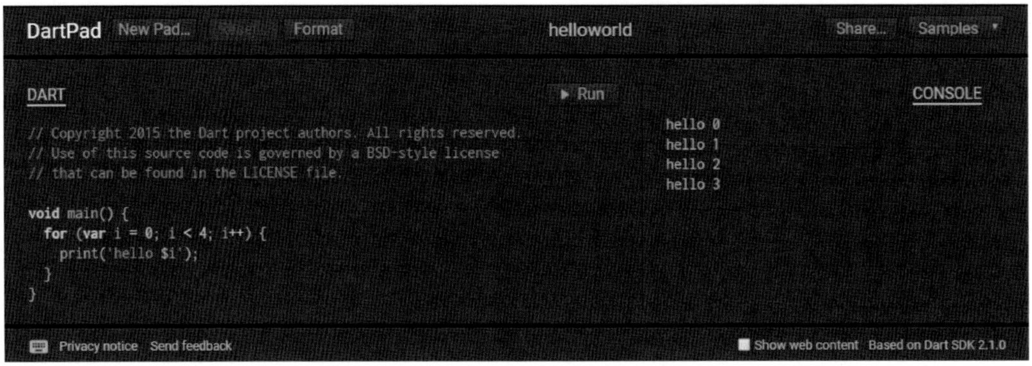

Figure 2.2 – Initial view of the DartPad tool

When you open DartPad, you are presented with an initial piece of code.

If it isn't already in the DartPad tool, replace the code in the tool with the following code so that you can run your first piece of Dart code:

```dart
void main() {
    for (int i = 0; i < 5; i++) {
        print('hello ${i + 1}');
    }
}
```

We will explore this preceding piece of code in the next section, so don't worry if it looks a little complicated. However, try running it in the DartPad tool by pressing the Run button, and you should see console output similar to this:

```
hello 1
hello 2
hello 3
hello 4
hello 5
```

> **Running locally**
>
> If you choose to run this code locally on your machine, then save the contents
> to a Dart file and run it with a Dart tool in a terminal—for example, save it
> to a file named `hello_world.dart` and then run the `dart hello_`
> `world.dart` command. This will execute the `main` function of the
> Dart script.

Let's look at the code you have in DartPad in more detail.

Hello world Dart style

The code you are presented with in DartPad looks similar to this:

```dart
void main() {
  for (int i = 0; i < 5; i++) {
    print('hello ${i + 1}');
  }
}
```

This code contains some basic language features that need highlighting. In this chapter,
we will explore the fundamentals of the Dart language that will allow someone already
experienced in basic programming to apply that knowledge to Dart.

If you feel you need a deeper introduction to the basics of programming, then the perfect
complementary book is *Learning Dart,* by Dzenan Ridjanovic.

Main function

As with most modern languages, Dart uses functions and methods as a way to break up
code. A function or a method is a chunk of code that (optionally) receives some data, runs
the code, and then (optionally) returns some data.

The function from the hello world example looks like this:

```dart
void main() {
  ...
}
```

The first line has several important pieces of information, outlined as follows:

- The data type that is returned from the method is defined first. In this case, `void` denotes that the method does not return any data when it has completed execution. `void` is a keyword in the Dart language that can only be used in specific circumstances to denote the absence of data. We will look at data types in the next section.

- The name of the function comes next—in this case, `main`. The name is used by other pieces of code to reference this method, and, in this specific case, `main` is the function name that the Dart VM searches for when it first starts running code. Every Dart application must have an entry point top-level function so that the Dart VM knows where to start code execution. The `main` function serves this purpose.

- The empty parentheses are where a function defines the data it expects to receive. This `main` function does not receive any data, hence the empty parentheses. We will look at the way a function can define the expected data later in the chapter.

- Finally, a curly bracket at the end of the first line specifies where the function code starts, and the closing curly bracket several lines later specifies where the function code ends. Unlike with some languages such as Python, the indentation or layout of the code is irrelevant to how the code is executed.

> **Function versus method**
>
> Functions and methods have identical syntax (the rules about how they are structured), and often the terms **function** and **method** are used interchangeably, so what is the difference? Specifically, a **function** exists outside of a class (we will look at classes later in the chapter). The `main` function is an example of this. Conversely, a **method** is tied to an instance of a class and has an implicit reference to the class instance via the `this` keyword.

So, you now know that the code is executed because the Dart VM searches for a `main` function, finds the one written above it, and then calls that function. We've also learned about the `void` data type. Let's take a look at the other data types available in Dart.

Variables and data types

Variables are key to any programming language, holding application state so that the correct execution flow can be followed, displaying the correct information to the user, and interacting with other systems through defined data structures.

Unstructured data can be dangerous, though, and may lead to bugs and difficult-to-maintain code. Therefore, a rich set of data types is required in a modern programming language. Let's explore this area of the Dart language, starting with the basics of declaring a variable.

Variable declaration

Variables store references to data and are key to decision making within your application. Variables have to be declared before they can be used.

A variable declaration follows many of the rules of similar programming languages, but due to type inference, Dart variable declaration can be looser.

The structure of a variable declaration is shown here:

```
type identifier = value;
```

`type` defines the data type that the variable can hold, such as a number or piece of text. If the variable can hold any type of data then it can be declared with the `dynamic` type. The type can simply be set to `var` if the Dart analyzer can infer the variable's type from the assigned value or later code. If the Dart analyzer is unable to infer the type, then the variable becomes the `dynamic` type.

`identifier` is a name you give to the variable that describes the data it is holding. There are rules defining what an identifier must be, and these are outlined here:

- Cannot be a keyword such as `new` or `class`
- Must contain alphabetical characters and numbers
- Cannot contain spaces and special characters except the underscore (_) and dollar ($) characters
- Cannot begin with a number

`value` is an initial value that the variable holds from a declaration.

Variables can receive new values at any point. The type is already known, so a change in variable value is simply achieved with the following code:

```
identifier = value;
```

Let's look at some examples of variable declarations, as follows:

```dart
var inferredString = "Hello"; // Type inferred as String
String explicitString = "World";
```

In these variable declarations, we show the following:

- An inferred declaration of `inferredString` where the type is inferred from the assigned value, the `"hello"` string
- A variable declaration where we use the explicit type of `String` for the `explicitString` variable

Both declaration approaches are acceptable because the types of both variables are unambiguous.

Null safety

Dart has support for a variable to have no value, called `null`. The use of the `null` value has been restricted in the latest releases of Dart; previously, you could assign any variable a `null` value at declaration or any later point. Now, you need to declare that a variable can accept the `null` value by specifying this on the variable's type when the variable is declared.

You may see older code that allows `null` without the explicit type declaration, simply because the change is very recent. In previous releases, this code would have been acceptable:

```dart
int newNumber; // newNumber is initialized to null
print(newNumber); // Prints null
newNumber = 42; // Update the value of newNumber
print(newNumber); // Prints 42
```

In Dart 2.12.0 and later, this code would no longer be allowed, showing errors within your IDE. There are two options available to declare the nullability of a variable. Let's look at both options.

? declaration

To specify that a variable can be set to the null value, you can add a ? character to the type of the variable. Therefore, to fix the preceding code example, we only need to add one character and the errors will be removed, as illustrated in the following code snippet:

```
int? newNumber; // newNumber type allows nullability
print(newNumber); // Prints null
newNumber = 42; // Update the value of newNumber
print(newNumber); // Prints 42
```

If you didn't spot it, we added a ? character after the int type. Now, the newNumber variable can either take an int or a null value.

Late variables

There are times when you know a variable will have a value set before that value is accessed, but the variable's value cannot be initialized immediately at variable declaration. An example of this in Flutter is where a variable is declared with no value, but immediately at widget initialization, it is given a value. If we were forced to do null checks every time we accessed the variable, our code would be harder to read and maintain.

To solve this problem, Dart has the late type modifier. This tells Dart that you are completely confident that at the point the variable's value is accessed, the variable will have already been set to a value.

Let's update the example to show that in action, as follows:

```
late int newNumber; // newNumber type allows nullability
// Do some initialisation stuff
newNumber = 42; // Update the value of newNumber
print(newNumber); // Prints 42
```

In the updated example, we declare newNumber with no value, but this is allowed because we have said, using the late modifier, that the value will be set before it is accessed. Later, we do set the value as we promised, and then the value access (within the print method) happens after the value is set.

Accessing nullable variables

As you would expect, if a variable can have a `null` value, then you will need to check if it is `null` before you use it. For example, suppose we have a variable that stores how many goals a team has scored, but before the match starts, it is set to `null`. The following code would show errors:

```
int? goals;
// Other code
print(goals + 2);
```

The `goals` variable is still potentially `null` at the point of the `print` statement, so adding 2 to `null` is not a valid operation—hence the errors from the Dart compiler.

To solve this problem, you can explicitly check if the variable is `null` and only access the value if it is not `null`. If it is not `null`, then Dart remembers this and will treat the variable as if it is no longer nullable. For example, the following code is allowed:

```
int? goals;
// Other code
If (goals != null) {
    print(goals + 2);
}
```

During the `if` statement, you have checked that the `goals` variable is not `null`. Dart then remembers that this check has taken place and allows for the `print` statement to show `goals` with 2 added to it.

Null-aware methods

Sometimes, you will need to call a method on a variable where the variable's type specifies that it can be null. The same approach of checking whether the variable is null will allow you to call the method without the compiler giving an error, as shown here:

```
String? goalScorer;
// Other code
if (goalScorer != null) {
    print(goalScorer.length);
}
```

In this code sample, we're checking if `goalScorer` is null, and only if it isn't null do we call the `length` method on it.

Another option that's available to you is to use the ? . null-aware method operator. This will only call the method if the variable is not null; otherwise, it will simply return null.

We can then rewrite the previous code sample so that it looks like this:

```
String? goalScorer;
// Other code
print(goalScorer?.length);
```

If this code sample runs and the goalScorer value is null, then the length method doesn't get called, and the print statement prints "null." However, if the goalScorer value is not null, then the length method does get called, and the length of String is printed.

Null-assertion operator

As we saw previously, if we can prove to the compiler that a variable is not null, then we can use the value of the variable or call methods on it. However, there are some situations where the business logic denotes that a variable is not null, but the compiler does not know that.

For example, take a look at this code:

```
int? goalTime;
String? goalScorer;
bool goalScored = false;
// Other code
if (goalScored) {
    goalTime = 21;
    goalScorer = "Bobby";
}
// More code
if (goalTime != null) {
    print(goalScorer.length);
}
```

In this (somewhat convoluted) example, the goalScorer value always gets set at the same time as the goalTime value. Therefore, we know that if goalTime is not null then goalScorer is not null. However, we haven't proved that to the compiler; we only know this is the case because our business logic determines that if there is time for a goal, then someone must have scored it.

To cope with these situations, we can use the ! (exclamation point) null assertion operator, which tells the compiler that we are confident that the variable is not null, so go ahead and use it. Note that if we are wrong, it will cause an exception, so use the ! operator carefully.

Let's look at it in action by modifying the final `print` statement so that it's compile safe:

```
if (goalTime != null) {
    print(goalScorer!.length);
}
```

In this example, we have added ! to say that we are confident that the `goalScorer` variable is not null. The compiler trusts that we are right about this.

When Dart moved to null safety, it was interesting that the team behind Dart decided to change the language's default behavior. Instead of allowing existing code to work without changes (backward compatibility), they decided that forcing all code developers to re-evaluate their code with regard to null safety was important enough that it should be forced upon them. Although at the time this was a relatively painful process, many bugs and code improvements have happened throughout the Flutter ecosystem (applications, plugins, tooling), meaning Flutter is in an even better position after the switch to null safety.

Built-in types

Dart is a type-safe programming language, which means that when the code is written and compiled, each variable must have a defined type. This is in contrast to languages such as JavaScript where the variable's type is not defined and can change while the code is running. This can lead to issues at runtime, where the expected type of a variable doesn't match the actual type.

Although types are mandatory, type annotations are optional, which means that you don't need to specify the type of a variable when you declare it, as long as Dart can infer the type.

First, let's look at how a variable is declared, and then we can look at the types a variable can take.

Here are the built-in data types in Dart:

- Numbers (such as num, int, and double)
- Booleans (such as bool)
- Collections (such as lists, arrays, and maps)
- Strings and runes (for expressing Unicode characters in a string)

Let's explore each built-in data type in detail, starting with numbers.

Numbers

Dart represents numbers in two ways, outlined as follows:

- `int`: 64-bit signed non-fractional integer values such as -263 to 263-1.
- `double`: Dart represents fractional numeric values with a 64-bit double-precision floating-point number.

Both of them extend the `num` type. Additionally, we have many handy functions in the `dart:math` library to help with calculations, such as the following ones:

- `Random` to generate a random bool or number
- `Min` or `Max` to find the larger or lesser of two numbers
- Trigonometric functions (sine, cosine, tangent)

In JavaScript, numbers are compiled to JavaScript numbers and allow the values -253 to 253-1.

> **BigInt**
>
> Dart also has the `BigInt` type for representing arbitrary precision integers, which means that the size is only limited by your computer's **random-access memory** (**RAM**). This type can be very useful depending on the context; however, it does not have the same performance as `num` types, so you should carefully consider when to use it.

Booleans

Dart provides two well-known literal values for the `bool` type: true and false.

Boolean types are simple truth values that can be useful for any logic. Unlike in JavaScript where everything with a value is true and everything without a value is false, Dart is strict about Boolean types and does not follow the same *truthy* and *falsy* approach.

Lists

In Dart, lists bring together the functionality of array and `List` types present in other programming languages, with some handy methods to manipulate elements. These types are outlined here:

- The `[index]` operator allows convenient access to the elements at a given index.
- The + operator can be used to concatenate two lists by returning a new list with the left operand followed by the right one.

Note that Dart lists are not naturally length-constrained, as arrays in some languages can be. Lists grow and shrink as needed through the use of the add and remove methods.

Note that a list should be created using the square brackets literal. In fact, creation of a list using the List type name is now deprecated. Here are some examples of the creation of a List:

```dart
List dynamicList = [];
print(dynamicList.length); // Prints 0
dynamicList.add("Hello");
print(dynamicList[0]); // Prints "World"
print(dynamicList.length); // Prints 1
List preFilledDynamicList = [1, 2, 3];
print(preFilledDynamicList[0]); // Prints 1
print(preFilledDynamicList.length); // Prints 3
```

> **Semicolon**
>
> In the preceding example, each line of code ends with a semicolon. This is required in Dart to show the end of a statement. Statements can be written across multiple lines but must terminate with a semicolon.

During list creation, a length can be set to enforce a fixed size. Lists with a fixed size cannot be expanded, so you need to ensure it is clear that a List has been created with a fixed size. The code to accomplish this is illustrated in the following snippet:

```dart
List fixedList = List.filled(3, "World");
fixedList.add("Hello"); // Error
fixedList[0] = "Hello";
print(fixedList[0]); // Prints "Hello";
print(fixedList[1]); // Prints "World";
```

> **The new keyword**
>
> In many OO languages, instances of classes such as Lists are created using the new keyword. This was also true in the Dart language but is now no longer used. However, note that it is still a reserved keyword, so you cannot name variables new.

Maps

Dart Maps are dynamic collections for storing key-value pairs, where the retrieval and modification of a value are always performed through its associated key. Both the key and value can have any type. You can see an example of this here:

```
Map nameAgeMap = {};
nameAgeMap["Alice"] = 23;
print(nameAgeMap["Alice"]); // Prints 23
```

Strings

In Dart, strings are a sequence of characters (**Unicode Transformation Format-16 (UTF-16)** code) that are mainly used to represent text. Dart strings can be single or multiple lines and use matching single or double quotes to wrap the text. You can see an example here:

```
String singleQuoteString = 'Here is a single quote string';
String doubleQuoteString = "Here is a double quote string";
```

Additionally, multiline strings can be created using matching triple single quotes or triple double quotes, as illustrated in the following code snippet:

```
String multiLineString = '''Here is a multi-line single
   quote string''';
```

Note that the indentation on the second line will be included in the created string.

Strings can be concatenated (stuck together) using the plus (+) operator, as illustrated in the following code snippet. In addition, the multiplier (*) operator is used where the string gets repeated a specified number of times, and the [index] operator retrieves the character at the specified index position:

```
String str1 = 'Here is a ';
String str2 = str1 + 'concatenated string';
print(str2); // Prints Here is a concatenated string
```

String interpolation

String interpolation (or, as I prefer, variable expansion) is the action of evaluating placeholders within a string and then concatenating the results. Dart has a simple syntax for string interpolation: ${ }.

The dollar ($) symbol identifies the placeholders to be evaluated. If this evaluation is a single variable, then the curly brackets can be omitted (and if not omitted, then a warning is shown). For a placeholder that involves more than the evaluation of a single variable, the curly brackets denote the boundary of evaluation.

Here are some examples to explain this concept further:

```
String someString = "Happy string";
print("The string is: $someString");
// prints The string is: Happy string
// No curly brackets were required
print("The string length is: ${someString.length}");
// prints The string length is: 16
// Curly brackets were required
print("The string length is: $someString.length");
// prints The string length is: Happy string.length
// Omitting the curly brackets meant only the variable was
evaluated, not the method on the variable.
```

Dart also has the runes concept to represent UTF-32 bits. For more details, check out the Dart language tour at https://dart.dev/guides/language/language-tour.

Literals

A literal is a notation to represent a fixed value. You have likely already used some of these before. Here is a quick recap of literal examples for the common types:

Type	Literal example
int	10, 1, -1, 5, and 0
double	10.1, 1.2, 3.123, and -1.2
bool	true and false
String	"Dart", 'Dash', and """multiline String"""
List	[1, 2, 3] and ["one", "two", "three"]
Map	{"key1": "val1", "key2": "val2"} and {"Sarah": 1, "Lisa": 2}

Const and final

If you have a variable that will not change in value then you can define it as a constant. If the value of the variable can be defined at compile time, for example, if it has a literal value, then you would use the const modifier to specify the variable as a constant. For example:

```
const String someString = "Happy string";
```

However, if the value will be set once, but that value is not known as compile time, then use the final modifier instead. For example:

```
final String someString = DateTime.now().toString();
```

Although, you do not need to use these modifiers, when we look at widgets in future chapters, and specifically stateless widgets, you should set your variables as final because a stateless widget should not, by definition, be able to mutate its state. Using final variables ensures this cannot happen.

With that, you have learned how to store data in a type-safe and null-safe way. Now, let's see how we can use that data within our code.

Control flows and looping

Before we can finish exploring the `main` method in DartPad, we need to know how to control the flow of code execution. This is done through a series of control flow statements. These are very similar to other programming languages, so let's see what they look like in Dart.

If/else

Dart supports the standard `if`, `else if`, `else` decision structure. It also supports `if` statements without curly brackets, which are especially useful during Flutter widget definitions. In these `if` statements, the next expression is evaluated if the condition is `true`. You can see an example of this in the following code snippet:

```
String test = "test2";
if (test == "test1") {
  print("Test1");
} else if (test == "test2") {
  print("Test2");
} else {
```

```
    print("Something else");
}
// Prints Test2
If (test == "test2")
    print("Test2 again"); // Prints Test 2
```

In the first example, we have initialized a variable called `test` and assigned it the `String` value `"test2"`. We then use an `if/else` statement to compare the value against the `String` literal `"test1"`, which will fail the comparison.

The code execution then moves to the first `else` statement because the first comparison evaluated to the `false` Boolean value and will evaluate the `if` statement defined in that `else` statement to check against the `String` literal `"test2"`. This combination of `else` followed by `if` is called an **else-if** statement, and you can have as many of these in an **if-else** statement as you require.

The `test == "test2"` condition evaluates to the `true` Boolean value, so code execution enters that branch of the code and prints `"Test2"` and then ends execution of the `if/else` statement, moving execution below the final `else` statement.

However, if this comparison had also been evaluated as the `false` Boolean value, then we would finally have had a catch-all `else` statement that would have been executed regardless of the variable's value.

In the second `if` statement, we evaluate the `test == "test2"` condition again, but this time we do not wrap the code branch in curly brackets. The line immediately after the `if` statement is run, printing `"Test2 again"`.

These `if/else` structures should be familiar to you if you have worked with other programming languages.

As mentioned previously, Dart does not deal with *truthy* and *falsy* concepts, unlike JavaScript. All conditions must evaluate to Boolean values, as illustrated in the following code snippet:

```
String test = "true";
if (test) { // Creates a compilation error
    print("Truthy");
}
```

The example will not compile because `test` is not a **Boolean**, so the condition does not evaluate to a Boolean value.

> **Equality checking and type coercion**
>
> In languages such as JavaScript, the equality of two variables can be checked either with the double equals or the triple equals operator, where the former checks whether the values match after attempting to coerce them to a similar type and the latter checks whether both the values and their type match. For example, in JavaScript, "7" == 7 evaluates to true, but "7" === 7 evaluates to false. This can lead to unexpected bugs and is not an approach that many programming languages follow because of this. Dart only has the double equals operator and does not do type coercion.

While and do-while loops

While and do-while control flows loop on a specific piece of code while their condition evaluates to true, and then when their condition evaluates to false, the loop is exited and code execution continues after the loop.

A do-while loop differs from a while loop by having the condition evaluate at the end of the first loop, therefore ensuring at least one execution of the code contained inside.

Let's look at some examples, as follows:

```
int counter = 0;
while (counter < 2) {
   print(counter);
   counter++;
}
// Prints 0, 1
do {
   print(counter);
   counter++;
} while (counter < 2);
// Prints 2
```

The counter variable is initialized as an int type and is assigned the value of 0. The code flow then enters the while loop and the condition is evaluated. At this point, the counter variable has a value less than 2, so the flow enters the loop, printing the counter value and incrementing the counter variable.

After completing the loop code, the loop condition is re-evaluated, and again the counter variable has a value less than 2, so the flow enters the loop again.

Finally, the value of the `counter` variable is 2, so the loop condition evaluates to `false` and the code flow moves to after the end of the loop.

The flow then enters the `do/while` loop. There is no conditional check at the start of the `do/while` loop, so the code in the loop is executed. At the end of the loop, the condition is checked and evaluates to `false`, meaning the loop is exited.

For loops

For loops follow this standard structure:

```
for (initialize; loop_condition; modify) {}
```

This is broken down into the following:

- `initialize`, where variables are initialized to manage the iteration
- `loop_condition`, where looping continues only if the condition evaluates to true
- `modify`, where variables can be modified on each loop to track progression

The following example will help make this clearer:

```
for (int index = 0; index < 2; index++) {
    print(index);
}
// Prints 0, 1
```

In the preceding example, the `index` variable is initialized to 0, and the `loop_` condition is evaluated to `true`. On each subsequent iteration, the `index` variable is incremented by 1 and then the `loop_` condition is re-evaluated, first to `true` and then to `false` when `index` reaches 2.

break and continue

Sometimes, it can be tricky to break out of a loop or start the next iteration of a loop without creating confusing code to manipulate the condition.

Adding a `break` statement to a loop allows you to jump out of the loop immediately, and adding a `continue` statement allows you to start the next iteration of the loop immediately.

Here is an example to help clarify this:

```
int counter = 0;
while (counter < 10) {
  counter++;
  if (counter == 4) {
    break;
  } else if (counter == 2) {
    continue;
  }
  print(counter);
}
// Prints 1, 3
```

In the preceding example, on the first iteration, the counter variable is incremented to 1; neither of the `if` conditions evaluate to true, so the value is printed.

On the second iteration, the counter variable is incremented to 2, so the `continue` statement is called before the `print` statement.

On the third iteration, the counter is incremented to 3; neither of the `if` conditions evaluate to true, so the value is printed.

On the fourth iteration, the counter variable is incremented to 4 and the `break` statement is called, breaking out of the loop and ending the code.

Hands-on continued

Let's look back at the DartPad `main` method. More of that should make sense to us now. You can see a representation of this here:

```
void main() {
  for (int i = 0; i < 5; i++) {
    print('hello ${i + 1}');
  }
}
```

We have explored the surrounding `main` function, but the code inside the function should now also be familiar.

We have learned about `for` loops, and in this code snippet, the `for` loop initializes the `i` variable to 0 and then loops until `i` reaches the value of 5, incrementing the value of `i` on each iteration.

Within the `for` loop, we have a `print` function. This function simply prints text to the terminal. As a `print` statement argument, we can see some string interpolation. This evaluates the value of `i + 1` and then concatenates it on the end of `hello` to make a **String** for printing to the screen.

We briefly looked at the `main` function and how that is structured. We've now encountered the `print` function as well, so now is a good point to look at functions and their parameters.

Functions and methods

As we discussed previously, functions and methods are self-contained chunks of code that work on a specific task. Note that the syntax of methods and functions is identical, so where I refer to functions in this section, I am also referring to methods. Let's look at another example of a function, as follows:

```
String sayHello() {
    return "Hello world!";
}
```

This `sayHello` function structure is very similar to the `main` function we explored previously but also includes a return type of `String`, so the function must have a `return` statement at the end that returns a value of the expected type. In this example, the function returns a `String` literal of `"Hello world!"`. If the function could return a `String` literal or `null` then, as we saw in the *Null safety* section, we would mark the function's return type as `String?`.

Note that the function return type can be omitted because the Dart analyzer can infer the return type from the `return` statement. If no `return` statement is provided, it assumes the function returns a **dynamic** type. If you want to tell the analyzer that the function will never return anything, you should mark it as `void`, as we saw in the `main` method earlier. Note that it is preferable to include the return type on the function signature to ensure that the code is easily understood and maintainable long term.

Try adding the `sayHello` function in DartPad, and then, in the `main` method, replace the `for` loop with a call to the `sayHello` function so that it looks something like this:

```
void main() {
    String helloMessage = sayHello();
    print(helloMessage);
```

```
    }
String sayHello() {
    return "Hello world!";
}
```

In this example, the `sayHello` function is a top-level function—in other words, it does not need a class to exist. Although Dart is an OO language, it is not necessary to write classes to encapsulate functions.

Run this in DartPad and you should see the output `"Hello world!"`. Congratulations—you just wrote your first Dart code and ran it successfully!

In Dart, `Function` is a type, like `String` or `num`. This means that it can also be assigned to fields or local variables or passed as parameters to other functions. Consider the following change to the `main` method:

```
void main() {
    var helloFunction = sayHello();
    String helloMessage = helloFunction();
    print(helloMessage);
}
```

It feels as though we've been saying hello to the world a lot in this chapter, but we've learned a lot about the Dart language. However, we still haven't explored what can go in those brackets defining the input data for the function. Let's take a look at that now.

Function parameters

A function can have two types of parameters: optional and required. Additionally, these parameters can be named instead of positional to make the code more readable. This is especially true in Flutter where widgets can have lots of optional parameters, so identifying which argument is for which parameter is critical to understanding the code and diagnosing issues.

> **Parameter versus argument**
>
> The term **parameter** refers to the entries in the function signature defining the input data types and names. An argument is the data passed to the function when it is called from another point in the code. The argument types when calling the function must match the parameter types on the function definition, either directly or through polymorphism.

A parameter's type doesn't need to be specified; in this case, the parameter assumes the **dynamic** type. Again, for long-term code readability and maintainability, adding parameter types is highly preferable.

Required positional parameters

This simplest function definition is achieved by defining positional parameters. This is the most common approach in other programming languages, so you will probably already be confident with this approach. The parameters are listed in order, and the arguments supplied when calling the function simply match the same ordering.

In the following function, both `name` and `age` are required positional parameters, so the caller must specify matching arguments in the same order when calling it:

```
sayHappyBirthday(String name, int age) {
   return "$name is ${age.toString()} years old";
}
```

To call this function, you would have something similar to this:

```
sayHappyBirthday("Laura", 21);
```

Optional positional parameters

Sometimes, not all parameters need to be mandatory for a function, so you can specify optional parameters on the function signature as well. The optional positional parameter definition is specified using the [ ] syntax. Optional positional parameters must go after all of the required positional parameters, as follows:

```
sayHappyBirthday(String name, [int? age]) {
   return "$name is $age years old";
}
```

If you run the preceding code without passing a value for `age`, you will see `null` in the returned string. When an optional parameter is not specified, the default value is `null`, hence the type definition needs to include a ? character to show it could be `null`. To help with this, you can specify default values for optional positional parameters.

To define a default value for a parameter, simply initialize the parameter value directly in the parameter definition, as illustrated in the following code snippet. This will be overwritten if the caller supplies an argument for that parameter:

```
sayHappyBirthday(String name, [int age = 21]) {
    return "Happy birthday $name! You are $age years old.";
}
```

Not specifying the parameter results in printing the default message, as follows:

```
void main() {
    var hello = sayHello('Robert');
    print(hello);
}
// Prints Happy birthday Robert! You are 21 years old.
```

Named parameters

Named parameter definitions are specified using the { } syntax. These definitions must also go after all the required parameters. As with optional positioned parameters, named parameters can have a default value, as illustrated in the following code snippet:

```
sayHappyBirthday(String name, {int age = 7}) {
    return "Happy birthday $name! You are $age years old.";
}
```

To specify a value for age, the caller must include the name of the optional named parameter, as follows:

```
sayHappyBirthday("Laura", age: 21);
```

By default, named parameters are optional; the calling function does not need to include an argument to match the parameter. However, named parameters can be specified as required by marking them with required, as illustrated in the following code snippet:

```
sayHappyBirthday(String name, {required int age}) {
    return "Happy birthday $name! You are $age years old.";
}
```

If the caller does not include the age named parameter in its arguments, then the Dart analyzer will show an error against the calling code.

Anonymous functions

Dart functions are objects and they can be passed as parameters to other functions, as we saw previously.

An anonymous function is a function that doesn't have a name; it is also called a lambda or closure. The forEach() function on a List is a good example of this; we need to pass a function to it that will be executed with each of the list collection elements, as follows:

```dart
void main() {
  List = [1, 2, 3, 4];
  list.forEach((number) => print('hello $number'));
}
```

Our anonymous function receives an item but does not specify a type; then, it just prints the value received by the parameter.

Lexical scope

Dart is lexically scoped, meaning that the layout of the code determines the scope for variables. So, inner functions can access variables all the way up to the global level, as illustrated in the following code snippet:

```dart
globalFunction() {
  print("Top-level globalFunction");
}
simpleFunction() {
  print("SimpleFunction");
  globalFunction() {
    print("Nested globalFunction");
  }
  globalFunction();
}
main() {
  simpleFunction();
  globalFunction();
}
```

When main calls simpleFunction, then the nested globalFunction function is defined, blocking access to the top-level globalFunction function. When globalFunction is called, it is the nested version that is called.

In contrast, when the main function calls the globalFunction function, the top-level globalFunction function is called because, in this scope, the nested globalFunction function from simpleFunction is not defined.

Hence, the output from calling the main method is this:

```
simpleFunction
Nested globalFunction
Top-level globalFunction
```

Summary

In this second chapter, we presented the available tools to start your Dart language studies, discovered what a basic Dart program looks like, and learned about the basic Dart code structure.

We demonstrated how the Dart SDK works and the tools it provides that help with Flutter application development and making the Flutter framework succeed in its objectives.

We reviewed some important concepts of the Dart language, introduced Dart OOP, looked at the data types available, saw how null safety is a key part of variable data types, investigated functions and their range of parameter specifications such as named/positional and optional/required, and explored how to control code execution flow.

There are still areas of the Dart language that we haven't yet explored, and these will be introduced as we progress through the book. However, you now have sufficient knowledge of Dart to get up and running and build your first Flutter application—exciting, isn't it?

In the next chapter, we will look at how Flutter compares to the other frameworks available to application developers.

3
Flutter versus Other Frameworks

Making a technology choice is rarely simple, and generally requires understanding the pros and cons of the different options, and eventually a leap of faith. You may be at the point where you are deciding whether your next project is going to be Flutter based, you may have dabbled with Flutter and want to solidify your knowledge before pushing forward with it, or you may be experienced and want a knowledge refresher. Regardless of your experience, it is always useful to understand the technology landscape and understand the synergies between different frameworks.

In this chapter, you will see how Flutter compares to other frameworks: the similarities and differences, the pros and cons of the different options, and how existing knowledge of another framework can be applied to Flutter. Even if you are fully decided on using Flutter in the future, it is worth reviewing this chapter as it gives context to some of the design decisions that have been made.

The following topics will be covered in this chapter:

- Native development
- Cross-platform frameworks
- Flutter community
- Flutter strengths and weaknesses

Native development

Often cited as the purest solution, **native development** refers to writing apps in the language common to the platform of the device. For iOS this is Swift (or previously, Objective-C), for Android it is Kotlin (or previously, Java), and for the web it is generally HTML/JavaScript:

Figure 3.1 – Swift and Kotlin logos

Native is seen as the purest solution because there is no bridge between the app and the platform, or no transpilation of code. Therefore, the code that is developed is the code that is run and talks directly to the features available from the platform, be that iOS, Android, or the web browser. Once you move away from native development, you introduce certain risks, such as the following:

- The software bridge having slow performance or deep, difficult to diagnose, bugs

- The transpilation process having deep, difficult to diagnose, bugs

- A lack of access to key platform features

It is therefore critically important that the quality of alternatives is assessed when moving away from native programming as a fundamental problem in an alternative framework can block and even invalidate an app.

> **Learning from experience 1**
>
> A real-world example of a framework problem invalidating an app happened to me a few years ago. We were using a cross-platform solution and were developing and testing on iOS. The framework effectively used a software bridge by embedding a web browser in the app, with the app running within the embedded web browser (we will see examples of this later). Once the app was nearing completion, we started testing on Android and found that the software bridge had serious performance issues that were fundamental and could not be worked around. After much heartache, the app was eventually only released on iOS, and an important lesson had been learned!

So, if native development is likely to have the best performance, the least chance of fundamental issues, and is the least likely to have deep bugs, why would you ever move away from native? There are many reasons, but like I said earlier, a technology decision is rarely clear-cut. Let's explore the many factors that can contribute to taking the decision to move away from native programming.

Developers

Many software projects have their technology choices decided not by careful consideration of the different technology options, cross-referenced against expected development timelines, with performance benchmarks and UI studies brought to bear. Let's be honest, most technology choices are either based on the skillset available, or the skillset that developers would like to learn next.

Learning a new programming language and framework will delay a project, sometimes seriously, and the code developed early in the project will be rewritten many times as developers learn to structure their code better, encounter different design methodologies, and optimize the execution flows.

This initial delay has to be taken into account when assessing technology choices; the best technology choice may not be the best project choice. If you already have a pool of developers, then the benefits of a technology change may be more than consumed by the reduction in productivity.

On the flip side, native developers tend to be more expensive and in higher demand than developers for other technologies. Additionally, learning a new skillset may initially reduce productivity, but for longer-running projects you would expect productivity to recover.

Project management

Unless you are developing for one platform, you will need several teams of developers to develop natively. This is because a Swift developer is generally not also a Kotlin developer, or if they are, the context switching between the two languages and development environments can seriously impact productivity.

Project managing several development teams where the resources are not fungible (that is, you cannot move a developer from one team to another) can lead to complications in ensuring feature parity and defect resolution.

For example, suppose that there is an iOS development team and an Android development team working on the same backlog of features for an app, aiming for a shared release date.

Imagine that the iOS development team encounters a defect that is complex to diagnose and fix, while the Android development team continues development at a high velocity. As the release deadline approaches, the Android team has many more features completed than the iOS team. At this point, the project manager has to earn their money by deciding whether to do the following:

- Release the apps without feature parity. This can be a confusing experience for users who have multiple devices.

- Delay release until the iOS team catches up. What do you do with the Android team during this time? They are likely to tidy up their code, fixing more minor bugs, and doing more extensive testing, leaving the Android code base in a much better state than the iOS code base, leading to further productivity differences going forward.

- Disable features on the Android version. Not necessarily an easy option if, as is normally the case, the features are not completely disconnected, and also likely to introduce bugs going forward unless disabling the feature is given time to be coded fully.

None of these options are optimal and are exacerbated if you are also developing for other platforms such as the web.

Contrast this with a single code base where one, or many, development teams are working in the same language, development environment, and backlog of features. If there are multiple teams, then the developers are much more fungible; if one team is struggling with a feature, then a developer can more easily switch teams and assist with the development.

Defect reports

Similar to the project management considerations, having native apps will lead to disparities in defect reports. One development team may have done less testing than the other, so on release, one app may be inundated with defect reports, while the other app may be relatively free of defects.

Additionally, you now need to know which platform the user is using to know which app has the bug. In some circumstances, such as crash reporting, this isn't such an issue. However, the vaguer identification of defects, such as a comment on a forum or social media, will likely not reveal that information, leading to a more complex identification and resolution of the defect.

Performance

Measuring performance is notoriously difficult. Do you look at benchmarks that only exercise certain parts of the framework or programming language, or higher-level performance, which can highly depend on the app structure, how the framework has been employed, and the kinds of tasks the app is doing? Therefore, in this chapter, generalities will be used simply as a guide.

However, it is generally accepted that native apps are the fastest and it is pretty clear why. The language and framework are optimized for the platform and vice versa.

Also, and equally importantly, there are no cross-platform compromises that need to be made. To make a framework completely cross-platform means that the app code may interact with the platform in a suboptimal way so that a single piece of code can work with all platforms.

For example, to use a feature, there may only need to be a single method call, but to use the same feature on Android may require several method calls. Depending on how this interaction is revealed to the developer, it may lead to suboptimal performance.

However, it is worth noting that in some situations, Flutter has been seen to be comparable with native apps in terms of performance, and it definitely doesn't appear to be an issue that is mentioned within the Flutter community.

Platform features

Native apps have access to all the features of the platform, otherwise, by definition, they can't be a feature of the platform because they would never be used.

Cross-platform solutions such as Flutter generally expose platform features through plugins. We will explore Flutter plugins later in the book, but as a quick overview, many plugins will interact directly with platform features and expose them to the app developer in a platform-agnostic way. In Flutter, there is a vibrant community creating plugins and these can be viewed at the package repository at `https://pub.dev`.

> **Plugin versus package**
>
> In Flutter, you can add plugins and packages to your project from the package repository. Both plugins and packages are simply a way to share code, but for clarity, a plugin is a special type of package that includes wrappers of native code. You will often use a mix of plugins and packages in your Flutter projects, but the terms "plugin" and "package" are somewhat interchangeable, so don't worry about the difference.

However, there will not necessarily be plugins created for every platform feature, or the plugins available may not support the platform that you require. This was true in the early days of Flutter, but is generally not an issue anymore. In this instance, you may need to write your own plugin.

Another consideration is that some platforms offer features that are not available on other platforms. In this case, a plugin may have been created, but will obviously not be platform agnostic. In this instance, you will need to include platform-specific code in your app.

Hot reload

One of the most awesome features of Flutter is hot reload; the ability to make changes to the code and see it instantly update on the device without your state being changed. This is hugely beneficial in software development; anything that reduces the time between code and feedback allows the developer to achieve flow more easily.

Android has a feature that appears similar, called Instant Run. However, under the covers, it works in a quite different way. Instead of using the JIT approach of Flutter, Android studio will compile the changes and then try to update as little as possible on the device. Often this leads to large changes and sometimes a full rebuild of the whole app.

iOS development with Swift does not currently have an equivalent to Flutter hot reload. There are ways to preview in XCode without running the full app, but this is obviously much more limited than the Flutter approach.

User experience

There are certain expectations of design that differ between users of different platforms. For example, many apps have design differences between iOS, Android, and the web. Developing native apps allows you to design your code around these considerations, whereas in cross-platform development, you may need to have platform-specific code.

Flutter caters for this to some degree by having platform considerations embedded in the built-in widgets. For example, the back button on the **AppBar** (the top bar on the app) changes styling depending on the platform.

However, if you want the actual user experience to be different on different platforms (that is, the flow and interactions), then platform-specific code will need to be added. This is relatively pain-free on Flutter (we will see this in later chapters) but can lead to platform-specific bugs, so this must be a consideration.

App size

A very basic native app can often be less than 1 MB.

A minimal Flutter app has to hold the core engine (circa 3 MB), framework + app code (circa 1 MB), and other files (circa 1 MB), meaning a basic Flutter app starts at 5 MB.

For larger apps, this is unlikely to be an issue because the relative size of the core engine and framework will be relatively smaller, but for very lightweight apps, it should be a consideration.

New platforms

There have been and will probably continue to be attempts to enter the mobile devices market with new platforms. An example of this is Huawei (a prolific mobile device seller), who are attempting to move from the Android platform to their own Harmony platform. Additionally, they are planning to share this platform with other device makers.

Creating a development team to develop apps for a new platform can be a hugely expensive risk because the platform may not get much traction and it may be a development dead-end. However, the benefits of getting onto a platform early can be huge because there is likely to be a lack of competition.

With a cross-platform framework, if the solution is updated to support the new platform, then it can be incredibly easy to release on the new platform with very little development needed. It hugely reduces the risk of moving to the new platform while keeping the potential upside.

Unfortunately though, if the framework is not updated to support the new platform, then you have no path to move your cross-platform app to the new platform. Note though that in this situation, you are not in a worse position than having native apps; in both scenarios, you would need to create a new app natively for the new platform.

Retired platforms

On the flip side, platforms can look promising and then fail. The most notable of these was the Windows Phone by Microsoft, which struggled to get market share due to a lack of apps on its store and was eventually retired when Microsoft changed its priorities.

Being locked into a platform as it begins to fail not only impacts the success of the app on that platform, but also leads to complicated political discussions:

- Should we continue to develop on that platform to keep feature parity?

- Will the platform recover? Constant analysis of the platform sales and market share distracts from product creation.

- Should we retire the app from the platform? Will that lose us customers who will eventually move to a platform that we still support?

With a cross-platform solution, these discussion points become relatively redundant. You can continue to release new versions of your app on the failing platform for a much longer period of time because the features developed will be used for all platforms. There is a requirement to test on the platform, but again this is somewhat alleviated because a lot of the testing will be carried out on other platforms anyway.

> **Learning from experience 2**
>
> When Windows Phone first arrived, I was keen to release a football (soccer) app into what I believed to be a fast-growing market. I used the native Microsoft framework **XNA** for the app development and produced **SoccerTime**. As mentioned previously, there was initially a lack of competitors, so the app grew quickly. Sadly, as we all know, the platform failed, and the lock-in meant I couldn't port to iOS and Android. **SoccerTime** was no more! Interestingly, it looks like the community converted XNA into a cross-platform solution called **Monogame**, an interesting twist on the native versus cross-platform debate.

Overview

Let's take a quick recap of the pros and cons of using native over cross-platform.

Pros:

- Performance
- Full platform feature access
- Closer alignment with expected user experience

Cons:

- Multiple code bases
- Multiple development teams
- Lack of fungibility
- Disparate defect reports
- Feature parity complexities and alignment on product vision
- Expense to move to a new platform
- Complexities of moving off a failing platform
- Different platforms having different features

Hopefully, you are sold on the idea of developing cross-platform but now understand the considerations. So what alternatives are there to Flutter?

Cross-platform frameworks

Let's look at a few alternative frameworks. There are quite a few options, but many are based around three core approaches: React Native, Cordova, and Xamarin.

React Native

The most common cross-platform framework before Flutter was released was React Native. Like Flutter, React Native is open source, and like Flutter, it is backed by a big software development company in the form of Facebook:

Figure 3.2 – React Native logo

It is a popular framework mainly because it reuses the technologies and methodologies of the React web framework. There is a very healthy React Native community that takes the framework forward and produces plugins for the different platforms. Also, given the greater maturity of the framework, there is likely to be a greater wealth of plugin support and documentation available.

Technology wise, React Native uses JavaScript for the general app look and feel, and then Java or Swift to write native modules for the more complex features such as image editing. The motto of the framework is "Learn once, write anywhere," unlike the Flutter vision of writing once and running everywhere. This is because the native modules are not reusable across the platforms, leading to different code bases.

Like Flutter, React Native has hot reloading, allowing fast development and iterations of app code.

Performance wise, the general view seems to be that React Native is slower than Flutter. There are many reasons for this, but the fact that Flutter is compiled to native libraries whereas React Native has a JavaScript layer seems to be a key contributor. However, with such a variety of app designs, it is hard to make anything other than generalizations.

Interestingly, in the 2020 Stack Overflow survey, React Native was noted as the 10th most dreaded framework, yet Flutter was noted as the third most loved framework. Enjoyment of coding is a huge aspect of productivity, so this is an important aspect to take into account.

Moving to Flutter from React Native

Flutter uses reactive-style views, with widgets being comparable to React components. This similarity makes it relatively easy for a React Native (or general web React) developer to understand the state, build, and `setState` aspects of Flutter.

Some key language differences between JavaScript and Dart, the programming language used by Flutter, are the following:

- Variables: Unlike JavaScript, Dart is a type-safe language, so variables must be declared with a type or the type system can infer the type.

- Dart has no concept of `undefined`. Either a variable has a value or it is null.

- Dart has no concept of truthy. Only the Boolean value of `true` is treated as a true value.

- The JavaScript **Promise** is represented by the Dart **Future** object. The async and await operators act on Futures like they do on Promises in JavaScript.

- Printing to the console uses the `print()` method instead of `console.log()`.

For more details, the Flutter documentation gives a great overview of transitioning from React Native to Flutter: `https://flutter.dev/docs/get-started/flutter-for/react-native-devs`.

Xamarin

Much like React and Flutter, Xamarin is open source and backed by a big technology company, in this case Microsoft:

Figure 3.3 – Xamarin logo

Xamarin uses .NET technologies and the C# programming language. When using Xamarin Native, you get all the performance benefits of native apps, but the user interface code is platform specific, so roughly 75% of the code base is shared. This means knowledge of native languages is required in addition to Xamarin.

With Xamarin.Forms, a separate product that replaces the platform-specific user interface code, code sharing can be increased. However, note that Xamarin.Forms is being retired soon and replaced with the Multi-platform App UI (MAUI).

Like React Native and Flutter, Xamarin supports hot reloading to allow faster rebuild and testing.

Considerations for the Xamarin approach are that the licenses can be expensive, especially for an enterprise. Additionally, the Xamarin community is much smaller than the React Native and Flutter communities, which can restrict available developers and also community support.

Moving to Flutter from Xamarin.Forms

The Xamarin.Forms Page concept is similar to the Route concept in Flutter. So a Route will lead from one Page to another Page.

However, the key difference is that everything is a widget in Flutter. So, whereas a `ContentPage` will contain elements such as `Entry` or `Button`, in Flutter, the page is a widget that contains nested widgets. One of the nested widgets may draw an input field or a button.

Again, the Flutter documentation does a great job of explaining how to migrate to Flutter: `https://flutter.dev/docs/get-started/flutter-for/xamarin-forms-devs`.

Cordova

Apache Cordova takes the web technologies of HTML, CSS, and JavaScript and allows them to run on mobile apps. Formerly PhoneGap, Cordova is itself more of a platform that allows frameworks to run within it, such as Ionic:

Figure 3.4 – Apache Cordova logo

Effectively, the Cordova app runs within a WebView, which is like a built-in browser for each platform. This means that, unlike React Native and Xamarin, all the code is cross-platform. However, a major issue is that the WebView implementations for different platforms can be subtly different, leading to inconsistencies and bugs in the user interface.

Additionally, depending on WebView performance, the app can run slowly, especially on graphic-intense apps. As an added complication, the WebView can be different on different versions of the platform, so performance and user interfaces can be different on different versions of the platform. This can be especially true on the Android platform.

Moving to Flutter from Cordova

One key difference you will notice immediately is that Flutter styling is embedded within the widget, rather than declared in a separate style document like CSS.

This has many benefits, a main one being the mental load that is put on the developer is hugely reduced as there is one less language to contend with.

The layout of widgets does not quite match the expectations of web developers. The number of times I've caused overflows because I've reverted to the web layout way of thinking is painful.

Again, there is excellent documentation on the Flutter site to guide you through the differences: `https://flutter.dev/docs/get-started/flutter-for/web-devs`.

Popularity

When choosing a framework, it is important to know the popularity so that you can assess whether the framework will have long-term support.

A common way to assess popularity is to look at the Stack Overflow trends report. This shows how many Stack Overflow questions were asked about a specific framework:

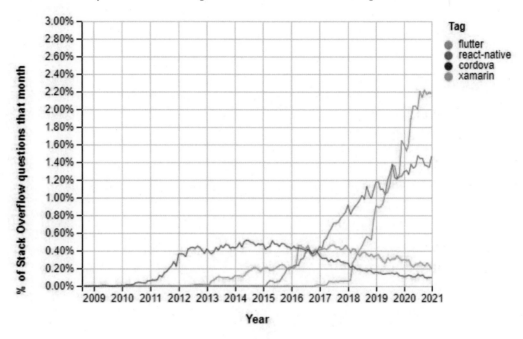

Figure 3.5 – Stack Overflow trend report

A simple comparison of the frameworks mentioned previously shows the following:

- Questions about the older frameworks of Cordova and Xamarin are reducing slowly.
- React Native and Flutter are seeing fast growth in questions asked.
- Flutter has become the most popular framework to ask about, especially since Flutter 1.0 was released in 2018.

It can be argued that fewer questions need to be asked about the older frameworks because they have already been asked, so feel free to interpret the chart as you wish, but it clearly shows that there is currently a lot of interest in Flutter.

Stack Overflow is a great resource, but a framework not only needs a healthy set of Stack Overflow questions for it to grow and develop; it also needs a strong community.

Flutter community

Flutter has a vibrant community, which is key to the long-term success of any software project that relies on community contributions. Google is very active in this, involving Flutter in conferences and organizing Flutter events.

Events

Flutter Engage is an event dedicated to the Flutter framework. It shares best practices, new developments, feature overviews, and the chance to interact with Flutter experts.

The first *Flutter Engage* took place on March 3, 2021 and introduced a whole raft of new Flutter features, including Flutter 2.0, dual-display widgets from Microsoft, first-class Google AdMob integration, and tooling to help with Flutter migration to newer versions, among many other features and bug fixes. Flutter 2.0 also introduced full support for the web platform, which was previously a beta release. In addition, stability on all desktop platforms was announced, which led to an announcement from Canonical, publisher of Linux distribution Ubuntu, that "*Flutter is the default choice for future mobile and desktop apps created by Canonical.*"

Google I/O, a general Google event for developers, often features Flutter talks. It is useful to attend these as not only can you learn about the new features being developed, you can also get a feel for the strategic direction of the project. It was at Google I/O that an early preview of project Hummingbird, the move of Flutter to the web, was shown.

There are regular **meetups** around the world where groups will discuss the latest Flutter technology, share their learning, and help newcomers join the Flutter bandwagon. It is worth noting that Flutter communities are not just English speaking, with great communities such as Flutterando in Brazil (with over 8,000 members) allowing you to have Flutter meetups in your native tongue. Check out the `https://meetup.com` site to find a meetup near you.

News and discussion

The Flutter **Google group** is a great place to raise questions and discuss issues. It is a very active group, generally with answers given within hours of questions being asked: `https://groups.google.com/g/flutter-dev`.

An alternative when having issues is to head to **Stack Overflow** for assistance. Many of the issues you encounter will have already been answered on there, and if not then it is very easy to ask your own question.

Two excellent email subscriptions will give you a weekly update on all things Flutter:

- **Flutter Weekly** provides links to useful libraries, code examples, and highlights future events. Subscribe at `https://flutterweekly.net/`.

- **Flutter Tap** gives more general news and event updates, alongside tutorial videos and useful packages. Subscribe at `https://fluttertap.com/`.

Resources

All of the Flutter code is on GitHub. You can view code here, track defects, and follow new releases. The main repository is at `https://github.com/flutter/flutter`, but all plugins will have their own repositories and issue tracking as well.

All of the plugins/packages created for Flutter and Dart are listed on the `https://pub.dev/` site. The site includes a powerful search that will list all the plugins and packages that are relevant. Importantly, the vitality of plugins and packages is reported through a series of metrics, allowing you to find the best plugin or package for your project:

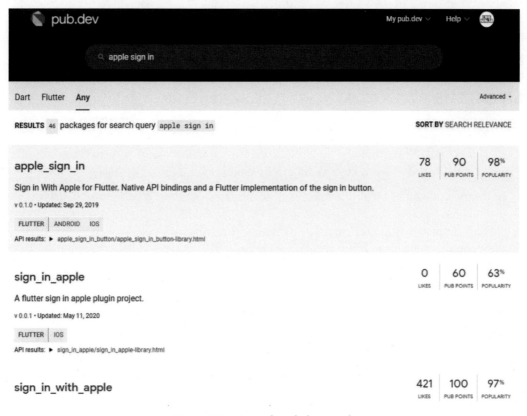

Figure 3.6 – Example pub.dev search

As you can see in the example, a search for `apple sign in` returns at least three options. Deciding between them used to be complicated, but now the likes, pub points (how well the project adheres to the standards such as documentation, code style, and platform support), and popularity help you get a feel for which plugin might have the best longevity and support.

The main **Flutter website** holds huge amounts of documentation, including the latest links to the community and news of events. I strongly suggest you take a look around the site to see what is available: `https://flutter.dev/`.

So, Flutter has a vibrant community that is helping drive the framework forward and make it even better. Let's bring together the key parts of this chapter from the point of view of Flutter itself.

Flutter strengths and weaknesses

So, we've had a look at the other options available to you for your mobile project, and looked at the vitality of the Flutter community. This book is not designed to brainwash you into thinking Flutter is the best option (though it probably is), but given the context of the technology landscape, let's recap the strengths and weaknesses of Flutter so that you can make an informed decision.

Strengths

The following are some of the strengths of Flutter:

- **Hot reload**: Flutter has the best hot reload functionality (equal to React Native and Xamarin), and this is a huge productivity benefit.

- **Single code base**: Of all the options available, only a couple (Flutter and Cordova) truly have a single code base that will work across platforms. As discussed, this helps hugely with project management, defect resolution, and new platforms becoming relevant or old platforms being retired.

- **Project vitality**: Flutter has a very active community with a huge range of community plugins, easy ways to ask questions, and the most activity on Stack Overflow. If this was a concern, it should have been mitigated somewhat by our exploration of the community.

- **Performance**: Dart compiling to native and the lack of a software bridge ensure that Flutter, if not as performant as native, is more than sufficient for apps.

- **Documentation**: The documentation on Flutter is excellent. Compared to some other cross-platform frameworks, the Google team, and the plugin writers, have worked hard to ensure that Flutter is very well documented.

Weaknesses

The following are some of the weaknesses of Flutter:

- **New framework**: Flutter is relatively new and although that means it can learn from what has come before, it also means that there are lots of changes that can impact backward compatibility. This means developers often need to migrate their code to cope with the changes, sometimes holding up new releases.

> **Flutter migration examples**
>
> A big Flutter change was the introduction of **null safety** to the language. Null safety had to be introduced to Dart and Flutter carefully as it required migration of code, and it made sense to work on dependencies, such as plugins, before developers migrated their app code. Another example is that Flutter widgets regularly get deprecated and replaced to improve consistency in the framework; for example, `FlatButton` became `TextButton` and `RaisedButton` became `ElevatedButton`.

- **App size**: As mentioned in the native discussion, a minimal Flutter app is already 5 MB. This is comparable with other cross-platform frameworks, but significantly bigger than native apps.

Summary

In this chapter, we looked at how Flutter compares to other mobile app development options. Initially, we explored native development options and using them versus general cross-platform solutions. We saw many of the advantages and disadvantages of the native approach.

We then looked at some common cross-platform frameworks and how they compare to Flutter. We saw that although they are trying to solve the same problem, they are doing so in different ways, leading to different trade-offs against the other options.

Next we explored the Flutter community and highlighted some useful resources. This helped us to understand that the Flutter community is very active, which is a huge positive for the future of Flutter.

One of the key aspects of the community is the plugins that are created. We will explore these further in later chapters.

You should now start to see why Flutter is so awesome, and why it is fast becoming one of the main development options for new app projects.

In the next chapter, you will have a proper play with Flutter, building on the Hello World! app you started in *Chapter 2, An Introduction to Dart*. We will particularly focus on widgets and how to use them to create your user interface.

4
Dart Classes and Constructs

In this chapter, we will look at **object-oriented programming (OOP)** and how it is supported by the Dart language. We will start by looking at the core principles of OOP with relation to the Dart language, and then explore how to use OOP within Dart.

We will then take a deeper look at class definitions and how instances of a class are created, including an exploration of the constructor types available, which forms a key part of the way Flutter apps are coded. Additionally, we will look at how we store our code in files, and how to import code from other files.

Finally, we will look at some key Dart topics that are used throughout Flutter—generics and asynchronous programming. These will help with your understanding of the Flutter topics we will cover later in the book.

On completion of this chapter, you will have a solid foundational knowledge of Dart, which will set you in good stead as we move to a deeper exploration of Flutter.

We will cover the following topics in this chapter:

- Object orientation in Dart

- Understanding classes in Dart

- The enum type

- Using generics

- Asynchronous programming

Technical requirements

In this chapter, we will explore the Dart classes and constructs. You can do this via DartPad or within your chosen **integrated development environment** (**IDE**), as discussed in the first chapter.

Either option will allow you to experiment with your code. If you choose to use your IDE, then you will need to ensure your system is configured correctly to run Dart programs. Please refer to *Chapter 1, An Introduction to Flutter* for details on how to ensure your system is ready to do this.

You can find the source code for this chapter on GitHub at `https://github.com/PacktPublishing/Flutter-for-Beginners-Second-Edition/tree/main/hello_world/lib/chapter_04`.

Object orientation in Dart

As with most modern languages, Dart is designed to be **object-oriented** (**OO**). As initially mentioned in *Chapter 2, An Introduction to Dart*, OOP languages are based on the concept of **objects** that hold both data (called **fields**) and code (called **methods**). These objects are created from blueprints called **classes** that define the fields and methods an object will have.

For a deeper exploration of the fundamentals of OOP, it is worthwhile reading an excellent book named *Learning Object-Oriented Programming* by Gaston C. Hillar.

The terms discussed here may be new to you, but the key areas are covered in greater depth in the next sections of this chapter. Let's start with a brief overview of how Dart follows OOP principles.

Objects and classes

The starting point of OOP—objects—are instances of defined classes. In Dart, everything is an object—that is, every value stored in a variable is an instance of a class. Additionally, all objects also extend the Object class, directly or indirectly. The following also applies:

- Dart classes can have both instance members (methods and fields) and class members (static methods and fields).

- Dart classes do not support constructor overloading, but you can use the flexible function argument specifications from the language (optional, positional, and named) to provide different ways to instantiate a class. Also, you can have named constructors to define alternatives. Giving names to your constructors allows you to have multiple constructors for a class, and also gives a clearer meaning to the reason why your class has multiple constructors.

Other OOP artifacts

Besides class definitions, other important OOP artifacts are presented in the Dart language (we will delve deeper into each of these throughout this chapter), outlined as follows:

- **Interface**: This is a contract definition with a set of methods available on an object. Although there is no explicit interface type in Dart, we can achieve the interface purpose with abstract classes.

- **Enumerated class**: This is a special kind of class that defines a set of common constant values.

- **Mixin**: This is a way of reusing a class's code in multiple class hierarchies.

Encapsulation

Dart does not have explicit access restrictions on fields and methods, unlike the famous keywords used in Java—protected, private, and public. In Dart, encapsulation occurs at the library level instead of at the class level (this will be discussed further in this following chapter). The following also applies:

- Dart creates implicit getters and setters for all fields in a class, so you can define how data is accessible to consumers and the way it changes.

- In Dart, if an **identifier** (**ID**) (that is, a class, class member, top-level function, or variable) starts with an underscore (_), it's private to its library where a library is normally the contents of a single file.

Inheritance and composition

Inheritance allows us to extend a class definition to a more specialized type. In Dart, by simply declaring a class, we are implicitly extending the object type. The following also applies:

- Dart permits single direct inheritance. A class can only inherit from one other class, leading to a strict tree structure. This is similar in many other languages and can be very restrictive to class design, so Dart offers other options alongside inheritance, especially **mixins**.

- Dart has special support for mixins, which can be used to extend class functionalities without direct inheritance, simulating multiple inheritance and enabling easy reuse of code.

- Dart does not contain a **final** class directive, unlike other languages. This means that a class can always be extended.

Abstraction

Following inheritance, abstraction is a process whereby we define a type and its essential characteristics, moving to specialized types from parent ones. The following also applies:

- Dart contains abstract classes that allow a definition of what something does/provides, without caring about how this is implemented.

- Dart has the powerful implicit interface concept, which also makes every class an interface, allowing it to be implemented by others without extending it.

Polymorphism

Polymorphism is achieved by inheritance and can be regarded as the ability of an object to behave like another; for example, the int type is also a num type. The following also applies:

- Dart allows overriding parent methods to change their original behavior.

- Dart does not allow overloading in the way you may be familiar with. You cannot define the same method twice with different arguments. If required, you can simulate overloading by using flexible parameter definitions through optional and positional parameters, as was seen in the *Functions and methods* section of *Chapter 2, An Introduction to Dart*.

Functions as objects

Dart is called a true object-oriented language. In Dart, even functions are objects, which means that you can do the following:

- Assign a function as a value of a variable and pass it as an argument to another function

- Return it as a result of a function as you would do with any other type, such as `String` and `int`

This is known as having first-class functions because they're treated the same way as other types.

So, now we know some of the fundamental principles of Dart, let's look at the core structure of the language.

Understanding classes in Dart

If you are an experienced programmer or are already familiar with Java or similar languages, you can skip some parts of this chapter as it has many similarities with the typical OOP concepts, such as inheritance and encapsulation. Some ideas, in particular, are important to verify, even if you are already familiar with the majority of OOP features, such as how Dart manages and structures constructors.

In this section, we will look at what makes a Dart class, how you construct an instance of one using a constructor, and how your class can inherit from other classes. We will also explore ways to use classes such as abstract classes, interfaces, and mixins, and finally, look at how we share class code across our code base using files and imports.

Class structure

Dart classes are declared by using the `class` keyword, followed by the class name, ancestor classes, and implemented interfaces. Then, the class body is enclosed by a pair of curly braces, where you can add class members, which includes the following:

- **Fields**: These are variables used to define the data an object can hold.

- **Accessors**: Getters and setters, as the name suggests, are used to access the fields of a class, where `get` is used to retrieve a value, and the `set` accessor is used to modify the corresponding value.

- **Constructor**: This is the creator method of a class where the object instance fields are initialized.

- **Methods**: The behavior of an object is defined by the actions it can take. These are the object functions.

Refer to the following small class definition example:

```
class Person {
  String? firstName;
  String? lastName;

  String getFullName() => "$firstName $lastName";
}


main() {
  Person somePerson = Person();
  somePerson.firstName = "Clark";
  somePerson.lastName = "Kent";
  print(somePerson.getFullName()); // prints Clark Kent
}
```

Now, let's take a look at the `Person` class declared in the preceding code sample and make some observations, as follows:

- We have not defined a constructor for the class, but, as you may have guessed, there's a default empty constructor (no arguments) already provided for us.

- To instantiate a class, we call the constructor invocation. Unlike in many OOP languages, there is no need to use the `new` keyword (although it is a reserved word and will appear in older code).

- The class does not have an ancestor class explicitly declared, but it does implicitly inherit from `Object`, as do all classes in Dart.

- The class has two fields, `firstName` and `lastName`, and a `getFullName()` method that concatenates both by using string interpolation and returning the result.

- The class does not have any `get` or `set` accessor declared, so how did we access `firstName` and `lastName` to mutate it? A default `get`/`set` accessor is defined for every field in a class.

- The dot `class.member` notation is used to access a class member, whatever it is—a method or a field (`get`/`set`).

Note the use of arrow notation on the `getFullName()` method. This is equivalent to writing the following:

```
String getFullName() {
    return "$firstName $lastName";
}
```

However, the arrow notation is more succinct and probably easier to read. We can make this even more readable using field accessors.

Field accessors – getters and setters

As mentioned previously, getters and setters allow us to access a field on a class, and every field has these accessors, even when we do not define them. In the preceding `Person` example, when we execute `somePerson.firstName = "Clark"`, we are calling the `firstName` field's `set` accessor and sending `"Clark"` as a parameter to it. Also, in the following example, the `get` accessor is used when we call the `getFullName()` method on the person, and it concatenates both names.

For example, we can modify our `Person` class to replace the old `getFullName()` method and add it as a getter, as demonstrated in the following code block:

```
class Person {
    String? firstName;
    String? lastName;

    String get fullName => "$firstName $lastName";
    String get initials => "${firstName[0]}.
    ${lastName[0]}.";
}

main() {
    Person somePerson = new Person();
    somePerson.firstName = "Clark";
```

```
    somePerson.lastName = "Kent";


    print(somePerson.fullName);      // prints Clark Kent
    print(somePerson.initials);      // prints C. K.
    somePerson.fullName = "peter parker";
    // we have not defined a setter fullName so it doesn't
        compile
}
```

The following important observations can be made regarding the preceding example:

- We could not have defined a getter or setter with the same field names firstName and lastName. This would give us a compile error, as the class member names cannot be repeated.

- We do not need to always define a get and set pair together, as you can see that we have only defined a fullName getter and not a setter, so we cannot modify fullName. (This results in a compilation error, as indicated previously.)

We could have also written a setter for fullName and defined the logic behind it to set firstName and lastName based on that, as illustrated in the following code snippet:

```
class Person {
    // ... class fields definition
    set fullName(String fullName) {
        var parts = fullName.split(" ");
        this.firstName = parts.first; this.lastName =
            parts.last;
    }
}
```

This way, someone could initialize a person's name by setting fullName, and the result would be the same. (Of course, we have not carried out any checks to establish whether the value passed as fullName is valid—that is, not empty, with two or more values, and so on.)

Static fields and methods

As you already know, fields are nothing more than variables that hold object values, and methods are simple functions that represent object actions. In some cases, you may want to share a value or method between all of the object instances of a class. For this use case, you can add the `static` modifier to them, as follows:

```dart
class Person {
  // ... class fields definition
  static String personLabel = "Person name:";
  String get fullName => "$personLabel $firstName
    $lastName";
  // modified to print the new static field "personLabel"
}
```

Hence, we can change the `static` field value directly on the class, as follows:

```dart
main() {
  Person somePerson = Person();
  somePerson.firstName = "Clark";
  somePerson.lastName = "Kent";
  Person anotherPerson = Person();
  anotherPerson.firstName = "Peter";
  anotherPerson.lastName = "Parker";
  print(somePerson.fullName); // prints Person name: Clark
    kent
  print(anotherPerson.fullName); // prints Person name:
    Peter Parker
  Person.personLabel = "name:";
  print(somePerson.fullName); // prints name: Clark Kent
  print(anotherPerson.fullName); // prints name: Peter
    Parker
}
```

The `static` fields are associated with the class, rather than any object instance. The same goes for the `static` method definitions. For example, we can add a `static` method to encapsulate the name printing, as demonstrated in the following code block:

```dart
class Person {
  // ... class fields definition
  static String personLabel = "Person name:";
  static void printsPerson(Person person) {
    print("$personLabel ${person.firstName}
      ${person.lastName}");
  }
}
```

As you can see, `static` fields and methods allow us to add specific behaviors to classes in general.

So, now we've seen how to structure a class and how to use the default constructor, let's explore a bit deeper how to define and use class constructors.

Constructors

To instantiate a class, we call the corresponding constructor with parameters, if required. Now, let's change the `Person` class and define a constructor with parameters on it, as follows:

```dart
class Person {
  late String firstName;
  late String lastName;
  Person(String firstName, String lastName) {
    this.firstName = firstName;
    this.lastName = lastName;
  }
  String getFullName() => "$firstName $lastName";
}

void main() {
  // Person somePerson = Person(); No longer compiles
  Person somePerson = Person("Clark", "Kent");
  print(somePerson.getFullName());
}
```

The constructor is also a method in Dart, and its role is to initialize the instance of the class properly. As a method, it can have many of the characteristics of a common Dart method, such as arguments—required or optional, and named or positional. In the preceding example, the constructor has two mandatory arguments.

If you look in our constructor body, it uses the `this` keyword. Furthermore, the constructor parameter names are the same as the field ones, which could cause ambiguity. So, to avoid this, we prefix the object instance fields with the `this` keyword during the value assign step.

Notice that we have to use the `late` keyword because the fields have not been declared with an initial value, but we know that values of the fields will be set on instantiation of the class, so their values will not be accessed before they have a value set.

Dart provides another way to write a constructor—using a shortcut syntax, such as the one provided in the following example:

```
Person(this.firstName, this.lastName);
```

There is no need for the constructor body, as the field values are set directly in the constructor signature. It can take a little while to get used to this syntax, but it not only makes the constructor declaration more succinct but also removes a big opportunity for code errors. Additionally, you no longer require the `late` keyword because the compiler can see that the value of the fields will be set on class instantiation.

Have a look at the following code snippet:

```
class Person {
    String firstName;
    String lastName;
    Person(this.firstName, this.lastName);
    String getFullName() => "$firstName $lastName";
}
```

As you can see, this is a much cleaner way of defining a class constructor because it is succinct, less open to code errors, and removes the need to manage the `null` type on the fields.

Named constructors

Unlike with Java and many other languages, Dart does not have overloading by redefinition, so to define alternative constructors for a class, you need to use the named constructors. For example, we could add the following constructor to the `Person` class that takes no parameters:

```
Person.anonymous();
```

The only difference compared with a simple method is that constructors do not have a `return` statement, as the only thing they have to do is to initialize the object instance properly.

We will see named constructors throughout the rest of the book, as the framework uses these a lot to initialize widget definitions.

Factory constructors

A `factory` constructor can be used when the constructor doesn't always create a new instance of the class it is defined on. This may be used when data is being cached and we want to return an instance from the cache rather than construct a new instance.

For example, suppose we are caching `Person` instances. We could create a `factory` constructor that checks if the `Person` instance is already in a cache and returns either a value from the cache or, if there is no cache entry, constructs a new `Person` instance. For the following example, imagine we have some cache service we can ask for an instance:

```
factory Person.fromCache(String firstName, String lastName) {
  if (_cacheService.containsPerson(firstName, lastName)) {
    return _cacheService.getPerson(firstName, lastName);
  } else {
    return Person(firstName, lastName);
  }
}
```

Note that a `factory` constructor has no access to the `this` keyword, so it needs to access another constructor to create a new instance of the class.

Class inheritance

In addition to the implicit inheritance to the `Object` type, Dart allows us to extend defined classes using the `extends` keyword, where all of the members of the parent class are inherited, except the constructors.

Now, let's check out the following example, where we create a child class for the `Person` class:

```
class Student extends Person {
  String nickName;
  Student(
    String firstName,
```

```
    String lastName,
    this.nickName,
  ) : super(firstName, lastName);

  @override
  String toString() => "$fullName, aka $nickName";
}
main() {
  Student = Student("Clark", "Kent", "Kal-El");
  print(student);

}
```

There are some really interesting things going on here that will help us when we start to look at widgets.

Firstly, the Student class defines its own constructor. However, it passes some of the properties in the constructor up to the parent class. This is done with the super keyword, which is placed at the end of the constructor, following the : character.

Next, you see @override. This is an annotation and is metadata giving an additional description to the method definition. There's an overridden toString() method on the Student class. This is where inheritance makes sense—we change the behavior of a parent class (Object, in this case) on the child class.

> **Why bother with the @override annotation?**
>
> Annotations generally contribute to the readability of the code. In this instance, the @override annotation has been used to mark the toString() method as overriding the method from the parent class. You may think this is obvious and that any decent **integrated development environment** (IDE) could show this relationship perfectly easily. However, the main value of the annotation in this situation is for code checking. If you think you have overridden a method but have misspelled it, then by explicitly saying you wish to override the method, the compiler knows your intention and can validate it. Also, if someone changes the super class method and removes the method you are overriding, the compiler will complain that a subclass is no longer overriding the removed method.

Finally, the print(student) method is called in the main method. As you can see in the print(student) statement, we are not calling any method; the toString() method is called for us implicitly.

A common example of overriding parent behavior is the `toString()` method. The objective of this method is to return a `String` representation of the object and it is defined on the top-level `Object` class.

As you can see in the preceding code example, overriding the `toString` method makes the code cleaner, and we provide a good textual representation of the object that can aid in understanding logs, text formatting, and more.

Abstract classes

In OOP, abstract classes are classes that cannot be instantiated. For example, our `Person` class could be abstract if we want to make sure that it only exists in the context of the program if it is a `Student` instance or another subtype, as illustrated in the following code snippet:

```
abstract class Person {
    // ... the body was hidden for brevity
}
```

The only thing we need to change here is the beginning of the class definition, marking it as `abstract`. We can still instantiate the subclass, as shown in the following code snippet:

```
main() {
    Person student = new Student("Clark", "Kent", "Kal-El");
    // Works because we are instantiating the subtype
    // Person p = new Person();
    // abstract classes cannot be instantiated
    print(student);
}
```

As you can see, we can no longer instantiate a `Person` class itself, only concrete subclasses.

An abstract class may have abstract members without an implementation, allowing it to be implemented by the child types that extend them, as illustrated in the following code snippet:

```
abstract class Person {
    String firstName;
    String lastName;
    Person(this.firstName, this.lastName);
    String get fullName;
}
```

The `fullName` getter from the preceding `Person` class is now abstract, as it does not have an implementation. It is the responsibility of the child to implement this member, as follows:

```
class Student extends Person {
  //... other class members
  @override
  String get fullName => "$firstName $lastName";
}
```

The `Student` class implements the `fullName` getter because, if it did not, the `Student` class would itself be abstract (and would need the `abstract` keyword to allow the code to compile) and therefore could not be instantiated.

Interfaces

Dart does not have the interface keyword but does allow us to use interfaces in a subtly different way from what you may be used to. All class declarations are themselves interfaces, which means that when you are defining a class in Dart, you are also defining an interface that may be implemented and not only extended by other classes. This is called **implicit interfaces** in the Dart world.

On this basis, our previous `Person` class is also a `Person` interface that could be implemented, instead of extended, by the `Student` class, as illustrated in the following code block:

```
class Student implements Person {
  String nickName;
  @override
  String firstName;
  @override
  String lastName;
  Student(this.firstName, this.lastName, this.nickName);
  @override
  String get fullName => "$firstName $lastName";
  @override
  String toString() => "$fullName, also known as
    $nickName";
}
```

Note that, in general, the code does not change too much, but the members are now defined in the Student class. The Person class is just a contract that the Student class adopted and must implement. You can probably see that a pure interface can be created by simply defining a fully abstract class.

Mixins

In OOP, mixins are a way to include functionality on a class without an association between the parts, such as through inheritance.

Mixins are mainly used in places where multiple inheritance is needed, as this is an easy way for classes to use common functionality. One of the main examples of this in Flutter is when you want to create a widget that is animated. Defining a widget class requires inheritance, so to add animation capabilities to your class, a mixin is required.

As an example, let's look at using mixins for our Person class. People have a mix of specific skills, and mixins can be ideal for reflecting this because we can add skills to a person without the need to define a common superclass for each combination or interface definition, leading to code duplication. Here, we define two classes to be used as mixins, as follows:

```
class ProgrammingSkills {
  coding() {
    print("writing code...");
  }
}
class ManagementSkills {
  manage() {
    print("managing project...");
  }
}
```

We have created two skills classes, ProgrammingSkills and ManagementSkills. Now, we can use them by adding the with keyword to the class definition, as illustrated in the following code example:

```
class SeniorDeveloper extends Person with ProgrammingSkills,
ManagementSkills {
  SeniorDeveloper(String firstName, String lastName) :
    super(firstName, lastName);
```

```
}
class JuniorDeveloper extends Person with ProgrammingSkills {
  JuniorDeveloper(String firstName, String lastName) :
    super(firstName, lastName);
}
```

Both classes will have the `coding()` method, without the need to implement it in each class, as it is already implemented in the `ProgrammingSkills` mixin. Additionally, the `SeniorDeveloper` class will have the `manage()` method.

Files and imports

When you look at the project structure of the `HelloWorld` project, you will notice that there is a file named `main.dart` that contains a class named `MyApp`. Unlike with some other programming languages, the class name does not need to match the filename.

Additionally, it is normal to put multiple classes, enums, and functions into one file to form a library of constructs that are closely related. This can allow nice encapsulation through making some classes private to the library through the addition of an underscore at the start of their name (as with variables). Other classes in the file can access and instantiate the private class, but it is not visible outside of the file.

When we explore widgets, in the next chapter, you will see that it is quite common to have two classes within a file and they can both contribute to a single widget, one of which is private to the file.

However, you don't want all of your app's constructs in a single file as it would become harder to find the construct that you need, would hinder encapsulation, and would probably cause performance issues with your IDE. Therefore, you need a way to refer to constructs in other files, and you do this through `import` statements. As with virtually any other programming language, `import` statements allow you to reference code in other classes, packages, and plugins.

If you look at the `main.dart` file in the `HelloWorld` project, you will see the following `import` statement at the very top:

```
import 'package:flutter/material.dart';
```

In this example, the `material.dart` file is being imported, with all the classes and functions within that file being made available to your class. This file holds lots of the basic constructs needed to create Flutter widgets, so most files in a Flutter project will need this import.

In this section, we looked at the structure of a Dart class, including fields and methods. Then, we explored the different ways in which constructors can be used to instantiate a class. After that, we discussed some of the special ways to use classes, such as abstract classes, interfaces, and mixins. We finished off by learning how class code can be shared across your app through files and imports. Let's now look at a special type of construct called enums, which are used in very specific scenarios.

The enum type

The enum type is a common data type used by most languages to represent a set of finite constant values. In Dart, it is no different. By using the enum keyword, followed by the constant values, you can define an enum type, as illustrated in the following code snippet:

```
enum PersonType { student, employee }
```

Note that you only define the value names. enum types are special types with a set of finite values that have an index property representing their value. Now, let's see how it all works.

First, we add a field to our previously defined Person class to store its type, as follows:

```
class Person {
    ...
    PersonType? type;
    ...
}
```

Then, we can use it just like any other field, as illustrated in the following code snippet:

```
main() {
    print(PersonType.values);
    Person somePerson = Person();
    somePerson.type = PersonType.employee;
    print(somePerson.type);
    print(somePerson.type.index);
    print(describeEnum(PersonType.employee));
}
```

The first print statement prints [PersonType.student, PersonType. employee].You can see that we are calling the values getter on the PersonType enum directly. This is a static member of the enum type that simply returns a list with all of its values.

The second `print` statement prints `PersonType.employee`.

The next `print` statement prints 1. You can see that the `index` property is zero, based on the declaration position of the value. Generally, you should not rely on the `index` value because it can change if the enum values are reordered or a new value is added.

Additionally, Flutter supplies the `describeEnum` method, which returns just the value of the enum. In the final `print` method, the value printed will be `employee`.

The more you can add type safety to your code, the safer that code is. However, sometimes you also want to specify the type that a class can contain, and you do this with generics.

Using generics

The `<>` syntax is used to specify the type supported by a class. If you look at the examples of lists and maps in *Chapter 2, An Introduction to Dart*, you will notice that we have not specified the type that they can contain. This is because this type of information is optional, and Dart can infer the type based on elements during the collection initialization.

When and why to use generics

The use of generics can help a developer to maintain and keep collection behavior under control. When we use a collection without specifying the allowed element types, it is our responsibility to correctly insert elements of the expected type. This can lead to bugs when data of an incorrect type is placed in a collection or incorrect assumptions are made about the contents of a collection.

Consider the following code example, where we have named a `List` variable `placeNames`. We expect this to be a list of names and nothing else. Unfortunately, without generics, we can place anything into the list, including a number. This can lead to issues when retrieving values from the list:

```
main() {
  List placeNames = ["Middlesbrough", "New York"];
  placeNames.add(1);
  print("Place names: $placeNames");
}
// prints Place names: [Middlesbrough, New York, 1]
```

However, if we specify the string type for the list, then this code would not compile, therefore improving the robustness of the code, as illustrated in the following code snippet:

```
main() {
    List<String> placeNames = ["Middlesbrough", "New York"];
    placeNames.add(1);
    // add() expects a String so this doesn't compile
}
```

Generics and Dart literals

In the list and map examples provided in *Chapter 2, An Introduction to Dart*, you will see we used the [] and {} literals to initialize them. With generics, as an alternative to the previous approach, we can specify a type during initialization, adding an `<elementType>[]` prefix for lists and `<keyType, valueType>{}` for maps.

Take a look at the following example:

```
main() {
    var placeNames = <String>["Middlesbrough", "New York"];
    var landmarks = <String, String>{
        "Middlesbrough": "Transporter bridge",
        "New York": "Statue of Liberty",
    };
}
```

Specifying the type of list seems to be redundant in this case as the Dart analyzer will infer the string type from the literals we have provided. However, in some cases, this is important, such as when we are initializing an empty collection, as in the following example:

```
var emptyStringArray = <String>[];
```

If we have not specified the type of the empty collection, it could have any data type on it as it would not infer the generic type to adopt.

Nullability in generics

Just as we saw in the *Null safety* section in *Chapter 2, An Introduction to Dart*, if a variable can receive a null value, then that must be declared on the variable's type. This is also true in generics if the type of the collection can include null entries.

For example, suppose in our landmarks map we allowed some places to have no landmark. We would need to declare this so that when we access the map's entries, we would know that null was a possible value. Let's update the previous example to see what that might look like, as follows:

```
main() {
  var landmarks = <String, String?>{
    "Middlesbrough": "Transporter bridge",
    "New York": "Statue of Liberty",
    "Barnmouth": null,
  };
}
```

We have specified that the value of the map entry is String?, meaning that it holds either a String or a null value. We have then added a new entry to the map containing a null value.

We have now learned a lot about how to add type safety to our code, and we will finish the chapter with a slight change of focus. Sometimes, we want to call some code that will take a long time to complete, so how do we do this while maintaining a great **user experience** (**UX**) for our app? Let's look at asynchronous programming.

Asynchronous programming

Dart is a single-threaded programming language, meaning that all of the application code runs in the same thread. Put simply, this means that any code may block thread execution by performing long-running operations such as **input/output** (**I/O**) or **HyperText Transfer Protocol** (**HTTP**) requests. This can obviously be an issue if your app is stuck waiting for something slow such as an HTTP request while the user is trying to interact with it. The app would effectively freeze and not respond to the user's input.

However, although Dart is single-threaded, it can perform asynchronous operations through the use of **Futures**. This allows your code to trigger an operation, continue doing other work, and then come back when the operation has been completed. To represent the result of these asynchronous operations, Dart uses the Future object combined with the async and await keywords. Let's look at these concepts now so that we can learn how to write a responsive application.

Dart Futures

When our code calls a method that is a long-running task but we don't want to block execution of other parts of the app such as the **user interface** (**UI**), we can mark the method as asynchronous using the `async` keyword. This tells all code that calls that method that it may be long-running, so you shouldn't block thread execution while waiting for the result. We can then call the method and continue the execution of other code.

However, we may want to get a result from the long-running method, so we need to come back to the method call after the long-running method has returned. To do this, we specify that we want to return when there is a response, using the `await` keyword. A key distinction between `async` and `await` is that the method itself declares its asynchronicity using `async`, but it is the code calling the method that specifies it will return when there is a response through the use of `await`. We will see both of these keywords in use later in this section.

So, we've declared that the method should be called asynchronously using `async`, and we may have specified that we want to come back to the method call when there is a result using `await`, but what does the method actually return? The `Future<T>` object in Dart represents a value that will be provided sometime in the future. It can be used to mark a method, for example, with a future result; that is, a method returning a `Future<T>` object will not have the proper result value immediately but, instead, after some computation at a later point in time.

It is easiest to understand this when you look at code examples that initially are not asynchronous but are long-running. Consider the following code:

```
import 'dart:io';
void longRunningOperation() {
  for (int i = 0; i < 5; i++) {
    sleep(Duration(seconds: 1));
    print("index: $i");
  }
}
main() {
  print("start of long running operation");
  longRunningOperation();
  print("continuing main body");
```

```
    for (int i = 10; i < 15; i++) {
        sleep(Duration(seconds: 1));
        print("index from main: $i");
    }
    print("end of main");
}
```

Here, we have the main function, which calls a long-running operation. We have used the sleep() function, which pauses code execution. This function is available in the dart:io package, so we have added an import statement to give us access to the function.

If you execute the preceding code, the output looks like this:

```
start of long running operation
index: 0
index: 1
index: 2
index: 3
index: 4
continuing main body
index from main: 10
index from main: 11
index from main: 12
index from main: 13
index from main: 14
end of main
```

You will notice that it stops the main function execution while the longRunningOperation() function is running, printing out the index: statements before continuing the main() execution and printing out the index from main statements. This is synchronous execution of all of the code and it will likely not fit well in all use cases. If this were an app, then the UI would be unresponsive, leading to a bad UX, because the thread is stuck waiting for the longRunningOperation() function to complete, rather than looking after all the many other activities needed to keep an app responsive.

Now, let's say we change this example so that the `longRunningOperation()` function is an asynchronous function and `main()` can continue executing without waiting for it to complete, as follows:

```
import 'dart:io';
import 'dart:async';
Future<void> longRunningOperation() async {
  for (int i = 0; i < 5; i++) {
    sleep(Duration(seconds: 1));
    print("index: $i");
  }
}
main() { ... } // main function is the same
```

We have made one key difference to our code—the `longRunningOperation()` function now has the `async` modifier to indicate that this is an asynchronous function and will return a `Future`. Notice that we have marked that the `return` type of the function is a `Future`. To access these modifiers, we have also added a new `import` statement for `dart:async`. Specifically, we have marked it as `Future<void>` because there is no returned object when the function completes.

If you now execute the preceding code, you may notice something strange; the output is shown here:

```
start of long running operation
index: 0
index: 1
index: 2
index: 3
index: 4
continuing main body
index from main: 10
index from main: 11
index from main: 12
index from main: 13
index from main: 14
end of main
```

Nothing has changed—we are still waiting for the `longRunningOperation()` function to complete. The reason for this is the `sleep()` function. The `sleep()` function is synchronous yet it is also long-running, so the thread is actually getting stuck there and not being released to perform other duties. Thankfully, there is an alternative to the synchronous `sleep()` function, called `Future.delayed()`. This method is asynchronous and will allow us to release the thread.

Let's update our example to become properly asynchronous, as follows:

```
import 'dart:io';
import 'dart:async';
Future<void> longRunningOperation() async {
  for (int i = 0; i < 5; i++) {
    await Future.delayed(Duration(seconds: 1));
    print("index: $i");
  }
}
void main() { ... } // main function is the same
```

We are now calling the `Future.delayed()` function, which is asynchronous. We want our code execution to continue from that point when the function completes, so we have specified this by adding the `await` keyword. Now, the thread will be released to do what it needs to, but when the function completes, our code execution will continue from the `await` point.

Let's run the code and see if this works, as follows:

```
start of long running operation
continuing main body
index from main: 10
index from main: 11
index from main: 12
index from main: 13
index from main: 14
end of main
index: 0
index: 1
index: 2
index: 3
index: 4
```

We no longer have purely synchronous code where one piece of code strictly executes after another, as we did before; here, what changes is the order. In the preceding example, the change occurs when the `longRunningOperation()` function calls `await` in another `async` function. The function is suspended and will be resumed only after a delay of 1 second. After the delay, however, the `main()` function is already running again; it did not wait for the `longRunningOperation()` function to complete because we didn't specify `await`, so the `longRunningOperation()` code will be executed only after the `main()` function has finished.

If we make the `main()` function an `async` function and await the execution of `longRunningOperation()`, then the `main()` function will be suspended right when we call `await longRunningOperation()` and will only be resumed after its execution. This would then behave just like the first output we saw.

One other experiment to try is to stop thread blocking in the `main()` method by replacing the `sleep()` function with `Future.delayed()`. This will then release the thread to move back to the `longRunningOperation()` function and create an interlaced pattern. To do this, change the code as follows:

```dart
main() async {
    print("start of long running operation");
    longRunningOperation();
    print("continuing main body");
    for (int i = 10; i < 15; i++) {
        await Future.delayed(Duration(seconds: 1));
        print("index from main: $i");
    }
    print("end of main");
}
```

If you run the preceding code, you will get the following output:

```
start of long running operation
continuing main body
index: 0
index from main: 10
index: 1
```

```
index from main: 11
index: 2
index from main: 12
index: 3
index from main: 13
index: 4
index from main: 14
end of main
```

To understand this pattern of output produced, you need to appreciate that Dart executes both asynchronous methods in the same thread. Both functions run asynchronously in this case, but this does not mean that they are executed in parallel. Dart actually executes one operation at a time; as long as one operation is executing, it cannot be interrupted by any other Dart code. This execution is controlled by the Dart event loop, which acts as a manager for Dart Futures and asynchronous code.

So, in our example, the `longRunningOperation()` function is executed, and when it reaches the `Future.delayed()` call, it relinquishes control of the thread. The thread can then continue execution of the `main()` function until it reaches its own `Future.delayed()` call when it relinquishes control of the thread. After a second, thread execution continues from the `await` point in the `longRunningOperation()` function, printing the index and looping until it relinquishes control of the thread again, ready for the thread to continue execution from the `main()` function's `await` point. This continues until both loops complete.

You can refer to Dart's official documentation on event loops to understand how this works, at `https://dart.dev/articles/archive/event-loop`.

There is a way to truly execute Dart code in parallel (that is, at the same time). To do this, we use Dart Isolates.

Dart Isolates

So, you may have been wondering, how can you execute truly parallel code and improve the performance and responsiveness of your app? Dart **Isolates** are designed exactly for this purpose. Every Dart application is composed at least of one `Isolate` instance—the main `Isolate` instance where all of the application code runs. So, to create parallel execution code, we must create a new `Isolate` instance that can run in parallel with the main Isolate instance, as illustrated in the following diagram:

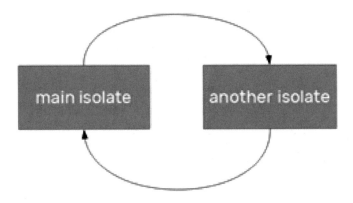

Figure 4.1 – Two Isolates in parallel

Isolates can be considered to be a sort of thread, but they do not share anything with each other, as the name suggests. This means that they do not share memory, so we do not need to use locks and other thread synchronization techniques here.

To communicate between isolates—that is, to send and receive data between them—we need to exchange messages. Dart provides a way of accomplishing this.

Let's change the previous implementation to use an `Isolate` instance instead, as follows:

```dart
import 'dart:io';
import 'dart:isolate';
Future<void> longRunningOperation(String message) async {
  for (int i = 0; i < 5; i++) {
    await Future.delayed(Duration(seconds: 1));
    print("$message: $i");
  }
}
void main() async {
  print("start of long running operation");
```

```
    Isolate.spawn(longRunningOperation, "Hello");
    print("continuing main body");
    for (int i = 10; i < 15; i++) {
        await Future.delayed(Duration(seconds: 1));
        print("index from main: $i");
    }
    print("end of main");
}
```

As you can see, there are some minor changes to the code, as outlined here:

- The `longRunningOperation()` function is almost identical, but we've added a `message` parameter to show how arguments can be passed on `Isolate` creation.

- To initiate the Isolate process to be executed, we use the `spawn()` method from the `Isolate` class. This takes two arguments—the function to be spawned and a parameter to be passed to the function.

- We have added the `import 'dart:isolate'` statement to gain access to the `Isolate` class.

Running the preceding code, you will note a very similar output to before, as illustrated here:

```
start of long running operation
continuing main body
index from main: 10
Hello: 0
index from main: 11
Hello: 1
index from main: 12
Hello: 2
index from main: 13
Hello: 3
index from main: 14
end of main
Hello: 4
```

Again, both functions run interleaved, but this time, the `main` function runs ahead of the `longRunningOperation()` function. This is because unlike the previous example where the thread did not relinquish control until it reached `await Future.delayed()`, the `spawn` operation creates an isolate asynchronously, allowing the `main()` function thread to immediately move to its `await Future.delayed()` function. Note additionally that there is not the dance we had in the previous example where each function relinquished thread control to the other at the `await` point. These are effectively two separate threads running independently.

Summary

In this chapter, we looked at how Dart fits with the OOP basics, which led to an exploration of Dart classes, including inheritance, abstraction, and mixins.

We took a deeper look at class constructors and the different types of constructors available in Flutter, including named and factor constructors.

We then explored enums and examples of how and when they would be used.

Finally, we looked at some more advanced Dart topics that are relevant to Flutter development. The first topic was generics, which allow you to specify type information for a class such as a collection or a Future. The second topic was asynchronous programming, the use of `Futures`, `async`, and `await`, and then a look at Isolates and how they can be used to allow parallel processing.

This chapter will have given you a strong foundational knowledge of Dart and the programming concepts that will be used throughout Flutter development. You may want to refer back to this chapter as we start to look at more advanced Flutter concepts that are built on these foundational principles.

In the next chapter, we will look at Flutter widgets, which will immediately make use of your new Dart knowledge!

Section 2: The Flutter User Interface – Everything Is a Widget

In this section, you will learn Flutter's way of working with the user interface, user data input, and the resources available to create rich user interfaces.

This section comprises the following chapters:

- *Chapter 5, Widgets – Building Layouts in Flutter*
- *Chapter 6, Handling User Input and Gestures*
- *Chapter 7, Routing – Navigating between Screens*

5
Widgets – Building Layouts in Flutter

In this chapter, you will learn what a widget is and the three different types of widgets: stateless, stateful, and inherited. You will explore some of the most common widgets in Flutter, view them in action, and learn how to add them to your application. Additionally, you will gain an understanding of how layout widgets can help you to structure your **user interface (UI)**.

Widgets are classes and objects within the Dart language. Therefore, this chapter will use a lot of the knowledge that you gained in *Chapter 4, Dart Classes and Constructs*, regarding Dart classes and enums. Armed with this knowledge, we will explore **Stateful** and **Stateless** widgets, which are classes that inherit from specific superclasses and are key to how you manage the UI of your app.

Next, we will take a closer look at the built-in widgets that come as part of the Flutter framework and cover most of your UI needs. It is useful to be aware of what is already available, including the layout widgets that control the positioning of their nested child widgets, which, in turn, gives you greater control of how your app looks to the user.

Finally, we will look at the concept of streams, which allows your code to react to changes in the data or state outside of your widget.

The following topics will be covered in this chapter:

- Stateful/stateless widgets
- Built-in widgets
- Understanding built-in layout widgets
- Using streams

By the end of the chapter, you should have a good idea of how Flutter apps are put together and why widgets are such an important part of the Flutter framework.

Technical requirements

You will need your development environment again for this chapter. Take a look back at *Chapter 1, An Introduction to Flutter*, if you require further information on how to set up your IDE or to refresh your knowledge regarding the development environment requirements.

You can find the source code for this chapter on GitHub at `https://github.com/PacktPublishing/Flutter-for-Beginners-Second-Edition/tree/main/hello_world/lib/chapter_05`.

Stateful/stateless widgets

In *Chapter 1, An Introduction to Flutter*, we learned that widgets play an important role in Flutter application development. They are the pieces that form the UI; they are the code representation of what is visible to the user.

UIs are almost never static; they change frequently, as you will have experienced when you have used a web page or an application. Although immutable by definition, widgets are not meant to be final – after all, we are dealing with a UI, and a UI will certainly change during the life cycle of any application. That's why Flutter provides two types of widgets: stateless and stateful.

> **Immutability**
>
> Most programming languages refer to the term "immutable." An immutable object is an object that never changes. That is, it cannot change itself, and it cannot be changed externally. Instead, if a change is needed, then the object is simply replaced. A stateless widget is immutable because it cannot change its properties or state, nor can something external change its properties or state. If the widget needs to change, then it is effectively replaced by a new widget that has different properties or state.

As you might expect, a stateless widget has no state, whereas a stateful widget holds state and adapts based on that state. This difference impacts the life cycle of the widget, how it is constructed, and how the code is structured. It's the developer's responsibility to choose what kind of widget to use in each situation. Generally speaking, a developer should look at stateless as the default option unless the widget needs to hold state. A stateful widget could be used for every scenario, but this will impact performance and code maintainability.

Additionally, Flutter uses the concept of inherited widgets (the **InheritedWidget** type), which is also a kind of widget, but it is slightly different from the other two types that we've mentioned.

Stateless widgets

A typical UI will be composed of many widgets, and some of them will never change their properties after being instantiated. They do not have a state; that is, they do not change by themselves through an internal action or behavior. Instead, they are changed by external events on parent widgets in the widget tree. So, it's safe to say that stateless widgets give control regarding how they are built to a parent widget in the tree. The following diagram shows a representation of a stateless widget:

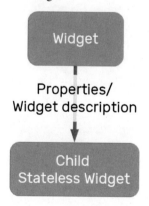

Figure 5.1 – A stateless widget

In the preceding diagram, the parent widget instantiates the child stateless widget and passes a set of properties during the instantiation. The child widget can only receive these properties from the parent widget and will not change them by itself. In terms of code, this means that stateless widgets only have final properties defined during construction, and these properties can only be changed through the update of a parent widget with the changes then rippling down to the child widgets.

Let's take a look at an example of a stateless widget from the Hello World! app that we explored in previous chapters.

Code example

The very first stateless widget inside the application is the application class itself:

```
class MyApp extends StatelessWidget {
  @override
  Widget build(BuildContext context) {
    return MaterialApp(
      title: 'Flutter Demo',
      theme: ThemeData(
        primarySwatch: Colors.blue,
      ),
      home: MyHomePage(title: 'Flutter Demo Home Page'),
    );
  }
}
```

As you can see, the MyApp class extends StatelessWidget and overrides the build(BuildContext) method. The build method is critical to all widgets and describes how the widget should appear on the screen. It does this by building a widget subtree below it. MyApp is the root of the widget tree; it is the top-level widget that is instantiated within the runApp method in the Dart main method. Therefore, it builds all the widgets down the tree. In this example, the direct child is MaterialApp. According to the documentation, MaterialApp can be defined as follows:

"A convenience widget that wraps a number of widgets that are commonly required for material design applications."

> **Material Design**
>
> Material Design is a standard set of designs and digital experiences that were created by Google to help teams build high-quality UIs. Apple has an equivalent named Cupertino, and we will look at examples of both throughout the remainder of this book.

In this example, the stateless widget does not receive any properties from its parent because it doesn't have a parent. We will view examples of properties being passed later.

`BuildContext` is an argument provided to the `build` method as a useful way to interact with the widget tree. It allows you to access important ancestral information that helps to describe the widget that is being built. For example, the theme data defined in this widget can be accessed by all child widgets to ensure there is a consistent look and feel to your application.

In addition to other properties, `MaterialApp` contains the `home` property. This is the first widget that is displayed within your application. Here, `home` refers to the `MyHomePage` widget, which is not a built-in widget, but rather a stateful widget defined within the Hello World! application.

You should now be able to understand how Flutter composes widgets to create the display. Let's take a look at the partner of stateless widgets, that is, the stateful widget.

Stateful widgets

Unlike stateless widgets, which receive properties from their parents that are constant throughout the widgets' lifetime, stateful widgets are meant to change their properties dynamically during their lifetimes. By definition, stateful widgets are also immutable, but they have a companion **State** class that represents the current state of the widget. This is shown in the following diagram:

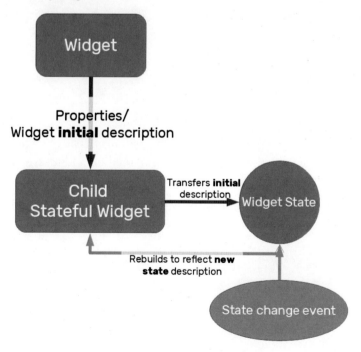

Figure 5.2 – A stateful widget

In the preceding diagram, a widget instantiates a child widget and, similar to the stateless widget example, passes properties to the child. These properties are, once again, final and cannot be changed within the widget. However, unlike the stateless widget example, a companion **State** object also has access to the widget properties and, additionally, is able to hold other properties that are not final.

By holding the state of the widget in a separate **State** object, the framework can rebuild the widget whenever necessary without losing its current associated state. The element in the elements tree holds a reference to the corresponding widget and also the **State** object associated with it. The **State** object will notify you when the widget needs to be rebuilt and then perform an update in the elements tree, too.

Code example

MyHomePage is a stateful widget, and so, it is defined with a **State** object named _MyHomePageState, which contains properties that affect how the widget looks. First, let's take a look at the widget:

```
class MyHomePage extends StatefulWidget {
    MyHomePage({Key key, required this.title}) : super(key: key);

    final String title;

    @override
    _MyHomePageState createState() => _MyHomePageState();
}
```

The first thing that you should pay attention to is that this extends the StatefulWidget, identifying, therefore, that this will have a State companion object. Stateful widgets must override the createState() method and return an instance of the companion object. In this example, it returns an instance of _MyHomePageState.

A valid widget state is a class that extends the framework **State** class, which is defined in the documentation as follows:

"The logic and internal state for a StatefulWidget."

Additionally, in this example, properties have been passed from a parent widget and these are surfaced in the widget constructor. Note that the `title` property has been passed in and is stored in the widget in the final field, which is named `title`. As discussed in *Chapter 4*, *Dart Classes and Constructs*, Dart has some clever shortcuts in the way it structures constructors, and by using `this.title` in this constructor body, we can automatically assign the value of the `title` property to the `title` field.

Normally, stateful widgets define their corresponding `State` classes in the same file. Additionally, state is typically private to the widget library, as external clients do not need to interact with it directly.

The following `_MyHomePageState` class represents the **State** object of the `MyHomePage` widget:

```
class _MyHomePageState extends State<MyHomePage> {
  int _counter = 0;

  void _incrementCounter() {
    setState(() {
      _counter++;
    });
  }

  @override
  Widget build(BuildContext context) {
    return Scaffold(
      appBar: AppBar(
        title: Text(widget.title),
      ),
      body: Center(
        child: Column(
          mainAxisAlignment: MainAxisAlignment.center,
          children: <Widget>[
            Text(
              'You have pushed the button this many times:',
            ),
            Text(
              '$_counter',
              style: Theme.of(context).textTheme.headline4,
```

```
            ),
          ],
        ),
      ),
      floatingActionButton: FloatingActionButton(
        onPressed: _incrementCounter,
        tooltip: 'Increment',
        child: Icon(Icons.add),
      ), // This trailing comma makes auto-formatting nicer for
      build methods.
    );
  }
}
```

Let's go through this code section by section.

First, there is only one class field, which is named _counter, so you can infer that the state of the MyHomePage widget is defined by that single property. The _counter property records the number of presses of the button in the lower-right corner of the screen. How this _counter property changes will be defined in your business logic.

> **What is business logic?**
>
> Business logic is the part of the code where you specify the business rules for your app. Unlike much of your app code, which is concerned with lower-level details, such as how to display widgets or connect to the database, the business logic determines how a user interacts with your app, and how that interaction impacts state data.
>
> For example, where a widget is placed on the screen, what color it is, and how it reacts when pressed is not business logic. However, if, by pressing it, the user can modify information about themselves, such as their gender, home address, or how many cakes they want to buy, then that is business logic.

The first method we encounter is the _incrementCounter method. This takes no arguments and has a **void** return code specifying that it returns no value. However, it does do something crucial that we should explore in further detail:

```
setState(() {
  _counter++;
});
```

A stateful widget is meant to change its appearance during its lifetime – that is, it defines what will change – and so it needs to be rebuilt to reflect such changes. In the **StatefulWidget** diagram (*Figure 5.2*), we saw that the framework rebuilds the StatefulWidget to reflect a new state. However, how does the framework know when something in the widget changes and that a rebuild is required?

The answer is the setState method. This method receives a function as a parameter that updates the widget's corresponding **State**. In this case, we have created an anonymous function, and in the function body, we have specified that the _counter variable should be incremented. By calling setState, the framework is notified that it needs to rebuild the widget. Once called, the widget will be redrawn with the new _counter value already set.

Finally, we reach the widget's build method. The method signature and intended function are identical to the build method of StatelessWidget that we discussed earlier. However, unlike StatelessWidget, we now have a state that will affect how we draw the widget, which could lead to far more complex code involving even more conditional statements.

The build method can look intimidating, and we will look at the individual widgets in more detail later in the chapter. However, at this point, try to get a feel for the composition structure shown. The method returns a Scaffold widget at the top level and is composed of three child widgets via three constructor arguments:

- appBar: This holds a widget of the AppBar type, which itself has one constructor argument named title. As you can guess, this describes the widget that will appear at the top of the screen as an app bar.

- body: This can hold any widget and appears in the main body of the application (that is, between the top app bar and any bottom menu bar). In this case, it holds a Center widget (which centers the child content). This, in turn, holds a Column widget (which creates a vertical column of widgets). Finally, this holds two Text widgets (which display a string of text).

- floatingActionButton: This holds a widget of the FloatingActionButton type, which is a button that floats above the app body in the lower-right corner (as the default configuration) and acts as a button.

Note that one of the arguments for the `FloatingActionButton` constructor is `onPressed`, and that the value is the `_incrementCounter` method. This ties the whole flow together:

1. The `MyHomePage` widget calls the `build` method of the companion state to display the app bar, body, and action button.

2. The user presses the action button.

3. The **onPressed** argument value is triggered, which calls the `_incrementCounter` method.

4. The `_incrementCounter` method calls the `setState` method with the anonymous function, specifying that the `_counter` variable should be incremented.

5. The framework calls the anonymous function, thereby incrementing the `_counter` variable.

6. The framework redraws the widget by calling the `build` method of the companion state again to display the updated app bar, body, and action button:

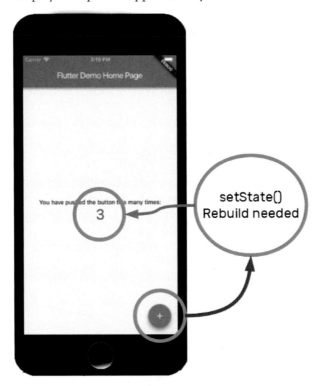

Figure 5.3 – The home page

As the preceding diagram shows, the `setState` method is crucial to this whole flow, and understanding this redrawn flow is central to how the Flutter framework works.

Let's complete this section by looking at a less well-known widget type, that is, the `InheritedWidget` type.

Inherited widgets

Besides `StatelessWidget` and `StatefulWidget`, there is one more type of widget in the Flutter framework, `InheritedWidget`. Sometimes, one widget might require access to data further up the widget tree. In such scenarios, one solution is to replicate the information down to the interested widget by passing it through all of the intermediate widgets. Let's view an example widget composition structure so that we can examine this in more detail:

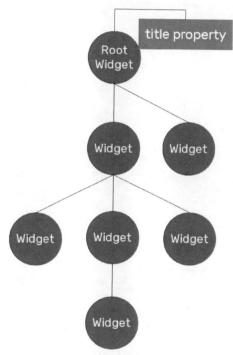

Figure 5.4 – A widget tree with a title property

In this scenario, let's suppose that one of the widgets down the tree requires access to the title property from the root widget. For this to happen in a world where there are only stateful and stateless widgets, we would need to pass the `title` property to every child widget via the constructors so that the child widget could, in turn, pass the `title` property to its child widgets. This can lead to lots of boilerplate code, can be error-prone if one of the widgets isn't coded quite right, and can be really painful if it is decided that the child widget needs another property, which means that all of the intermediate widgets need to be updated.

To address this problem, Flutter provides the `InheritedWidget` class. This is an auxiliary kind of widget that helps to propagate information down the tree, as shown in the following diagram:

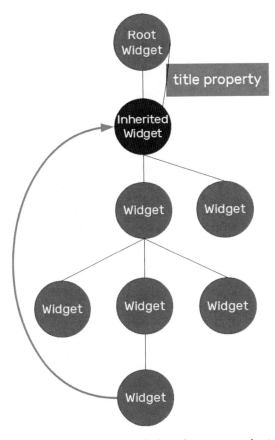

Figure 5.5 – A widget tree with the title property inherited

By adding an `InheritedWidget` to the tree, any widget below it can access the data it exposes by using the `of(InheritedWidget)` method of the `BuildContext` class that receives an `InheritedWidget` type as a parameter and uses the tree to find the first ancestral widget of the requested type.

There are some very common uses of `InheritedWidget` in Flutter. One of the most common uses is from the `Theme` class, which helps to describe colors for a whole application. We will explore this in *Chapter 6, Handling User Input and Gestures*.

Now, let's investigate something that you might have spotted in some of the previous code examples, that is, a constructor property with the name of **key**.

The widget key property

If you take a look at the constructors of the `StatelessWidget` and `StatefulWidget` classes, you will notice a parameter named **key**. This is an important property for widgets in Flutter.

The **key** property allows you to preserve the state of a widget between rebuilds. You might remember that the framework takes the widget tree and renders it to an element tree. The element tree is a very simple representation of the widget tree that only holds the widget's type and the references to its children widgets. When a change or rebuild occurs, the framework uses the widget's type and children references to determine whether a redraw is needed. In situations where there are many widgets of the same type as children of the same widget (for example, rows or columns), there can be situations where the ordering changes but doesn't invalidate the element tree. In this situation, the behavior of Flutter can be unexpected.

Without keys, the element tree would not know which state corresponds to which widget, as they would all have the same type. When a widget has a state, it needs the corresponding state to be moved around with it. Put simply, that is what a **key** helps the framework to do. By holding the key value, the element in question will know the corresponding widget state that needs to be with it.

In most situations, a key is not needed (and should not be used); however, if you see some strange behavior where you are sure your widget is changing state but this is not being correctly reflected on the UI, then it is worth checking whether the framework is misunderstanding the element tree and whether a key might be a suitable remedy for the situation. If you need more information regarding how a key affects the widget and the available types of keys, please check out the official documentation's introduction to keys: `https://flutter.dev/docs/development/ui/widgets-intro#keys`.

We have now explored the fundamental building blocks of Flutter: widgets. Specifically, we have looked at three types of widgets, stateless, stateful, and inherited, along with the situations that you would use them in. Now you have a basic knowledge of the fundamentals of widgets, let's take a look at some widgets you get for free when you start your UI.

Built-in widgets

Flutter has a big focus on the UI, and because of this, it contains a large catalog of widgets that allow you to get started with a high-quality UI relatively easily.

The available widgets of Flutter range from simple ones, such as the `Text` widget in the Flutter counter application example, to complex widgets that enable you to design dynamic UI with animations and multiple gesture handling.

In this section, we will go through these built-in widgets in more detail. We will start with the basic widgets of text and images, move on to more advanced widgets involving user interaction, such as buttons, and finish with a look at layout widgets, which control how other widgets are positioned on the UI.

Basic widgets

The basic widgets in Flutter are a good starting point, not simply because of their ease of use, but because they also demonstrate the power and flexibility of the framework, even in simple scenarios.

In this section, we will explore the most common widgets that you are likely to use as you get started with Flutter. However, there are many more widgets available that you can explore in the *Widget catalog* at `https://flutter.dev/docs/development/ui/widgets`.

The Text widget

The `Text` widget displays a string of text that can be styled as follows:

```
Text (
  "Some exciting text",
  style: TextStyle(color: Colors.red, fontSize: 14),
  textAlign: TextAlign.center
)
```

Pay attention to the structure of the `Text` constructor. The first parameter, that is, the string of text, is a positional parameter. It is then followed by a series of named parameters. Flutter leans heavily on the named parameter approach to keep widget trees readable, but where a parameter is fundamental to the widget, such as the text for a `Text` widget, this is often the first positional parameter.

The most common properties of the Text widget are as follows:

- style: This holds a TextStyle instance that controls how the text should be styled. The TextStyle constructor has properties that allow you to set the text color, background, font family (including the use of a custom font from the assets; please refer to *Chapter 1, An Introduction to Flutter*), line height, font size, and more.

- textAlign: This holds a value from the TextAlign enum describing how the text should be aligned. Options include center alignment and justified alignment.

- maxLines: This holds an integer specifying the maximum number of lines that the text can be wrapped over before it is truncated.

- overflow: This holds a value from the TextOverflow enum describing how the text should be shown that exceeds the available space. Options include fading, ellipsis, or clipping.

To view all of the available Text widget properties, please refer to the official Text widget documentation page at https://docs.flutter.io/flutter/widgets/Text-class.html.

The Image widget

The Image widget displays an image from different sources and formats. Currently, the supported image formats are JPEG, PNG, GIF, animated GIF, WebP, animated WebP, BMP, and WBMP:

```
Image(
  image: AssetImage(
    "assets/dart_logo.jpg"
  ),
)
```

The Image widget is not quite as simple to construct as the Text widget because it needs to know the source of the image file. This could be from the internet, from a file on the device, or from within the app as defined in the assets. To manage this, the widget has an image constructor property that specifies an ImageProvider type.

In this example, the image comes from an asset within the app. This is denoted by using an AssetImage provider that takes the location of the asset as a positional constructor parameter. To retrieve an image from the internet, instead of AssetImage, you should use the NetworkImage provider, which works in a similar way. To retrieve an image from a file on the device, you should use the FileImage provider.

The `Image` class contains convenience constructors to help you with the loading of images, such as the following:

- `Image.asset`: This creates an `AssetImage` provider, which is used to obtain an image from your assets using the asset key. For example, take a look at the following:

```
Image.asset(
    'assets/dart_logo.jpg',
)
```

- `Image.network`: This creates a `NetworkImage` provider to obtain an image from a URL. For example, take a look at the following:

```
Image.network(
    'https://picsum.photos/250?image=9',
)
```

- `Image.file`: This creates a `FileImage` provider to obtain an image from a file:

```
Image.file(
    File(file_path)
)
```

Note that this uses a `File` object to refer to the location of the file.

Now that we have explored the `Text` and `Image` widgets, you have the tools to display information to the user. However, your app will need to allow users to input data, so let's take a look at some of the built-in widgets that will allow this interaction.

Material Design and iOS Cupertino widgets

Many of the widgets in Flutter are descended, in some way, from a platform-specific guideline: Material Design or iOS Cupertino. This enables the developer to follow platform-specific guidelines in the easiest possible way.

For example, Flutter does not have a `Button` widget; instead, it provides alternative button implementations for Google Material Design and iOS Cupertino guidelines. However, you can quite easily just choose one set of implementations to use in the development of your app and use that for all releases (such as the Play Store, the App Store, or the web). There is definitely no need to switch between Material and Cupertino depending on whether the app is running on Android or iOS.

Buttons

Buttons are widgets that automatically accept a user interaction (such as a tap or a click) and call the relevant code or method supplied to them in their constructor.

On the Material Design side, Flutter implements the following button widgets:

- `ElevatedButton`: The `ElevatedButton` widget was previously named `RaisedButton`, but this name was deprecated for clarity. However, you might notice the use of the `RaisedButton` widget in old code examples, which is effectively the same widget. The `ElevatedButton` widget is a button that appears to hover slightly above the page.

- `FloatingActionButton`: As we mentioned earlier, a floating action button is circular, shows an icon, and hovers over the page, generally, in the lower-right corner, although the position can be configured. It is used to enact a primary action for the page it is shown on. For example, on a page showing email messages, the action button could have a plus icon on it denoting the ability to create a new email when it is pressed.

- `TextButton`: A text button is a string of text printed on a Material widget that will react to touch by showing the standard Material splash or ripple. Unlike an `ElevatedButton` widget, the `TextButton` widget does not appear to hover or looks raised above the page.

- `IconButton`: An icon button is a picture printed on a Material widget that, like the `TextButton` widget, will react to touch by showing a splash or ripple effect.

- `DropDownButton`: The `DropDownButton` widget is very similar to the drop-down buttons that you view on web pages. It shows a currently selected item alongside an arrow. Pressing the button will drop down a menu that allows the user to select another item.

- `PopUpMenuButton`: The `PopUpMenuButton` widget will pop up a menu of options to the user, allowing the user to take an action on the app.

For the iOS Cupertino style, Flutter provides the `CupertinoButton` class.

Scaffold

Scaffold implements the basic structure of a Material Design or iOS Cupertino visual layout. Generally, you would use this as the root widget of your page because it allows you to lay out your whole page in a somewhat standard format.

For Material Design, the `Scaffold` widget can contain multiple Material Design components, such as the following:

- `AppBar`: The `AppBar` sits at the top of the device screen. Generally, it will hold a child widget containing text (the title of the page), which appears on the left, and then some action widgets, generally buttons, which appear on the right.

- `body`: The body is the main chunk of the page. It will appear below the `AppBar` (if you have one) and cover the whole screen.

- `TabBar`: Generally, the `TabBar` is just below the `AppBar` and allows the user to switch horizontally between several sub-pages of your page. For example, you might have a chat client and want the user to be able to switch between live messages and pinned messages. The `TabBar` will allow this to happen with a horizontal swipe.

- `TabBarView`: To work with a `TabBar`, you will need to define the views that appear as the user moves between the tabs. `TabBarView` fits that need and will need to match.

- `BottomNavigationBar`: `BottomNavigationBar` sits at the base of the device screen, allowing the user to switch between the top-level app views via a single tap.

- `Drawer`: `Drawer` is a panel that slides in from the side of the screen, allowing the user to quickly navigate around the app. Generally, you would use a bottom navigation bar for the main context changes (for example, to switch from email to the calendar), and then possibly use `Drawer` to navigate within that context (for example, to choose the inbox or spam folder within the email section). However, Flutter is not opinionated in terms of how you should lay out your app, so you are free to choose how to use these widgets yourself.

In iOS Cupertino, the structure is different with some specific transitions and behaviors.

The available iOS Cupertino classes are `CupertinoPageScaffold` and `CupertinoTabScaffold`, which are typically composed of the following:

- `CupertinoNavigationBar`: A top navigation bar, which is typically used with `CupertinoPageScaffold`

- `CupertinoTabBar`: A bottom tab bar, which is typically used with `CupertinoTabScaffold`

As you can see, the Cupertino Scaffold is far more limited in terms of its structure and features than the Material Scaffold. Generally, a good starting point to get a page of your app up and running is to use the Material Scaffold because it covers most of the needs of a page right from the start.

Dialogs

A dialog pops over the top of the currently displayed UI as a modal window, and the display behind it is masked with a translucent gray mask. They are useful for popping short snippets of information, warnings, or errors.

Both Material Design and Cupertino dialogs are implemented by Flutter. On the Material Design side, they are `SimpleDialog` and `AlertDialog`; on the Cupertino side, there is `CupertinoAlertDialog`.

Text fields

Text fields allow a user of your app to enter text using their device's keyboard.

Text fields are implemented in both guidelines by the `TextField` widget in Material Design and by the `CupertinoTextField` widget in iOS Cupertino. Both of them display the keyboard for user input. Some of their common properties are as follows:

- `autofocus`: This indicates whether the `TextField` should be focused automatically when it is shown (if nothing else is already focused on).

- `enabled`: This sets the field as editable or not.

- `keyboardType`: This changes the type of keyboard that is displayed to the user when editing. For example, if you only want the user to enter numbers, then the number pad is shown, or if you want the user to enter a password, then autocorrect is disabled.

We will look at `TextField` widgets in much more detail in *Chapter 6, Handling User Input and Gestures*, especially their use within an input format.

Selection widgets

Selection widgets allow a user to select one or more answers to a question.

The available control widgets for selection in Material Design are as follows:

- `Checkbox` allows the selection of multiple options in a list.

- `Radio` allows a single selection in a list of options.

- `Switch` allows the toggle (on/off) of a single option.

- `Slider` allows the selection of a value in a range by moving the slider thumb.

On the iOS Cupertino side, some of these widget functionalities do not exist. However, there are some alternatives available, as follows:

- `CupertinoActionSheet`: This is an iOS-style modal bottom action sheet that enables you to choose one option among many.

- `CupertinoPicker`: This is a picker control that is used to select an item in a short list.

- `CupertinoSegmentedControl`: This behaves like a radio button, where the selection is a single item from an options list.

- `CupertinoSlider`: This is similar to `Slider` in Material Design.

- `CupertinoSwitch`: This is also similar to Material Design's `Switch`.

It is worth noting that there is no issue with mixing and matching widgets. If you decide that a Cupertino widget looks better than a Material widget, then feel free to use it within your app.

Date and time pickers

For Material Design, Flutter provides date and time pickers through the `showDatePicker` and `showTimePicker` functions, which build and display the Material Design dialog for the corresponding actions via a dialog.

On the iOS Cupertino side, the `CupertinoDatePicker` and `CupertinoTimerPicker` widgets are provided, following the previous `CupertinoPicker` style.

Other components

There are also design-specific widgets that are unique to each platform. Material Design, for example, has the concept of cards, which are defined in the documentation as follows:

"A sheet of Material used to represent some related information."

On the other side of things, Cupertino-specific widgets could have unique transitions present in the iOS world.

It is worth exploring further and then deciding on a design standard for your app. Consistency is probably more important for an app so that the user feels comfortable interacting with your app, so take the time to decide on your approach.

Now that you have an idea of the vast number of built-in widgets available in Flutter, the next natural question is to ask how you should control where they appear on the screen. We've seen a tiny glimpse of this through the Scaffold widget, but most of the content of the Scaffold is held in the body parameter, and that doesn't manage where its child widgets are shown on the screen. It seems we might need another type of widget, that is, a type that can manage the position of other widgets. So, let's take a look at those next.

Layouts

Some widgets initially do not appear to have an effect on how the UI appears to the user. However, if they are in the widget tree, then they will be there somewhere, which affects how a child widget appears (such as how it is positioned or styled).

For example, to position a button in the bottom corner of the screen, we could specify a positioning that is relative to the screen. However, as you might have noticed, buttons and other widgets do not have a position property.

So, you might be asking yourself, "How are widgets organized on the screen?" Well, the answer is more widgets! Flutter provides widgets that allow you to compose the layout itself, with positioning, sizing, styling, and more.

Displaying a single widget on the screen is not a good way to organize a UI. Usually, we will lay out a list of widgets that are organized in a specific way; to do so, we use container widgets.

Let's take a look at the most common built-in layout types.

Container

The simplest way to manage the layout of a widget is to place it as the child of a `Container` widget. Take a look at the following example:

```
Container(
  decoration: BoxDecoration(
    border: Border.all(),
  ),
  padding: EdgeInsets.all(14),
  child: Text(
    'Beautiful Teesside',
  ),
)
```

In this example, the `Container` widget will put 14 pixels of padding around itself, then place a border on all 4 sides, and then, finally, place the text of `'Beautiful Teesside'` within the border.

The `Container` widget holds useful attributes, such as the following:

- `padding`: This indicates how much space should be placed around the container when laying it within the widget tree.

- `margin`: This indicates the amount of space to place around the child widget.

- `decoration`: This allows you to choose whether the `Container` widget should have a background image or color, whether it should have borders around it, whether the borders should have sharp or curved corners, and much more.

- `height/width`: This allows you to decide how much space the `Container` widget should take up on the screen.

Note that there are more specialized widgets that build on the generality of the `Container` widget.

Styling and positioning

The task of positioning a child widget within a parent widget, such as a `Stack` widget, is done through other widgets. We've discussed the generic `Container` widget, but Flutter also provides widgets for very specific tasks.

Centering a widget inside a parent widget is achieved by wrapping the child inside a `Center` widget. Aligning a child widget relative to a parent can be done with the `Align` widget, where you specify the desired position through its `alignment` property. Another useful widget is `Padding`, which allows you to specify the amount of space around the given child.

The functionalities of these widgets are aggregated in the `Container` widget, which combines those common positioning and styling widgets to apply them to a child directly, making the code much cleaner and shorter.

Row and Column

The most common containers in Flutter are the `Row` and `Column` widgets. They have a `children` property that expects a list of widgets to display in some kind of direction (that is, a horizontal list for `Row` or a vertical list for `Column`). You viewed a `Column` widget in the Hello World! app, so let's take a look at a `Row` example:

```
Row(
    mainAxisAlignment: MainAxisAlignment.spaceBetween,
    children: [
        Text("Staithes"),
        Text("Saltburn"),
        Text("Whitby"),
    ],
)
```

In this example, a row of three pieces of text will be placed on the screen with an equal amount of space between them. Note that `Row` isn't great at managing overruns of space, so on a smaller device, you would need to add additional widgets or properties to ensure that the text is displayed correctly.

> **What is with that trailing comma?**
>
> You might have noticed that when declaring lists, or passing arguments to constructors, we often have a trailing comma. Dart doesn't care whether your list has a trailing comma: `[item1, item2]` versus `[item1, item2,]`. However, there are a few reasons why you might choose to include a trailing comma. Firstly, adding items to a list is easier if there is already a comma present. Secondly, copying and pasting become much easier because every entry in the list has the same syntax. Thirdly, the Dart formatter automatically places each list entry onto its own line if there is a trailing comma at the end of the list.

Stack

Another widely used widget is the `Stack` widget, which organizes children widgets in layers, where one child can overlap another child either partially or totally.

This appears similar to a `Row` or `Column` widget in that it takes a list of children widgets and layers them in the order they are defined. So, the first widget is effectively at the bottom of the stack, and the last widget is at the top, potentially covering the lower widgets.

ListView and GridView

If you have developed some kind of mobile application before, then you might have already used lists and grids. Flutter provides classes for both of them, namely, the `ListView` and `GridView` widgets.

`ListView` is very similar to a `Column` widget; however, it is designed to be scrollable and also draw widgets on demand. For example, if you have a list of more than 10 widgets, such as a list of songs or films, then for performance reasons, you might not want to draw all of the widgets to the screen. `ListView` allows you to draw these widgets as they arrive on the screen due to scrolling or orientation changes, using the `ListView.builder` constructor. We will look at this in more detail in later chapters.

`GridView` is also very similar but creates grids of widgets rather than simple lists. It also has the on-demand ability of `ListView`.

In addition to this, other less typical, but nonetheless important, container widgets are available, such as `Table`, which organizes children in a tabular layout.

Other widgets (gestures, animations, and transformations)

Flutter provides widgets for anything related to the UI. For example, gestures such as scroll or touch will all be related to a widget that manages gestures. Animations and transformations, such as scaling and rotation, are also all managed by specific widgets. We will be examining some of them in more detail in the following chapters.

Now that we've learned how to display a UI and interact with the user, there is another key concept to understand that allows your app to better react to other external changes, that is, streams.

Streams

As its name suggests, a **Stream** is simply a stream of data that your app can react to. For example, a stream is used to allow your app to respond to user authentication changes, which we will explore, in further detail, in *Chapter 9, Popular Third-Party Plugins*. That stream shares updates to a user's authentication status. To use the stream, you register to listen to the Stream instance and supply a function that will be called when there is new data added to the stream.

Throughout third-party plugins, especially Firebase plugins, you will see the regular use of streams so that the plugins can effectively call back into your code to tell you something has changed. They are very similar in concept to the use of a callback method, which is passed to the data source and called on data changes.

As a very brief example to give context to this idea, let's take a look at an example of a stream that gives updates when the weather forecast changes. Let's suppose a plugin supplies us with a `WeatherService` class. We might write some code like this:

```
WeatherService.onForecastChange().listen((Forecast fct) {
    if (fct.sunny) {
        print("Yay, beach weather!");
    } else {
        print("Time to get the board games out!");
    }
});
```

In this example, we call the `onForecastChange()` method on `WeatherService`, which returns a stream. Then, we call the `listen()` method on the returned stream and pass in an anonymous function as an argument to the `listen()` method. The anonymous function accepts a `Forecast` instance as a parameter.

Now, every time the forecast changes, `WeatherService` will put a new `Forecast` instance onto the stream, and the anonymous function will be triggered, printing out the "sunny" or "not sunny" message.

The use of streams is very powerful because it allows you to create a very reactive app. Your app will not only react to user inputs, but it will also react to other external changes such as database updates, authentication changes, third-party service updates (such as the Weather Forecast service), or device sensor updates (such as orientation), among many other things.

Summary

In this chapter, you looked at the different types of widgets, such as stateless, stateful, and inherited, which are classes that inherit from the built-in widget type of classes. You examined the differences between the types, when to use each type, and how to make use of the features of each type.

Next, you explored the built-in widgets that are available as part of the Flutter framework, including layout widgets that help structure the UI.

One of the key aspects of the Flutter community is the plugins and packages that are created. As part of this, we explored streams to demonstrate one of the ways that updates can be shared with your app. We will explore plugins and packages, in further detail, in later chapters.

You should now have a better understanding of how Flutter apps are put together; however, as you can imagine, there's still a lot to explore. In the next chapter, we will take a further look at how users interact with Flutter apps.

6
Handling User Input and Gestures

With the use of widgets, it is possible to create an interface that is rich in visual resources while also allowing user interaction through gestures and data entry. In this chapter, you will learn about the widgets used to handle user gestures and receive and validate user input, along with how to create your own custom inputs.

The following topics will be covered in this chapter:

- Handling user gestures
- A deeper look at the stateful widget life cycle
- Input widgets and forms
- Creating custom inputs

Technical requirements

You will need your development environment again for this chapter. Look back at *Chapter 1, An Introduction to Flutter*, if you need to set up your IDE or refresh your knowledge of the development environment requirements.

You can find the source code for this chapter on GitHub at `https://github.com/ PacktPublishing/Flutter-for-Beginners-Second-Edition/tree/ main/hello_world/lib/chapter_06`.

Handling user gestures

A mobile application would be very limited without some kind of interactivity. The Flutter framework allows the handling of user gestures in every possible way, from simple taps to drag and pan gestures. The screen events in Flutter's gesture system are separated into two layers, as follows:

- **Pointers layer**: This layer holds the raw information about how a pointer (for example, a touch, mouse, or stylus) is interacting with the screen. This raw data will include the location and movement of the pointer.

- **Gestures layer**: This layer takes multiple pointer actions and tries to assign them some meaning as a user action. These semantic actions (for example, a tap, drag, or scale) are often more useful to the application, and they are the most typical way of implementing user input handling.

Pointers

Flutter starts screen input handling in the low-level pointer layer. Generally, there is no need to use events from this layer in your application, but if you need to do some bespoke input handling, then you can use this layer to receive events on every pointer update and decide how to control it. For example, if you are coding a game, then you may need precise details on every pointer update rather than relying on the higher-level gesture events.

The Flutter framework implements pointer event dispatching on the widget tree by following a sequence of events:

- `PointerDownEvent` is where the interaction begins, with a pointer coming into contact with a certain location of the device screen. Here, the framework searches the widget tree for the widget that exists in the location of the pointer on the screen. This action is called a hit test.

- Every following event is dispatched to the innermost widget that matches the location and then raises the widget tree from the parent widgets to the root. This propagation of event actions cannot be interrupted. The event could be `PointerMoveEvent`, where the location of the pointer is changed, `PointerUpEvent`, indicating that the pointer is no longer in contact with the screen, or `PointerCancelEvent`, where the pointer is still active on the device but is no longer interacting with your app.

- The interaction will finish with one of the `PointerUpEvent` or `PointerCancelEvent` events.

Flutter provides the `Listener` class, which can be used to detect the pointer interaction events listed previously. You can wrap a widget tree with this widget to handle pointer events on its widget subtree.

Gestures

Although possible, it is not always practical to handle pointer events by ourselves using the `Listener` widget. Instead, the events can be handled on the second layer of the gesture system. The gestures are recognized from multiple pointer events, and even multiple individual pointers (multitouch). There are multiple kinds of gestures that can be handled:

- **Tap**: A single tap/touch on the device screen.

- **Double-tap**: A quick double-tap on the same location on the device screen.

- **Press and long-press**: A press on the device screen, similar to tap, but having contact with the screen for a longer period of time before release.

- **Drag**: A press that starts with a pointer having contact with the screen in some location, which is then moved, and stops having contact at another location on the device screen.

- **Pan**: Similar to drag events. In Flutter, they are different in direction; pan gestures cover both horizontal and vertical drag.

- **Scale**: Two-pointers are used for a drag move to employ a scale gesture. This is also similar to a zoom gesture.

Like the `Listener` widget for pointer events, Flutter provides the `GestureDetector` widget, which contains callbacks for all of the preceding events. You would use them according to the interaction you want to allow. Let's take a look at some examples of `GestureDetector`.

GestureDetector

We can create a stateless widget called `TapExample` to have a look at `GestureDetector` detecting a gesture event:

```
class TapExample extends StatefulWidget {
  TapExample({Key key}) : super(key: key);


  @override
  _TapExampleState createState() => _TapExampleState();
}


class _TapExampleState extends State<TapExample> {
  int _counter = 0;
  @override
  Widget build(BuildContext context) {
    return GestureDetector(
      onTap: () {
        setState(() {
          _counter++;
        });
      },
      child: Container(
        color: Colors.grey,
        child: Text(
          "Tap count: $_counter",
        ),
      ),
    );
  }
}
```

In this example, we have a stateful widget named `TapExample` and its companion state class, `_TapExampleState`. This follows the stateful widget structure we saw in the previous chapter. We need to have a state because we want the widget to react to user input, and this will involve changing the value of a variable and then redrawing the widget.

In the state object, we have a single _counter variable to show how many taps have been performed on the screen. The state object also has the obligatory build method, which holds the details of how the widget should be drawn to the screen. As previously, this is done by returning a child widget tree.

The top widget that is returned is GestureDetector, which in turn has a child constructor parameter into which we have passed a Container widget holding a Text widget. GestureDetector wraps the child widgets and reports on gestures that happen within the child widget tree. Let's look at how we listen to the different gestures.

Tap

A tap gesture involves a pointer contacting the screen at a location and then ending contact at a similar location, without moving away from the location.

In the preceding example, we have specifically used GestureDetector's onTap constructor parameter. Let's look closer at the key section of code:

```
GestureDetector(
  onTap: () {
    setState(() {
      _counter++;
    });
  },
  ...
```

The onTap parameter takes a function as the argument, and we have placed an inline function that increments the _counter variable within the setState method.

If you wish to listen to more fine-grained gestures around taps, there are also other constructor parameters on GestureDetector that can be used:

- onTapDown: A pointer that may be about to tap has come into contact with the screen.

- onTapUp: A pointer that has tapped the screen has finished touching the screen.

- onTapCancel: A pointer that triggered onTapDown (so the gesture layer thought there was a chance the full gesture was going to be a tap) did not actually do a tap.

Using GestureDetector to receive gestures is really that simple, so let's look at the other gestures available to us.

Double-tap

A double-tap has very similar constraints to tap but adds the stipulation that there must be two taps in quick succession.

The code will look very similar to the tap example:

```
GestureDetector(
  onDoubleTap: () {
    setState(() {
      _counter++;
    });
  },
  ...
```

The only difference from the previous example is that the `onDoubleTap` constructor parameter is used. We have passed in the same inline function as the argument and the function will be called every time double-taps are performed at the same location on the screen.

If you wish to listen to more fine-grained gestures around double-taps, there are also other constructor parameters on `GestureDetector` that can be used:

- `onDoubleTapDown`: A pointer that may be about to double-tap has come into contact with the screen.

- `onDoubleTapUp`: A pointer that has double-tapped the screen has finished touching the screen.

- `onDoubleTapCancel`: A pointer that triggered `onDoubleTapDown` (so the gesture layer thought there was a chance the full gesture was going to be a double-tap) did not actually do a double-tap.

Note that some of the more fine-grained, or partial, gestures may be triggered before the full gesture has been resolved, and therefore not align with the correct gesture. For example, `onTapDown` would be triggered on the first tap of a double-tap, but ultimately the tap gesture would not complete because the user did a double-tap rather than a single tap. So, be careful when you use these partial gestures.

Press and hold

A press on the device screen is similar to a tap but having contact with the screen for a longer period of time before release and with no movement away from the location.

The code will look very similar to the previous examples:

```
GestureDetector(
  onLongPress: () {
    setState(() {
      _counter++;
    });
  },
  ...
```

The only difference from the previous item is the property assigned, `onLongPress`, which will be called every time a tap is performed and held for some time before being released from the screen.

If you wish to listen to more fine-grained gestures around long-press, there are also other constructor parameters on `GestureDetector` that can be used:

- `onLongPressStart`: A pointer in contact with the screen has been recognized as enacting a long-press.

- `onLongPressEnd/nLongPressUp`: A pointer that has long-pressed the screen has finished touching the screen.

- `onLongPressMoveUpdate`: A pointer that triggered `onLongPressStart` has now been drag-moved.

It is possible to use many of the different gestures in the same `GestureDetector`. `GestureDetector` will decide which gesture, if any, is applicable to the touch and call the function supplied for that gesture.

Drag, pan, and scale

Drag, pan, and scale gestures are similar to each other, and we have to decide which one to use in each situation, as they cannot all be used together in the same `GestureDetector` widget.

Drag gestures are separated into vertical and horizontal gestures. Even the callbacks are separated.

Horizontal drag

A horizontal drag, as the name suggests, is where the pointer has been placed on the screen, dragged in a mainly horizontal direction, and then released.

Let's see how the detection of a horizontal drag looks in code:

```
GestureDetector(
  onHorizontalDragStart: (DragStartDetails details) {
    setState(() {
      _move = Offset.zero;
      _dragging = true;
    });
  },
  onHorizontalDragUpdate: (DragUpdateDetails details) {
    setState(() {
      _move += details.delta;
    });
  },
  onHorizontalDragEnd: (DragEndDetails details) {
    setState(() {
      _dragging = false;
      _dragCount++;
    });
  },
  ...
```

This time, we need a bit more work than for tap events. In the example, we have three properties present in the state:

- _dragging: Used to update the text viewed by the user while dragging.
- _dragCount: This accumulates the total number of drag events made from start to end.
- _move: This accumulates the offset of the dragging that is applied to the text using the translate constructor of the Transform widget.

As you can see, the drag callbacks receive parameters related to each event: DragStartDetails, DragUpdateDetails, and DragEndDetails. These contain values that may help at each stage of the dragging.

Vertical drag

A vertical drag, as the name suggests, is where the pointer has been placed on the screen, dragged in a mainly vertical direction, and then released.

The vertical version of drag is almost the same as the horizontal version. The significant differences are in the callback properties, which are onVerticalDragStart, onVerticalDragUpdate, and onVerticalDragEnd.

What changes for vertical and horizontal callbacks in terms of code is the delta property value of the DragUpdateDetails class. For horizontal, it will only have the horizontal part of the offset changed, and for vertical, the opposite is the case.

Pan

A pan is similar to a horizontal or vertical drag but the movement of the pointer when in contact with the screen is not predominantly only horizontal or vertical but is instead a mix of both.

The significant differences to the previous examples are that, in addition to the callback properties, which are now onPanStart, onPanUpdate, and onPanEnd. For pan drags, both axes' offsets are evaluated; that is, both delta values in DragUpdateDetails are present, so the dragging has no limitation on the direction.

Scale

The scale version is nothing more than panning on more than one pointer.

Let's see what the scale version of panning looks like:

```
GestureDetector(
  onScaleStart: (ScaleStartDetails details) {
    setState(() {
      _scale = 1.0;
      _resizing = true;
    });
  },
  onScaleUpdate: (ScaleUpdateDetails details) {
    setState(() {
      _scale = details.scale;
    });
  },
  onScaleEnd: (ScaleEndDetails details) {
```

```
setState(() {
  _resizing = false;
  _scaleCount++;
});
},
...
```

We have three properties in the state:

- _resizing: This is used to update the text viewed by the user while resizing using the scale gesture.

- _scaleCount: This accumulates the total number of scale events made from start to end.

- _scale: This stores the scale value from the ScaleUpdateDetails parameter, and that later is applied to the Text widget using the scale constructor of the Transform widget.

As you can see, scale callbacks look very similar to drag callbacks in that they also receive parameters related to each event: ScaleStartDetails, ScaleUpdateDetails, and ScaleEndDetails. These contain values that may help at each stage of the scale event.

Gestures in material widgets

While GestureDetector is a very useful widget, most of the time you will not need to use it because built-in widgets will already have gesture management built into them.

Material Design and iOS Cupertino widgets have many gestures abstracted to a constructor parameter by using the GestureDetector widget internally in their code.

For example, material widgets such as ElevatedButton embed a special widget named InkWell that, in addition to giving access to the tap gesture event, will also create a splash effect on the target widget. The onPressed property of ElevatedButton exposes the tap functionality that can be used to implement the action of the button.

Consider the following example:

```
ElevatedButton(
  onPressed: () {
    print("Running validation");
    ...
  },
  child: Text("validate"),
)
```

A child `Text` widget is displayed in `ElevatedButton` and a tap on the button is handled by the function passed as the argument to the `onPressed` constructor parameter.

So, now that you've had an introduction to gestures, we can move on to other input methods for users. In preparation for that, we first need to learn a little more about stateful widgets.

A deeper look at the stateful widget life cycle

In the previous chapter, we looked at how stateful widgets differ from stateless widgets and how the `build()` method can be called multiple times, triggered by the `setState()` method.

However, there are some additional parts of the life cycle of a stateful widget that we will explore at this point because they are important to how we manage input data and also become increasingly important throughout the rest of the book as we look at more advanced widget interactions.

Key life cycle states

There are several life cycle states that a stateful widget can pass through. In this section, we will look at the states that you will need in most situations. Later in the book, we will introduce additional life cycle states for specific scenarios and corner cases.

Creation of the state

The creation of a state happens at the very start of the stateful widget life cycle, just after the constructor is called. The stateful widget creates a companion `State` object to hold the mutable state by calling the `createState()` method and passing an instance of the companion `State` object. This is a required step in the life cycle; otherwise, the stateful widget will not have a state.

We saw an example of the `createState()` method in the previous chapter:

```
class MyHomePage extends StatefulWidget {
    MyHomePage({Key key, this.title}) : super(key: key);

    final String title;

    @override
    _MyHomePageState createState() => _MyHomePageState();
}
```

Initializing the state

The instance of `State` can initialize its state variables or other infrastructure requirements (such as database connections) in the `initState()` method. This method is only called once when the widget is added to the widget tree for the first time (that is, it becomes visible to the user) and is optional.

We will see some examples of this later in the chapter, but a basic example of the `initState()` method looks as follows:

```
@override
void initState() {
    super.initState();
    // Custom initialization logic here
}
```

In this example, we see that the first line of the method must be a call to initialize the state of the `super` class. This is followed by any custom logic that is required to initialize the widget.

Build

As you saw in the previous chapter, the build method is called when the widget is to be drawn to the screen. It is called after `initState()` and then called every time `setState()` is triggered.

Disposing of the state

When a widget is removed from the widget tree, the `dispose()` method is called. Any infrastructure clean-up needed, generally for activities that happened during `initState()`, such as setting up database listeners or internet connections, will be done in the `dispose()` method.

Again, we will see an example of this later in the chapter, but here is the skeleton structure of the method:

```
@override
void dispose() {
    // Custom clean-up code here
    super.dispose();
}
```

In this example, we see that the last line of the method must be a call to dispose of the state of the `super` class. However, before this, any custom logic that is required to dispose of the widget can be placed.

> **Not disposing of connections**
>
> A common source of errors in an application can be the failure to close connections to databases or other internet resources within the `dispose` method. If you do not close your connections, then they will remain active and continue to try to interact with your widget and use up valuable resources such as device memory and processing power. You will see errors in your logs if you have a connection that is trying to call `setState()` on a widget that is no longer mounted on the widget tree, and this is a big hint that you are not cleaning up connections.

Mounted

In addition to the life cycle states, there is an important field available to you, from the Stateful parent class of your widget, called mounted. This will tell you whether the widget is still mounted onto the widget tree. Specifically, when initState is called, then mounted is marked as true, and when dispose is called, mounted is marked as false.

You would use this for situations such as listening on a database or internet connection. If a change in database or internet connection state was coded to trigger an update of the widget (perhaps through setState()), then it is prudent to add a mounted check before calling setState() as the widget may have been removed from the widget tree between the time you set up the listener and the time it received an update.

Let's look at a simple example:

```
if (mounted) {
  setState(() {
    // Change state here
  });
}
```

In this example, we have wrapped a setState() call within a mounted check to ensure the widget is still on the widget tree and able to be redrawn.

So, now you know a lot more about the stateful widget life cycle, and have the knowledge of user input via gestures, let's look at another common way to receive user input, via input widgets and forms.

Input widgets and forms

The ability of your app to manage gestures is a good starting point for interaction with the user, but for many apps, you also need a way to get other types of input from a user. Getting user data is what adds custom content and customization to many apps.

Flutter provides many input data widgets to help the developer get different kinds of information from the user. We have already seen some of them in *Chapter 5, Widgets – Building Layouts in Flutter*, including TextField, and different kinds of Selector and Picker widgets.

A TextField widget lets the user enter text with a keyboard. The TextField widget exposes the onChanged method, which can be used to listen for changes on its current value, as we have seen previously with the TextField widget. However, another way to listen for changes is by using a controller.

Getting input through a controller

When using a standard TextField widget, we need to use its controller property to access its value. This is done with the TextEditingController class:

```
final _controller = TextEditingController.fromValue(
   TextEditingValue(text: "Initial value"),
);
```

As you can see, by setting the text property of the controller, we can specify the initial value of the widget it is controlling.

After instantiating TextEditingController, we set the controller property of the TextField widget so that it "controls" the widget:

```
TextField(
   controller: _controller,
);
```

TextEditingController is notified whenever the TextField widget has a new value. To listen for changes, we need to add a listener to our _controller:

```
_controller.addListener(() {
   this.setState(() {
     _textValue = _controller.text;
   });
});
```

We have to specify a callback function that will be called every time the TextField widget changes. In this case, we have made a simple inline function that sets a _textValue state variable to the value of the text in TextField as retrieved via the text property on the controller. Check the full example in the attached chapter files.

A similar approach is used for other input widgets. Often, though, you will want to construct a form that holds a group of input data widgets and have validation and feedback for users that work across the whole form.

FormField and TextField

Flutter provides two widgets to help organize the storing of input data, validation of it, and providing feedback promptly to the user. These are the Form and FormField widgets.

The FormField widget works as a base class to create our own input field within a form. Its functions are as follows:

- To help the process of setting and retrieving the current input value
- To validate the current input value
- To provide feedback form validations

FormField widgets often have a Form widget as an ancestor, but in some cases, this is not needed. For example, when we have a single FormField to take input, there is probably no need for a Form widget to manage the form updates.

Many built-in input widgets from Flutter come with a corresponding FormField widget implementation. One example of this is the TextField widget, which has the form-specific TextFormField widget. The TextFormField widget helps with access to TextField's value and also adds form-related behaviors to it, such as validation.

Accessing the FormField widget's state

If we are using the TextFormField widget, then there is an alternative approach to accessing the input data using the FormField widget's state:

```
final _key = GlobalKey<FormFieldState<String>>();

...

TextFormField(
  key: _key,
);
```

We can add a key to `TextFormField` that later can be used to access the widget's current state through the `key.currentState` value, which will contain the updated value of the field.

The specialized type of key refers to the kind of data the input field works with. In the preceding example, this is `String`, because it is a `TextField` widget, so the key type depends on the particular widget used.

The `FormFieldState<String>` class also provides other useful methods and properties to deal with `FormField`:

- `validate()` will call the widget's validator callback, which should check its current value and return an error message, or null if it's valid.

- `hasError` and `errorText` result from previous validations using the preceding function. In `material` widgets, for example, this adds some small text near to the field, providing proper feedback to the user about the error.

- `save()` will call the widget's `onSaved` callback.

- `reset()` will put the field in its initial state, with the initial value (if any) and clear validation errors.

Form

Having `FormFieldWidget` helps us access and validate its information individually. But when we have a set of input widgets in a form structure, then we can use the `Form` widget. The `Form` widget groups the `FormFieldWidget` instances logically, allowing us to perform operations including accessing field information and validating the whole set of fields in a more structured way.

The `Form` widget allows us to run the following methods on all descendant fields easily:

- `save()`: This will call the `save` method of all `FormField` instances, saving all the form data in the fields at once.

- `validate()`: This will call the `validate` method of all `FormField` instances, causing all the errors to appear at once.

- `reset()`: This will call the `reset` method of all `FormField` instances, resetting the whole form to its initial state.

Accessing the Form widget's state

Your app will need to be able to access the Form widget's state, much like we accessed the FormField widget's state, so that you can run validation, data saves, and resets from other parts of the user interface, not just within the form widget tree. For example, you may have a floating action button that allows you to save the form, or an app bar button to reset the form.

Let's look at two ways to access the form state.

Using a key

The Form widget must be used with a key of the FormState type. FormState contains helpers to manage all of the children of FormField:

```
final _key = GlobalKey<FormFieldState<String>>();
...
  Form(
    key: _key,
    child: Column(
    children: <Widget>[
      TextFormField(),
      TextFormField(),
    ],
  ),
);
```

In this example, we have a Form with a global key and, indirectly, two TextFormField widgets as children.

We can then use the key to retrieve the Form widget's associated state and call its validation with _key.currentState.validate().

Most of the time this is the best way to access the Form widget, but if you have a complex widget tree, then there is another option. Let's have a look at this alternative option.

Using InheritedWidget

The Form widget comes with a helpful class to dispense with the need to add a key to it and still get its benefits.

Each Form widget in the tree has an associated InheritedWidget with it. Form and many other widgets expose this in a static method called of(), where we pass BuildContext, and it looks up the tree to find the corresponding state we are looking for. Knowing this, if we need to access the Form widget somewhere below it in the tree, we can use Form.of(), and we gain access to the same functions as we would have if we were using the key property:

```
Widget build(BuildContext topContext) {
  return Form(
    child: Column(
      mainAxisSize: MainAxisSize.min,
      children: <Widget>[
        TextFormField(
          validator: (String value) {
            return value.isEmpty ? "Not empty" : null;
          },
        ),
        TextFormField(),
        Builder(
          builder: (BuildContext subContext) => TextButton(
            onPressed: () {
              final valid = Form.of(subContext).validate();
              print("valid: $valid");
            },
            child: Text("validate"),
          ),
        )
      ],
    ),
  );
}
```

Pay special attention to the Builder widget used to render TextButton. As we have seen before, the inherited widget can be used to look up the widget tree. When we use Form.of(subContext), it uses BuildContext from Builder, which is lower down the widget tree than the Form widget. Therefore, Form.of(subContext) will search the widget tree and find Form.

If the builder wasn't present and we used the context from the `build` method, then `Form.of(topContext)` would start the search on the widget tree above the `Form` widget and would not find the `Form` widget during that search.

Validating user input

Validating user input is one of the main functions of the `Form` widget. To ensure the data entered by the user is valid, it is fundamental to run validation checks as the user probably does not know all the allowed values or may have made a mistake.

The `Form` widget, combined with `FormField` instances, helps you show an appropriate error message if an input value needs to be corrected, before saving the form data through its `save()` function.

We have already seen, in the previous `Form` examples, how to validate the form field values. Let's look at the actual flow:

1. Create a `Form` widget with `FormField` on it.

2. Define the validation logic on each `FormField` validator constructor property by passing a validation function as the argument. Here is an example of an inline function:

```
TextFormField(
    validator: (String value) {
        return value.isEmpty ? "Cannot be empty" : null;
    },
)
```

3. When a user chooses to submit the form, call `validate()` on `FormState` by using its key, or the `Form.of` method discussed previously.

4. Each `FormField` that is a child of the form will have the `validate()` method called:

    A. Where the validation is unsuccessful, some error text is returned as a string. This error text is then displayed on `FormField` to the user so that they can correct the issue and submit the form again.

    B. Where the validation is successful, a `null` value is returned.

5. If the validation is successful, the `save()` method can be called on `FormState` to persist all of the data from the input fields.

Now that you have an understanding of forms, let's take a look at how we can go deeper on the customization of our form inputs.

Custom input and FormField widgets

We have seen how the `Form` and `FormField` widgets help with input manipulation and validation. Also, we know that Flutter comes with a series of input widgets that are `FormField` variants containing helper functions such as `save` and `validate`.

The extensibility and flexibility of Flutter is everywhere in the framework, so creating your own custom input fields is entirely possible.

Creating custom inputs

Creating a custom input in Flutter is as simple as creating a normal widget and including the methods described earlier. We normally do this by extending the `FormField<inputType>` widget, where `inputType` is the value type of the input widget.

So, the typical process is as follows:

1. Create a custom widget that extends `StatefulWidget` (to keep track of the value) and accepts input from the user by encapsulating another input widget, or by customizing the whole process, such as by using gestures.

2. Create a widget that extends `FormField` that basically displays the input widget created in the previous step and also exposes its fields.

Custom input widget example

Later, in *Chapter 9, Popular Third-Party Plugins*, we will see how to use a plugin to add authentication to our app. For now, we will be creating a custom widget that will be similar to the one used in that step.

In this example, we will ask the user for a phone number and then pretend they have been sent a six-digit verification code. We will then ask them to enter the verification code, which must match the server value in order to successfully log in.

For now, that's all the information we need to know for the creation of the custom input widget. This is what it's going to look like:

Figure 6.1 – Example of a custom input widget

The widget will start a simple six-digit input widget, which will later become a `FormField` widget and expose the `save()`, `reset()`, and `validate()` methods.

Creating an input widget

We start by creating a normal custom widget. Here, we expose some properties. Bear in mind that in a real application, we would probably expose more than the properties exposed here, but it's enough for this example:

```
class VerificationCodeInput extends StatefulWidget {
  final BorderSide borderSide;
  final onChanged;
  final controller;
  ...
}
```

The only important property exposed here is `controller`. We will see the reason in a few moments. Let's check the associated `State` class:

```
class _VerificationCodeInputState extends
State<VerificationCodeInput> {
  @override
  Widget build(BuildContext context) {
    return TextField(
      controller: widget.controller,
      inputFormatters: [
        FilteringTextInputFormatter.allow(RegExp("[0-9]")),
        LengthLimitingTextInputFormatter(6),
      ],
      textAlign: TextAlign.center,
      decoration: InputDecoration(
        border: OutlineInputBorder(
          borderSide: widget.borderSide,
        ),
      ),
      keyboardType: TextInputType.number,
      onChanged: widget.onChanged,
    );
  }
}
```

As you can see, the widget simply returns a `TextField` in the `build` method with some predefined customization:

- `FilteringTextInputFormatter` allows you to specify a regex with either the allowed or denied characters for the input. The `.allow` or `.deny` constructors can be used to create the relevant filter check. In this example, we have used the `.allow` constructor to specify a regex allowing numbers.

- By setting the `keyboardType` property with `TextInputType`, you can make sure the best keyboard is popped up to the user. We only want numbers, so popping up a full keyboard would be unhelpful to the user. In this example, we have ensured that just a number pad is popped up by using `TextInputType.number`.

- `LengthLimitingTextInputFormatter` specifies a maximum character limit for the input.

- Also, to make it look a bit fancy, a border has been added through the `OutlineInputBorder` class.

Take note of the important part of this code: `controller: widget.controller`. Here, we are setting the controller of the `TextField` widget to be a controller passed to our custom input from a parent widget so that the parent widget can take control of our custom input's value.

Turning the widget into a FormField widget

To turn the widget into a `FormField` widget, we start by creating a widget that extends the `FormField` class, which is `StatefulWidget` with some `Form` facilities.

This time, let's start by checking out the new widget's associated `State` object. Let's do this by breaking it into parts:

```
class _VerificationCodeFormFieldState extends
State<VerificationCodeFormFieldInput> {
  final TextEditingController _controller =
  TextEditingController(text: "");
  @override
  void initState() {
    super.initState();
    _controller.addListener(_controllerChanged);
  }
  ...
```

From the preceding code, you can see the state has a _controller field, which will represent the controller used by the FormField widget. It is initialized in the initState() function where we add a listener to it, so we can know when the value is changed in the _controllerChanged listener.

The remainder of the widget is as follows:

```
void _controllerChanged() {
  didChange(_controller.text);
}

@override
void reset() {
  super.reset();
  _controller.text = "";
}

@override
void dispose() {
  _controller?.removeListener(_controllerChanged);
  super.dispose();
}
```

There are also other important methods that we must override to make it work properly:

- With initState(), we now use its opposite in the dispose() method. Here, we stop listening to changes in the controller.

- The reset() method is overridden, so we can set _controller.text to empty, making the input field clear again.

- The _controllerChanged() listener notifies the super FormFieldState state via its didChange() method so it can update its state via setState() and notify any Form widget that contains it about the change.

Now, let's examine the FormField widget code to see how it works:

```
class VerificationCodeFormField extends FormField<String> {
  final TextEditingController controller;
  VerificationCodeFormField({
    Key key,
    FormFieldSetter<String> onSaved,
    this.controller,
```

```
      FormFieldValidator<String> validator,
  }) : super(
    key: key,
    validator: validator,
    builder: (FormFieldState<String> field) {
      _VerificationCodeFormFieldState state = field;
      return VerificationCodeInput(
        controller: state.controller,
      );
    },
  );
  @override
  FormFieldState<String> createState() =>
    _VerificationCodeFormFieldState();
  }
  ...
```

The new part here is in the constructor. The `FormField` widget contains the `builder` callback, which should build its associated input widget. It passes the current state of the object so we can build the widget and retain the current info. As you can see, we use this to pass the controller constructed in the state, so it persists even when the field is rebuilt. That's how we keep the widget and state synchronized, and also integrate with the `Form` class.

Summary

In this chapter, we have seen how gesture handling works in the Flutter framework, along with the methods for handling gestures, such as tap, double-tap, pan, and zoom, for example. We have seen some widgets that use `GestureDetector` by themselves to handle gestures.

We then looked deeper at the life cycles of stateful widgets so that we could use this new knowledge to explore input widgets and access their data.

Finally, we extended this knowledge of input widgets by exploring the use of the `Form` and `FormField` widgets to properly validate and handle user data.

In the next chapter, you will put together the widget knowledge you have gained from the previous two chapters to create full app pages and navigate between them using the `Route` concept.

7
Routing – Navigating between Screens

Mobile apps are typically organized into multiple screens or pages. You will have seen this when you use many mobile apps. For example, perhaps an app has an initial list view of items (such as groceries or films), and when you choose one of the items, you are taken to another screen or page where more details are shown about the item. When you do this, you have just navigated from one screen to another.

In Flutter, moving between screens is called a route and is managed by the `Navigator` widget of the application. The `Navigator` widget manages the navigation stack, pushing a new route onto the stack or popping a previous one off. In this chapter, you will learn how to use the `Navigator` widget to manage your app routes, how to add transition animations, and how to pass information (state) between screens.

The following topics will be covered in this chapter:

- Understanding the `Navigator` widget
- Understanding routes
- Screen transitions
- Passing data between screens

By the end of this chapter, you will be able to create an app with several screens and manage the routes between them. You will be well on the way to having the skills to create a useable Flutter app!

Technical requirements

You will need your development environment again for this chapter. Look back at *Chapter 1, An Introduction to Flutter*, if you need to set up your IDE or refresh your knowledge of the development environment requirements.

You can find the source code for this chapter on GitHub at the following link: `https://github.com/PacktPublishing/Flutter-for-Beginners-Second-Edition/tree/main/hello_world/lib/chapter_07`.

Understanding the Navigator widget

Mobile applications will often contain more than one screen. If you are an Android or iOS developer, you probably know about `Activity` or `ViewController` classes that represent screens on those platforms.

An important class for navigation between screens in Flutter is the `Navigator` widget, which is responsible for managing screen changes while maintaining a history of screens so that the user can move back through screens (if the app allows it).

A new screen in Flutter is just a new widget that is effectively placed on top of another. This is managed through the concept of routes, which define the possible navigable routes a user can follow through the app. As you may already have guessed, the `Route` class is a helper for Flutter to work on the navigation workflow.

The main classes in the navigation layer are as follows:

- `Navigator`: The `Route` manager.
- `Overlay`: `Navigator` uses this to specify the appearances of the routes.
- `Route`: A navigation endpoint.

We will explore these different classes in the next few sections, but first, we need to look at how the actual approach to navigation has changed as Flutter has evolved.

Navigator 1.0 and 2.0

As Flutter has moved to the web, and generally evolved to be a more complete app development framework, the way that app navigation between screens is structured has changed, and now there are two different available ways to navigate.

Navigator 1.0 worked in an imperative style; the code flow instructed the framework to add or remove screens from the stack. This works nicely for most apps, especially within iOS or Android environments, and is a simple approach that is easy to understand and follow.

However, the web introduces new challenges around direct links deep within the app that are designated through specific URLs. In an iOS or Android app, you generally expect a user to enter through the first screen of the app and navigate from there. However, on the web, you may share a web URL that links to a specific screen within the web app. For example, suppose you are browsing a book-selling website and share a link for a single book. You would expect the person you shared it with to be able to go directly to that web page while still having the stack of expected screens that they would have followed to get to that page (in this case, the book list page) available to them.

This is not a web-specific scenario; the same is true for deep links within iOS or Android apps, but it becomes more obvious in web apps that the Navigator 1.0 approach is not as well suited to a world where people can enter your app on any screen.

Navigator 2.0 follows a declarative style that is similar to the approach used within a widget tree; the screens available are declared upfront and the state decides which ones are shown to the user.

We will explore both approaches as both are supported and entirely acceptable ways to build your app. Many in the community believe that the naming was unhelpful because it implies that Navigator 2.0 supersedes the original navigator approach. This is generally not true and, additionally, Navigator 2.0 can be a much more complicated way to start your Flutter development.

> **Imperative versus declarative**
>
> Imperative and declarative are different ways of writing your code. There is no right or wrong choice, and different situations may suit a specific choice. In coding, you can specify code that becomes active based on the world state (declarative) or you can instruct code to run (imperative).
>
> A way to think about the difference is perhaps to think of a parent organizing lunch for a young child. The parent has effectively declared that at a set time of the day, they will make lunch. When the state of the world changes (that is, time passes), the parent assesses the state change and if it matches their declared intent, then they make lunch. Nothing has told the parent to make the lunch; it was a change in the world state that triggered their lunch-creating activity. On the flipside, the child is told to eat their lunch when it is ready, perhaps using a verb in the imperative form to instruct the child: "Eat your lunch."
>
> To complete the example and show that either option is fine, imagine an alternative scenario where the adult has set an alarm to instruct them to make the lunch (imperative) and the child has declared that they will eat food whenever it is placed on the table (declarative). This is also an acceptable scenario.

Navigator

The `Navigator` widget is the key to moving a user from one screen to another. Most of the time, the user will change screens and need their data to be passed along to the new screen. This is another important task for the `Navigator` widget.

Navigation in Flutter is conceptually a stack of screens:

- We have one element at the top of the stack. In Navigator, the topmost element on the stack is the currently visible screen of the app.

- The last element inserted is the first to be removed from the stack, commonly referred to as **last in first out** (**LIFO**). The last screen visible is the first that is removed.

- The `Navigator` widget has `push()` and `pop()` methods to add and remove screens from the stack. This is the imperative, Navigator 1.0 style; the navigator is being told to add or remove screens.

- The `Navigator` widget has a `pages` property where, much like a stack containing a list of widgets, the pages are listed and shown or removed based on the state of the containing widget. This is the declarative, Navigator 2.0 style; the screens listed in the `pages` property are shown or not based on state rather than being told to show or not.

Let's take a look at the Navigator 1.0 approach.

Navigator 1.0

The Navigator 1.0 approach has been in use since Flutter was created, and the vast majority of code examples available use the Navigator 1.0 approach to navigate between screens. Therefore, it is important to know this approach to navigation, and in many cases, it will be the best fit for your app anyway due to its simplicity.

Let's look at how we would use this approach to navigation, first by understanding what a **Route** is.

Route

The navigation stack elements are Routes, and there are multiple ways to define them in Flutter.

When we want to navigate to a new screen, we define a new Route widget to it, in addition to some parameters defined as a `RouteSettings` instance.

RouteSettings

This is a simple class that contains information about the route relevant to the `Navigator` widget. The main properties it contains are as follows:

- `name`: Identifies the route uniquely. We will explore this in detail in the next section.
- `arguments`: With this, we can pass anything to the destination route.

MaterialPageRoute and CupertinoPageRoute

The **Route** class is a high-level abstraction, but different platforms may expect screen changes to behave differently. In Flutter, there are two main alternative implementations that align with platform expectations: `MaterialPageRoute` and `CupertinoPageRoute`, which adapt to Android and iOS respectively.

So, you must decide when developing an application whether to use the Material Design or iOS Cupertino transitions, or both, depending on the context.

Putting it all together

It is time to check out how to use the `Navigator` widget in practice. Let's extend the hello world! example to have a basic flow that navigates to a second screen and back.

Firstly, let's create a widget that we can use as the second screen. In your `main.dart`, add a new widget that looks something like this:

```dart
class AnotherScreen extends StatelessWidget {
  AnotherScreen({required this.title});
  final String title;
  @override
  Widget build(BuildContext context) {
    return Scaffold(
      body: Center(
        child: ElevatedButton(
          child: Text(title),
          onPressed: () {
            // To be added
          },
        ),
      ),
    );
  }
}
```

This is a simple `Stateless` widget that takes a single `String` parameter named `title` and has the `build` method defined. You should be starting to get familiar with widget trees, but let's step through this `build` method as a refresher.

The `Scaffold` widget is at the top level and can be used to specify the app bar at the top of the screen, the body of the screen, and other items such as floating action buttons. It also has the benefit of being a Material widget, which means that child widgets can also be Material widgets.

We then have a `Center` widget, which simply centers the child widget within the **Center**'s parent widget, and finally, we have an `ElevatedButton` widget, which is where the magic will happen. It has a simple `Text` widget as a child (which takes the `title` parameter as the text to display), and the `onPressed` handler, which we will look at shortly.

Let's now add a route to this new page. Within the `build` method of the `_MyHomePageState` class, you will see the `Column` widget. Make a change to its `children` property to add an `ElevatedButton`, as shown here:

```
children: <Widget>[
  ... // Text widgets
  ElevatedButton(
    child: Text('Press this'),
    onPressed: () {
      Navigator.of(context).push(
        MaterialPageRoute(builder: (context) {
          return AnotherScreen(title: "Go back");
        }),
      );
    },
  ),
],
```

Much like the `ElevatedButton` we looked at before, this `ElevatedButton` has a child `Text` widget and an `onPressed` handler. This time we have added code to the handler that will change the screen. Let's look at that line by line:

```
Navigator.of(context).push(
```

You may recognize this structure from *Chapter 5, Widgets – Building Layouts in Flutter*, where we explored `InheritedWidgets`. The `Navigator` widget is an inherited widget, which means you can find it by searching the context to retrieve it. There is an implicit Navigator created within the `MaterialApp` widget, so this is looking up the tree and finding the `Navigator` associated with the `MaterialApp` widget and returning it.

We then choose to `push()` an entry onto the Navigator. As you saw previously, the Navigator is like a stack, so we are pushing a new screen onto the stack so that it appears over the existing screen.

We pass the push method a `MaterialPageRoute`:

```
MaterialPageRoute(builder: (context) {
```

This holds the information about the new screen that we want to draw, and the contents of the new screen are returned as part of the `builder` property on the `MaterialPageRoute`.

Finally, we return the widget for the new screen:

```
return AnotherScreen(title: "Go back");
```

This specifies that when the route is drawn using the `builder` property, we want the `AnotherScreen` widget to be drawn.

With this all in place, you can try your first navigation to a new screen! Click the **Press this** button and you should navigate to a new screen with the **Go back** button showing. However, the **Go back** button has no code within its `onPressed` method, so let's go back and fix that. If you leave the code running, then you can take advantage of hot reloading.

Set the following code as the `onPressed` method on the `ElevatedButton` of the `AnotherScreen` class:

```
onPressed: () {
    Navigator.of(context).pop();
},
```

This looks similar to the use of `Navigator` above, but instead of the push method, we now use the `pop()` method to remove the current screen from the navigator stack and effectively go "back" to the previous screen.

Save this change, enjoy the wonder of hot reloading, and then check whether you can get back from the second screen to the first.

Getting the Navigator

You may see code examples where the Navigator call looks slightly different. Instead of `Navigator.of(context).pop()`, you may see `Navigator.pop(context)`. These are effectively equivalent because the first line of code in `Navigator.pop(context)` is to find the Navigator using `Navigator.of(context)`. Use whichever approach feels more comfortable to you.

Well done – you've set up your first navigation. The world is now your oyster! Hopefully, you can now see how a multi-screen app can be built and that, although the syntax can seem a little intimidating at first, it actually all makes sense. Note that this is clearly an imperative approach to navigation; you are instructing the navigator to change pages through the use of push and pop.

There is another way to use the imperative approach, which uses named routes.

Named routes

The route name is an important piece of navigation. It is the identification of the route with its manager, the `Navigator` widget.

We can define a series of routes with names associated with each of them. It provides a level of abstraction to the meaning of a route and a screen. In addition, they can be used in a path structure; in other words, they can be seen as subroutes in the same way a web URL is structured.

Moving to named routes

Our previous example of navigating was very simple, but we can better organize the navigation structure through the use of named routes, allowing us to do the following:

- Organize the screens in a clear way
- Centralize the creation of screens
- Pass parameters to screens

Named routes are specified on the `MaterialApp` widget, so let's modify the hello world code to use named routes.

Firstly, update the `MaterialApp` widget so that it has a `routes` property that looks like this:

```
routes: {
  '/': (context) => MyHomePage(title: 'Flutter Demo Home
    Page'),
  '/screen2': (context) => AnotherScreen(title: "Go back"),
},
```

In this code, we have specified that there are two routes available within the app. The `'/'` route, which will use the `MyHomePage` widget to draw the screen, and the `'/screen2'` route, which will use the `AnotherScreen` widget to draw the screen.

If you try to run the code as it is now, you will get an error because you now have both the `'/'` route and the home property set on the `MaterialApp`. The `'/'` route is a special route that is equivalent to the home of the app, so you are effectively defining home twice and Flutter doesn't know which one should be used.

So, go ahead and remove the home property and try running the app; it should work now. Note that the navigation still works without routes because ultimately you are still adding and removing screens to the navigation stack, whether you choose to use routes or not.

Finally, let's change the navigation so that it uses the route. In the `ElevatedButton` of `_MyHomePageState`, edit `onPressed` so that it looks like this:

```
onPressed: () {
    Navigator.of(context).pushNamed("/screen2");
},
```

Notice how much cleaner the code feels, and the intent of the navigation is clearer. The creation of a `MaterialPageRoute` is now implicit.

Save the update, let the hot reload work its magic, and then check that the navigation flow still works correctly. `pop()` continues to work as before; `pushNamed` still just adds a screen to the stack, so the pop will simply remove that screen as expected.

Arguments

You may notice that now our title for `AnotherScreen` is always going to be the same. This often isn't the behavior you would want; you would expect the calling screen to be able to set the arguments of the screen that is being navigated to.

To solve this problem, the `pushNamed` method also accepts arguments that are passed to the route. Make the following change to your `onPressed` method in the `ElevatedButton`:

```
Navigator.of(context).pushNamed('/screen2', arguments: "Go back again");
```

However, life is not so simple now, and the `routes` parameter of `MaterialApp` can no longer be used. Instead, we need to use the `onGenerateRoute` parameter to pass the settings to the `AnotherScreen` widget.

On your `MaterialApp` widget, remove the `routes` parameter and add `onGenerateRoute` so it looks like this:

```
onGenerateRoute: (settings) {
  if (settings.name == '/') {
    return MaterialPageRoute(builder: (context) =>
    MyHomePage(title: "Flutter Demo Home Page"));
  } else if (settings.name == '/screen2') {
    return MaterialPageRoute(builder: (context) =>
    AnotherScreen(title: settings.arguments as String));
  }
},
```

The `onGenerateRoute` code looks at the `settings.name` to see which route was selected and then returns a `MaterialPageRoute` with the details required for that route. This looks very similar to the code that we had when we were using the `push` method instead of `pushNamed`, but has the obvious disadvantage that we've lost type safety on `settings.arguments` and have to hope the cast to `String` works correctly.

Should I use named routes?

Whether you choose to use named routes is your choice – there is no right answer because the choice will be based on personal opinion.

Personally, I prefer to use the `push()` method because it has strong type safety on the constructor parameters of the widget within the route. However, if you are not passing arguments to the routes, or you prefer the style of having central route management, then you may choose named routes.

So, we've seen how to move to a route using `push` and `pushNamed`, and how to pass arguments to those routes. However, there will be situations where we want to return a result to the calling screen during a `pop()`, so let's look at that next.

Retrieving results from Route

When a route is pushed to the navigation, we may want to expect something back from it—for example, when we ask for something from the user in a new route, we can take the value returned via the `pop()` method's `result` parameter.

The `push` method and its variants return a Future. The Future resolves when the route is popped and the value of Future is the `pop()` method's `result` parameter.

We have seen that we can pass arguments to a new **Route**. As the inverse path is also possible, instead of sending a message to the second screen, we can take a message when it pops back.

Let's update `AnotherScreen` so that the user can make a choice. In the `build` method, update the `Center` widget so that the child is a `Column` holding two `ElevatedButtons` like this:

```
Widget build(BuildContext context) {
  return Scaffold(
    body: Center(
      child: Column(
        mainAxisAlignment: MainAxisAlignment.center,
        children: [
          ElevatedButton(
            child: Text(title),
            onPressed: () {
              Navigator.of(context).pop(true);
            },
          ),
          ElevatedButton(
            child: Text("Cancel"),
            onPressed: () {
              Navigator.of(context).pop(false);
            },
          ),
        ],
      ),
    ),
  );
}
```

You will notice that, apart from the slight widget tree change to accommodate the extra `ElevatedButton`, `pop()` now takes an argument. In this case, it is a bool, but any type can be returned via the pop method.

Now we need to update the code in `onPressed` of `ElevatedButton` in `MyHomePage` so that it can receive the returned value.

Let's look at how we could do that with this example code. Note that the example has moved back to use push rather than pushNamed for navigation. Feel free to revert your code back to the earlier example of routes using push:

```
ElevatedButton(
  child: Text('Press this'),
  onPressed: () async {
    bool? outcome = await Navigator.of(context).push(
      MaterialPageRoute(builder: (context) {
        return AnotherScreen(title: "Go back");
      }),
    );
    ScaffoldMessenger.of(context).showSnackBar(
      SnackBar(content: Text("$outcome")),
    );
  },
),
```

The result of push is a **Future**, so our code will need to wait for the result and it specifies this through the await keyword. That means we also need to update the method signature of the anonymous function we are supplying to onPressed to specify that it is an asynchronous function. We do this with the async keyword between the parameters list in the round brackets (which is empty) and the method body in the curly brackets.

Finally, we use a very useful Flutter feature, SnackBar, to pop the result to the screen. ScaffoldMessenger is an InheritedWidget, so we use the now-familiar <type>. of() syntax to find it, and then use it to show a snack bar (a notification that slides up from the bottom of the screen). The showSnackBar method simply takes a SnackBar widget as its parameter, which we have specified as having a child widget of the Text type containing the outcome value.

If you need to refresh your knowledge of working with Futures, take a look back at *Chapter 4, Dart Classes and Constructs.*

As you can see, Navigator 1.0 is a fully featured and intuitive navigation system that you can easily add to your app to allow users to navigate around easily. The use of the inherited Navigator widget, alongside routes, is simple to understand and implement. I'll be honest and say I have used Navigator 1.0 for all my apps and have only occasionally found a limitation. However, there are some situations when Navigator 1.0 doesn't quite fit the requirements, especially in the world of the web, so let's take a look at Navigator 2.0.

Navigator 2.0

As mentioned previously, the Navigator 1.0 approach had some limitations around building screen stacks on deep linking, and this is most apparent on web-based apps. Therefore, Navigator 2.0 was created and takes a different, declarative, approach to navigation.

Let's start by looking at Pages, the key part of Navigator 2.0.

Pages

The **Navigator** has a parameter called `pages` that takes a list of **Page** widgets. As this list changes, due to changes in state, the stack of routes is updated to match the **pages** list.

This is very similar to how other widgets that compose a list of children widgets work. For example, a `Column` widget will have children widgets that it composes into a column to display on the screen. If the state changes, and this means the children widgets in the **Column** change, then Flutter will redraw the column on the screen with the updated widgets.

The big advantage of this approach is that if you start with a pre-defined state that involves a stack of several screens (for example, a deep web URL link into your app), then this will work automatically by having several **Page** entries in the `pages` parameter right from the start. Previously, bespoke solutions , such as passing the initial state from parent to child widgets, would be needed with a potentially clunky startup as the app worked its way through the routes to the page that was requested.

Navigator 2.0 in action

As it is generally considered a more complicated approach to app navigation, we will not go into too much depth on the Navigator 2.0 approach, but it is useful to know it exists and to get a general feel for it so that once you are more confident in your Flutter knowledge, you can investigate the approach more fully.

In this example, we will pick out how the hello world! app would be changed to suit a Navigator 2.0 approach. We will add some simple changes to allow someone to see a list of towns and to click a button to view further details on that town.

The first change will be to the `MyApp` widget. In the hello world! app, it is currently a stateless widget, but with Navigator 2.0, the navigation uses state to determine which pages should be on the stack, so we need to convert it to a stateful widget:

```
class MyApp extends StatefulWidget {
  @override
  State<StatefulWidget> createState() => _MyAppState();
}
```

```
class _MyAppState extends State<MyApp> {
  String? _selectedTown;

  ...
}
```

We've also introduced a class field named _selectedTown. Note the underscore at the start of the name to ensure the field cannot be accessed outside of the class. This field will hold the name of the town selected, or null if no town is selected.

Next, we need to create a widget that will form the page shown when a town is selected. The widget is pretty standard; it has a title parameter and displays the title and a **Close** button within a column:

```
class TownScreen extends StatelessWidget {
  TownScreen({required this.title});
  final String title;
  @override
  Widget build(BuildContext context) {
    return Scaffold(
      body: Center(
        child: Column(
          mainAxisAlignment: MainAxisAlignment.center,
          children: [
            Text(title),
            ElevatedButton(
              child: Text("Close"),
              onPressed: () {
                Navigator.of(context).pop();
              },
            ),
          ],
        ),
      ),
    );
  }
}
```

Additionally, it has a navigator pop() method, as you would expect in Navigator 1.0. What this does in the navigator is very different, as we will see next.

Next, because the state is on MyApp and not on MyHomePage, when a town is selected, the buttons on MyHomePage will need to have a way to update the state on MyApp, and specifically to set the _selectedTown field to the correct value.

To achieve this, we need to add a callback method within MyApp that can be passed to MyHomePage as a parameter:

```
void _setTownName(String townName) {
  this.setState(() {
    _selectedTown = townName;
  });
}
```

This method simply takes townName as a parameter and uses the value to set the state of the MyHomePage widget.

We then need to make use of this callback in MyHomePage by adding it as a parameter within the constructor and a field on the class:

```
MyHomePage({required this.title, required this.
townNameCallback});
final void Function(String) townNameCallback;
```

Then, use this parameter within the new town buttons to correctly set the state. These two buttons have been added to the column within MyHomePage:

```
ElevatedButton(
  child: Text('Whitby'),
  onPressed: () {
    widget.townNameCallback("Whitby");
  },
),
ElevatedButton(
  child: Text('Scarborough'),
  onPressed: () async {
    widget.townNameCallback("Scarborough");
  },
),
```

They both call the callback method and specify the name of the town that has been selected, therefore setting the state on MyHomePage.

Finally, we need to update `MaterialApp` to use two new parameters – pages and onPopPage:

```
MaterialApp(
  title: 'Flutter Demo',
  home: Navigator(
    pages: [
      MaterialPage(
        child: MyHomePage(
          title: "Press this",
          townNameCallback: _setTownName,
        )),
      if (_selectedTown != null)
        MaterialPage(
          child: BookScreen(title: _selectedTown!),
        ),
    ],
    onPopPage: (route, result) {
      if (!route.didPop(result)) {
        return false;
      }
      setState(() {
        _selectedTown = null;
      });

      return true;
    },
  ),
  ...
);
```

Let's look at the pages parameter first. As you can see, it holds a list of two pages: one containing the `MyHomePage` widget, which takes in the callback as a parameter, and one containing the `BookScreen` widget, which takes in the `_selectedTown` value as a parameter.

What is important to note here is that the page containing `BookScreen` is only added to the pages list if the `_selectedTown` value is not null. Therefore, when the `_setTownName` callback is called and a town name is set, the flow is very much like the build flow within a widget where the pages list is re-evaluated and the `BookScreen` page is added to the list.

Now let's look at `onPopPage`. In this method, we tell the navigator what to do when a page is popped. The first action has to be to check whether the pop was successful. Assuming that is the case, then we can assume the pop came from `BookScreen` and by nulling the `_selectedTown` value, the `BookScreen` page will be removed from the pages list and `MyHomePage` will be visible again.

> **Further Navigator 2.0 learning**
>
> The example shared here is incomplete because the use of the back button and changes to the route from the underlying platform are not handled. If you want to complete the example, then good documentation can be found here: `https://medium.com/flutter/learning-flutters-new-navigation-and-routing-system-7c9068155ade`.

There are plugins that can simplify the Navigator 2.0 approach and we will look at those in *Chapter 9, Popular Third-Party Plugins*.

For the examples within the rest of the book, we will focus on Navigator 1.0 as it is simpler and will allow us to focus on the area being explored without being confused by Navigator 2.0 boilerplate code.

Now that we have explored moving users between screens at the code level, let's next explore the move between screens at the user interface level.

Screen transitions

Changing screens needs to look smooth for the user. You want the user to enjoy their experience within your app, and jarring screen transitions can impact their enjoyment and flow.

As we have seen, `MaterialPageRoute` and `CupertinoPageRoute` are classes that add a route to the navigator and you may have noticed as we experimented with the example app that they add a transition between the old and new Route. These transitions align with the platform defaults but can be customized as well.

On Android, for example, the entrance transition for the page slides the page upward and fades it in. The exit transition does the same in reverse. On iOS, the page slides in from the right and exits in reverse.

Flutter lets us customize this behavior by adding our own transitions between screens. To do this, we need to look a little deeper at routes.

PageRouteBuilder

PageRouteBuilder is a helper class that can be used for custom Route creation, instead of using the pre-built route subclasses of MaterialPageRoute and CupertinoPageRoute.

PageRouteBuilder contains multiple callbacks and properties to help in the PageRoute definition. Here are its key parameters:

- transitionsBuilder: This is where we specify the callback for the transition animation. Specifically, a builder function that returns a widget.

- pageBuilder: This is where we specify the callback that draws the page we are transitioning to, specifically, a builder function that returns a widget.

- transitionDuration: The duration of the transition.

- barrierColor and barrierDismissible: These define partially covered routes of the model and not for the fullscreen of the app.

Using these parameters, you can create your own route instance with your own custom transitions.

Custom transitions in practice

Let's first modify ElevatedButton on _MyHomePageState so that instead of creating a MaterialPageRoute, we use PageRouteBuilder.

As a reminder, this is what the button looks like with a standard MaterialPageRoute:

```
ElevatedButton(
    child: Text('Press this'),
    onPressed: () {
        Navigator.of(context).push(
            MaterialPageRoute(builder: (context) {
                return AnotherScreen(title: "Go back");
            }),
```

```
    );
  },
),
```

Within the onPressed parameter, we passed an anonymous function that returned a MaterialPageRoute. Within the MaterialPageRoute, we returned the base widget of the next screen – in this case, the AnotherScreen widget.

Let's change the onPressed argument so that it creates a custom route:

```
ElevatedButton(
  child: Text('Press this'),
  onPressed: () async {
    Navigator.of(context).push(
      PageRouteBuilder(
        pageBuilder: (context, animation, secondaryAnimation)
        => AnotherScreen(title: "Go back"),
        transitionsBuilder: (context, animation,
        secondaryAnimation, child) {
          return child;
        },
      ),
    );
  },
),
```

Instead of simply pushing a MaterialPageRoute onto the navigator stack, we have now pushed the PageRouteBuilder onto the stack, which extends **Route**.

We have added the AnotherScreen widget as the return value from the pageBuilder anonymous function, and simply return the child widget from the transitionsBuilder anonymous function.

If you run this code, you will see that there is no transition between pages because our `transitionBuilder` anonymous function doesn't do anything. So, let's change the default transition to use a slide transition. To do this, we need to change the `transitionsBuilder` anonymous function:

```
PageRouteBuilder(
  pageBuilder: (context, animation, secondaryAnimation) =>
  AnotherScreen(title: "Go back"),
  transitionsBuilder: (context, animation, secondaryAnimation,
  child) {
    return SlideTransition(
      position: Tween<Offset>(
        begin: const Offset(-1, 0),
        end: Offset.zero,
      ).animate(animation),
      child: child,
    );
  },
)
```

Here, instead of simply returning the child widget, we return a `SlideTransition` widget that encapsulates the animation logic for us: a transition from left to right, until it becomes fully visible. The child widget is nested inside `SlideTransition`, so the contents of your new page slide over the previous screen because it is contained within the `SlideTransition` widget. Note that when you go back to the previous screen (by popping the top route off the navigator stack), the animation runs in reverse.

You will see a little complication around the `Tween` and `Offset` classes. We have not checked out animations in detail yet, so they will look new to you. We will explore this in more detail in *Chapter 10, Using Widget Manipulations and Animations*.

If you are planning to use the same transition for every page, then a useful approach would be to extend the `PageRouteBuilder` class and create a reusable transition that you could add to the code as easily as a `MaterialPageRoute` or `CupertinoPageRoute`. This will allow you to avoid duplicated code, and make app-wide changes to transitions if you need to.

For example, suppose you wanted to use `SlideTransition` throughout your app. Then, you could make your custom `MySlideTransition` class and extend `PageRouteBuilder`:

```dart
class MySlideTransition extends PageRouteBuilder {
  final Widget transitionPage;
  MySlideTransition({required this.transitionPage})
      : super(
          pageBuilder: (
            BuildContext context,
            Animation<double> animation,
            Animation<double> secondaryAnimation,
          ) => transitionPage,
          transitionsBuilder: (
            BuildContext context,
            Animation<double> animation,
            Animation<double> secondaryAnimation,
            Widget child,
          ) => SlideTransition(
              position: Tween<Offset>(
                begin: const Offset(-1, 0),
                end: Offset.zero,
              ).animate(animation),
              child: child,
            ),
        );
}
```

In this class, we have a single constructor parameter named `transitionPage`, which is the widget of the page we are transitioning to. As part of the constructor, the class sets the argument of the parent `PageRouteBuilder` parameter, `pageBuilder`, to simply return `transitionPage` and sets the `transitionsBuilder` argument as the `SlideTransition` we experimented with before.

Therefore, whenever an instance of `MySlideTransition` is created, it will automatically call the superclass constructor of `PageRouteBuilder` and set the two parameters to the anonymous functions we were previously specifying on each individual transition.

Now, within our `ElevatedButton` code, we can very easily specify the `onPressed` function to be the following:

```
ElevatedButton(
    child: Text('Press this'),
    onPressed: () {
      Navigator.of(context).push(
        MySlideTransition(
          transitionPage: AnotherScreen(title: "Go back"),
        ),
      );
    },
),
```

We just need to add our own custom route widget to the navigator stack and we automatically get `SlideTransition`.

There are many different transitions you can try that have built-in classes, such as the following:

- `ScaleTransition`: The new screen enlarges over the previous screen.
- `RotationTransition`: The new screen spins as it overlaps the previous screen.
- `FadeTransition`: The new screen fades in over the previous screen.

You would simply replace the `SlideTransition` widget with one of these other widgets to get the desired effect.

Now we have looked a lot at how we move between screens, we also need to explore how we take application state with us.

Passing data between screens

In almost all apps, there is the concept of application state. This is larger than the state within one widget as it travels with the user throughout the app. If you have worked with other frameworks, you will have seen varying ways to hold application state, and Flutter doesn't have a single way to hold and share state.

We will look at options for how to store application state long term in *Chapter 9, Popular Third-Party Plugins*, but once the state has been retrieved from storage, how should you share that state among your many different application screens?

It's worth noting that there is no right or wrong answer for state management, but every approach has benefits and weaknesses and you will need to decide which approach suits you from a maintenance, code readability, and app usage perspective.

Passing state in widget parameters

The simplest way to share state around your app, and probably the way most developers start managing state with Flutter, is simply to pass it to each screen within the constructor parameter.

For example, suppose that when a user logs in to your app, you create an instance of your own User class that holds important information. You can then simply pass that instance to any screen through a constructor parameter.

The obvious benefit of this approach is that it is very simple to get up and running a prototype of an app. When you want to try out a new framework or try out an app idea, then this approach is fine.

There are, however, many drawbacks with this approach:

- If you decide a screen needs some extra state information that is currently not available to it, then all intermediate screens will need to be updated to pass that state to the screen.

- You cannot naturally listen for changes to the state and make the pages (including those already on the stack but not active) automatically update and reflect the changes.

- Long-running asynchronous activities such as listening on database updates do not have a natural place to live and may get bundled into the state classes.

For the examples within this book, we will follow this approach as it keeps the code simple and clear, but as you create a more complex app and become more comfortable with Flutter and Dart, here are a few recommendations on where to look next for state management.

InheritedWidget

We've seen the use of InheritedWidgets several times within this chapter and previous chapters. Specific examples have been for finding the Navigator and ScaffoldMessenger. You achieve this using the <type>.of(context) syntax, which searches the context for the first instance of the specified type.

This approach can be used with state, allowing you to search the context for the state information you require. This specifically alleviates one of the drawbacks of the parameter-based approach previously mentioned because intermediate screens that have no interest in specific state information do not need to accept it in their parameters just so they can pass it to a child widget.

BLoC

The **BLoC (Business Logic Components)** approach uses a streams approach to sharing state information. Your widgets listen to their chosen state information streams and are told when the state has changed so that they can choose how to deal with that state change when it happens.

This fits very nicely with the Flutter declarative approach because when the app state changes, the widget is notified and can choose to update its own internal state if the app state change is relevant. By updating its internal state, it will then trigger a build call and render any changes to the user.

Personally, I use the BLoC pattern for all my apps that have gone beyond proof of concept. Additionally, the BLoC pattern works really well for listening on external systems such as databases or network requests because the listener logic sits within the BLoC and manages updates to the app state as needed.

Redux

The key difference between Redux and BLoC is that Redux has one state object that manages all the app states, whereas BLoC has a set of BLoCs that deal with different areas of the app state.

There are three main concepts in Redux:

- **Store** – This is where the app state is stored.

- **Action** – Information about an intention to change the state.

- **Reducer** – Calculates the next app state based on an action.

Other options

As you can see, there are already many app state management solutions available, but for completeness, here are some other key ones if you don't prefer to use the ones listed previously:

- Binder

- Flutter commands

- GetIt

- MobX

- Riverpod

The latest options available are listed on the Flutter site at the following link:

`https://flutter.dev/docs/development/data-and-backend/state-mgmt/options`

Summary

In this chapter, we have explored the concept of screens within an app and seen how to add navigation between them. First, we got to know the `Navigator` widget, the main player when it comes to navigation in Flutter. We have seen how it composes the navigation stack or history by using the `Overlay` class.

We have also seen another important piece of navigation, `Route`, and how to define it for use in our applications. We checked out different approaches to implement the navigation, with the most typical way being with the `MaterialPageRoute` widget.

We also explored the new Navigator 2.0 approach to get a feel for how this declarative approach to screen management contrasts with the Navigator 1.0 imperative approach.

Finally, we briefly explored app state management and some of the common approaches. This is a rich area that you should explore when you become more confident with Dart and Flutter.

In the next chapter, we start to look at another part of the framework that allows Flutter developers to get an app up and running quickly – the wonderful world of Flutter plugins.

Section 3: Developing Fully Featured Apps

In this section, you will learn how to develop a professional app. The developer needs to add features that encompass a lot of advanced and custom mechanisms, as well as using plugins to extend the framework as per their needs.

This section comprises the following chapters:

- *Chapter 8, Plugins – What Are They and How Do I Use Them?*
- *Chapter 9, Popular Third-Party Plugins*
- *Chapter 10, Using Widget Manipulations and Animations*

8
Plugins – What Are They and How Do I Use Them?

Flutter is lucky to have an amazing community of developers who share code with each other via plugins. It is this kind of open source approach that allows frameworks such as Flutter to thrive and allows for innovation across the platform. It also means you generally don't need to re-invent the wheel, allowing you to focus on the unique aspects of your app, rather than spending a lot of time working on basic functionality.

This chapter will start by explaining what a plugin is and how you can add them to your app. There is a wide range of plugins available, from user interface widget libraries to low-level messaging tooling and music management classes, so the setup is somewhat bespoke for each plugin. However, there are general rules to follow and best practices for managing versions.

Finally, we will look at some common challenges with plugins and how to resolve them.

The following topics will be covered in this chapter:

- What is a plugin?
- Where can I find plugins?
- How do I add a plugin to my project?
- How do plugins work on iOS and Android?
- Common issues

By the end of the chapter, you will be able to add plugins to your app, allowing you to really explore some of the exciting capabilities of Flutter.

Technical requirements

You will need your development environment again for this chapter as we will add a plugin to the hello world project. Look back at *Chapter 1, An Introduction to Flutter*, if you need to set up your IDE or refresh your knowledge of the development environment requirements.

You can find the source code for this chapter on GitHub at the following link: `https://github.com/PacktPublishing/Flutter-for-Beginners-Second-Edition/tree/main/hello_world/lib/chapter_08`.

What is a plugin?

Many programming frameworks and software tools have the concept of plugins. They may go by another name, such as third-party libraries, extensions, or add-ons, but they are effectively the same thing – a self-contained, modular code deliverable that can be "plugged in" to your existing app code to provide extra functionality.

Within this chapter, you will see references to the term packages, a chunk of Dart code, and assets. A plugin is a special type of package that makes functionality available to your app and this is what we are looking at in this chapter.

There are many benefits as well as drawbacks to the plugin approach. So let's take a look and understand why Flutter would choose to use plugins within the framework and then we will move on to the drawbacks.

Benefits

As you would expect, Flutter uses plugins because they bring many benefits. This is especially true of code reuse; creating a great Flutter app would be much harder if you had to create everything from scratch. Let's look at the benefits.

Code reuse

As a developer, you will understand that nobody wants to recreate code if they can help it. Not only does it waste time, but it can also introduce bugs when the recreated code contains mistakes or doesn't take into account all the different execution flows that the original code considered. Additionally, the recreated code can cause maintenance headaches when fixes are required because you need to double fix your code.

Plugins alleviate this problem by solving a specific issue (for example, linking to the device calendar) and all your app code can reference that single plugin. If an issue is found, the plugin can be updated, and all users of the plugin will gain the benefit of the fix.

Many eyes

One of the great things about plugins is that because many people use them and find issues with them, the plugins become very stable and feature-rich.

You may feel that in some cases it is easier just to write your own code, but it is almost impossible to test your code on all the different devices out there, all the different screen ratios, or used in all the weird and wonderful ways that users manage to find. Plugin code is effectively tested for free across devices, screen ratios, and usage patterns, so why not take advantage of that.

Low-level integration

For some functionality, you will need to integrate with the base **operating system** (**OS**) of the device. This could require Java, Swift, JavaScript, or some other language that can interface with the OS, and unless you are proficient in those languages and also knowledgeable about the APIs available within the OS, this could be quite a challenge.

Plugins take care of that need to understand low-level integration, so you can spend your time becoming an expert in Dart and Flutter.

There are, as you would expect, some downsides to using plugins, so let's take a quick look at those now, and then explore how to alleviate them later in the chapter.

Drawbacks

As with any software decision, especially on such a huge scale as plugins, there will be drawbacks that you need to consider when using them. The benefits massively outweigh the drawbacks, but you should still be aware of them so that you can decide how to mitigate their impact.

Version management

Like any good plugin system, all plugins in Flutter are versioned using the semantic versioning scheme. This means it is easy to manage which version of a plugin you are using, and ensure that you have the latest or best (not always the same) version of the plugin for your app.

However, with any versioning system, there is the potential for incompatibility, especially when you have a large number of inter-dependent plugins. This can cause problems, and in rare cases, block you from releasing your app.

Semantic versioning

Versioning software is generally required in any software project for lots of good reasons. Semantic versioning standardizes the way versioning is done.

It uses three digits separated by a dot, for example, 1.2.3.

These follow the *major.minor.patch* structure. The major number is incremented when there is a breaking change or big update to the software. The minor number is incremented when new code that is backward compatible is released, and the patch number is incremented when a fix is added that is low risk.

Difficult to diagnose bugs

Some plugins can be quite complicated, and when something doesn't quite work as you would expect, it can be difficult to resolve the problem. Generally, plugin writers are happy to assist if you find an issue, but sometimes issues can be hard to recreate, or worse, only happen on release versions rather than debug versions, so you only have second-hand information about the problem.

In many ways, the issue isn't that the plugin has a bug, it's that it is hard to diagnose because you didn't write the code. On the flip side, if you did write the code, instead it would probably also contain the same bug and you would have a lot more code to maintain, so you may not have time to look at resolution.

Breaking changes

Sometimes, a plugin developer will make a breaking change because they want to fundamentally change the way the plugin works, or they want to standardize their plugin with the approach of other plugins, or for one of many other reasons.

The plugin developer will create a new version of the plugin with the major version incremented and warn developers of the change. You don't have to take the new version of the plugin, but the developer is unlikely to maintain older versions, so it is preferable to stay on the latest version so that you can receive any bug fixes.

This can sometimes have a large impact on your code, especially if you rely heavily on that plugin.

So now you have a feel about what a plugin is and the pros and cons of using them, let's take a look at where you can find them and what they look like.

Where can I find plugins?

Flutter has a very easy way to find the plugins that you may need via the `https://pub.dev` site that they maintain. This is where all plugins are registered and the primary way that developers find plugins.

This site not only allows you to search for plugins but also includes useful sections such as the following:

- **Flutter favorites**: Plugins that demonstrate the highest levels of quality.
- **Most popular packages**: The most downloaded plugins.
- **Package of the week**: This is a series of animated videos that introduce some of the plugins available. Flutter has been very successful in the use of short videos to introduce the widget of the week and has rolled out the concept of package of the week.

Let's now take a look at the individual entries for a plugin at `pub.dev`.

Plugin entry

One of my personal favorite plugins is the one that introduces a new widget, the `AutoSizeText` widget. Just like the name suggests, this widget will resize the text it contains so that it fits within the bounds.

To find the plugin, simply type `auto size text` in the search bar and your results will look something like this:

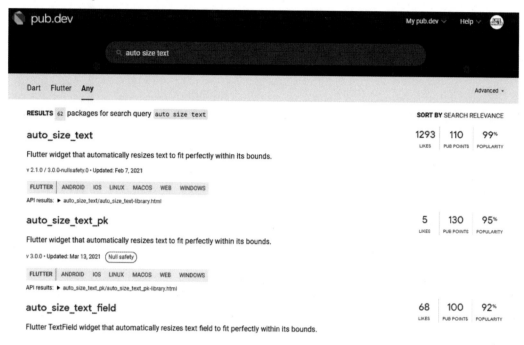

Figure 8.1 – Pub.dev search results

The first thing you will notice is that there are lots of plugins that do similar things, so it used to be very tricky to work out which plugin was best maintained and most used. As you can imagine, accidentally using a plugin that is no longer maintained means that bug fixes are not actioned and upgrading transient dependencies (other plugins that this plugin depends on) does not happen. Additionally, choosing a plugin that nobody else uses means it may not have been tested as thoroughly as the other plugins that are available.

However, `pub.dev` now shows a series of metrics and other information so that you can make a more informed choice. It may feel like we are focusing a little too much on plugin searching, but making the right choice can make a huge difference to your project, and potentially make or break it.

Key information to take from this page is obviously the metrics on the right (which we will look at soon), but also the following:

- The updated date: Is the code still being maintained?
- The list of supported platforms: For `auto_size_text`, the supported platforms are Android, iOS, Linux, macOS, Web, and Windows.

- Tags: When Flutter has a big change, plugins are tagged to show whether they have completed the change. In this example, the move to *Null safety* is very important, and only the second result has been tagged as having made the transition to Null safety. However, note that `auto_size_text` actually has two versions available, the second of which is named `nullsafety.0`, suggesting that the work is ongoing to move to a null safe release.

If we click on **auto_size_text**, we can see further details about the plugin:

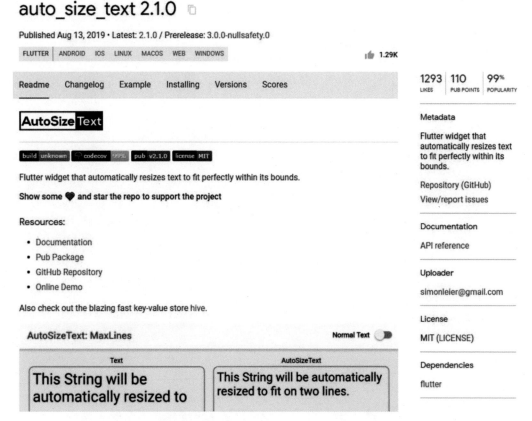

Figure 8.2 – The auto_size_text details page

Much of the details from the search page are replicated, including the metrics:

- **Likes**: As you would expect, if people like the plugin, then they can "like" it.

- **Pub points**: The plugin is analyzed and assigned points (out of 110) on code maintainability, documentation, platform support, up-to-date dependencies, and so on.

- **Popularity**: A measure of how many apps rely on the plugin.

Used together, these are a very powerful way to assess the maturity of the plugin and how likely it is to be maintained in the future.

Other useful information on the page includes the following:

- **Readme**: This is where the information about the plugin is kept, often including installation and project configuration instructions.

- **Changelog**: This is where you can look at why a plugin version has been increased. This is especially useful when you need to upgrade a major version and want to know what breaking changes there were.

- **Example**: Most plugins come with a small example app so you can see how the plugin is used.

- **Installing**: A high-level guide to how to install this plugin. Generally, you wouldn't need to look closely at this section as all plugins are installed in the same way.

- **Repository (GitHub)**: Most plugins are developed via a GitHub repository and link to it from this page. If you want to see how the plugin works, then this is the place to look.

- **View/report issues**: A hugely important link because you can see what issues other people have reported and how the resolution is progressing, and also raise your own issues. Note that most plugin maintainers volunteer to maintain their plugin and therefore have other jobs, so please be understanding if they are unable to respond to any issues immediately.

Due to the huge size of the Flutter community, there are also many video and text tutorials available for plugins across the web, on publications such as Medium and YouTube, that can give additional guidance.

So now that we've seen how to access key information about a plugin, let's try adding the `auto_size_text` plugin to our hello world project.

How do I add a plugin to my project?

Adding a plugin to your project is generally surprisingly easy. However, it is crucially important that you read the **readme** fully because for some plugins, there can be platform-specific configuration that you need to set up before the plugin will run. In some extreme cases (such as `google_mobile_ads`), your app will completely fail to start unless the plugin setup has been completed correctly.

We will use the example of `auto_size_text` as a plugin we wish to add. We saw above the readme for this plugin, but let's look at the **Installing** section now. The following screenshot shows the instructions for installation:

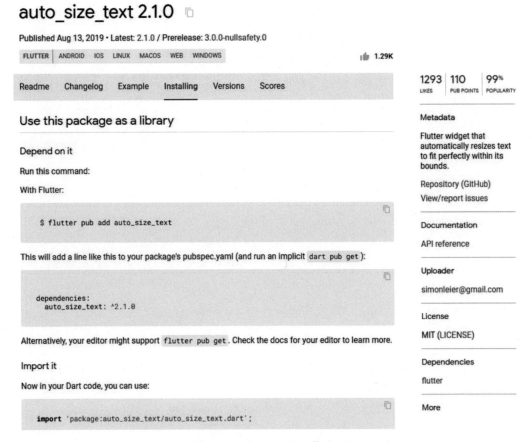

Figure 8.3 – The auto_size_text installation instructions

There are two ways to add a plugin to your project, but the outcome is the same.

The first option is to run a `flutter` command on the command line to do all the work for you:

```
flutter pub add auto_size_text
```

The other option is to replicate what that command does under the covers. I suggest that you follow the steps in the next section to begin with so that you understand what is happening.

The pubspec.yaml file

The `pubspec.yaml` file is where dependencies and assets are configured. There is a specific section called **dependencies** that holds information about plugins that your project depends on.

It will look something like this:

```
dependencies:
  flutter:
    sdk: flutter


  # The following adds the Cupertino Icons font to your
  application.
  # Use with the CupertinoIcons class for iOS style icons.
  cupertino_icons: ^1.0.1
```

The indentation is crucial here and is what **YAML** files rely on to understand the contents. Note that `cupertino_icons: ^1.0.1` is indented by two spaces. This denotes that it is under the `dependencies` header and therefore is a dependency of the project.

Under `cupertino_icons`, add another line, indented by two spaces, which says the following:

```
auto_size_text: ^2.1.0
```

You have now declared that your project depends on the `auto_size_text` plugin. If you are sharing your project with other developers, then they will instantly see the dependency and be able to update the project accordingly.

You have also specified the version of the plugin using the plugin's semantic version. This locks your app to a specific version of the plugin, allowing you to test and release without dependency changes sneaking in. You may have noticed the ^ character before the version number. This specifies that you are happy to receive any patch version updates to the plugin.

For example, if you specify version `2.1.0`, then only version `2.1.0` will be used by you and any other developers that are using this source code. If you specify version `^2.1.0`, then any version `2.1.x` where `x >= 0` can be used. This means you will automatically receive patch updates (when you download the plugin). There is a risk that you may have a slightly different version of the plugin to your colleagues, but there will only be disparities at the patch level.

The plugin isn't yet downloaded and available to your project. To do this, we will use a very useful command called `flutter pub`, which is used to manage plugins.

flutter pub

Within the `flutter` command, there is a `pub` command that is specifically used for plugin management. There are several ways you can use it, so let's look at some of the most used ones.

flutter pub get

The `flutter pub get` command will read through all the dependencies in `pubspec.yaml`, retrieve the relevant plugins from `pub.dev`, and download them to a central repository on your computer, ready for your project to access it.

We need to use the following command at this point to download the `auto_size_text` plugin that our project depends on:

```
PS C:\Flutter\hello_world> flutter pub get
Running "flutter pub get" in hello_world...          2,142ms
```

Occasionally, `flutter pub get` will fail due to inconsistent dependencies and we will look at how to resolve that in the *Common issues* section later in the chapter.

At this point, the plugin dependency has been declared and downloaded to your computer. You are ready to go, but let's just look at some other useful `flutter pub` commands.

flutter pub outdated

This command will check whether any of your dependencies have newer versions that you may want to upgrade to. Running this command will give you output like the following:

```
PS C:\Flutter\hello_world> flutter pub outdated
Showing outdated packages.
[*] indicates versions that are not the latest available.

Package Name   Current    Upgradable   Resolvable   Latest

direct dependencies: all up-to-date.

transitive dev_dependencies:
crypto         *3.0.0     *3.0.0       *3.0.0       3.0.1
```

```
vm_service     *6.1.0+1   *6.1.0+1     *6.1.0+1    6.2.0
You are already using the newest resolvable versions listed in
the 'Resolvable' column.
Newer versions, listed in 'Latest', may not be mutually
compatible.
```

Although this looks quite intimidating, the key part to note is that your direct dependencies are all up to date, so you don't need to do anything further.

If the command shows that there are newer dependencies, then you will first need to understand what the changes are, by going to pub.dev and reading the changelog. Then, you can update pubspec.yaml to specify the new version, and finally run flutter pub get to download the latest version to your computer.

flutter pub upgrade

It was mentioned earlier that the version can include the ^ symbol to specify that you are happy to receive patch updates.

These patch updates do not magically appear on your computer; you still need to tell Flutter to retrieve the updates. You can do this with the flutter pub update command. It is much like flutter pub get, but you give it permission to get the latest plugins within the constraints of the versions specified in pubspec.yaml.

So now that you understand a bit more about Flutter plugin management, we can explore how you would use the plugin within your code next.

Using a plugin in your code

Now that the plugin code has been downloaded to your computer, and you have specified that your project depends on that plugin, the next step is to import the code into the classes where you need it.

Import statements

If you look at the main.dart file, you will see the following import statement at the very top:

```
import 'package:flutter/material.dart';
```

Like virtually any other programming language, `import` statements allow you to reference code in other classes, packages, and plugins. In this example, the `material.dart` file is being imported, with all the classes and functions within that file being made available to your class. We will use an `import` statement to access the plugin code, but first, let's create a new file to hold a new stateless widget.

Adding Dart files

In your IDE, create a new file within the `lib` folder named `red_text_widget.dart` and open it up. It will initially be empty, so let's put some code in there.

You may have a shortcut in your IDE that allows you to generate the stateless widget code. Try typing `stless` and see if the IDE gives you any hints. If it does, set the widget name to `RedTextWidget`. If not, simply copy the following code into the file:

```
class RedTextWidget extends StatelessWidget {
  @override
  Widget build(BuildContext context) {
    return Container();
  }
}
```

You may notice that there are errors on the page. This is because you need to add an `import` statement. In isolation, the class name `StatelessWidget` doesn't exist, it isn't within the same Dart file, so the compiler has no idea what it is.

We need to add the same `import` that we saw on the `main.dart` file to import all the standard Flutter framework classes, so at the very top, add the following:

```
import 'package:flutter/material.dart';
```

Ta da! The errors disappeared. You now have a stateless widget that returns an empty **Container** widget from the `build` method.

Let's add a constructor parameter that takes a `String` named `text`. We will pass the contents of this parameter down to the `AutoSizeText` widget when we add it.

Your widget will look like this:

```
import 'package:flutter/material.dart';


class RedTextWidget extends StatelessWidget {
  final String text;


  RedTextWidget({required this.text});


  @override
  Widget build(BuildContext context) {
    return Container();
  }
}
```

In this example, we have used a named parameter, text, used a shortcut assignment within the constructor using this.text, and specified that it is a required parameter using the required keyword.

Using the plugin

Now let's use the AutoSizeText widget in our shiny new widget. Firstly, we need to tell the compiler that we want to access the **AutoSizeText** widget classes, so add the following import statement to the top of your file:

```
import 'package:auto_size_text/auto_size_text.dart';
```

Now that the code is available, we can use the widget within our build method. Let's simply return AutoSizeText with the String value from our text parameter, which will look like this:

```
  @override
  Widget build(BuildContext context) {
    return AutoSizeText(
      text,
      style: TextStyle(color: Colors.red),
    );
  }
```

You'll notice that the `AutoSizeText` widget looks just like any other built-in widget because it is just like any of the built-in widgets. The widget takes one required positional constructor parameter (`text`) and one optional named constructor parameter (`style`). It has many other optional named constructor parameters so that you can further control the look of the widget.

Putting it all together

Finally, let's add our new widget to the `MyHomePage` widget so that it is visible. We need to add the `import` statement for our new file so that, just like how we imported the `AutoSizeText` widget code, the code of our `RedTextWidget` is available to this class:

```
import 'package:hello_world/red_text_widget.dart';
```

We can then change the first **Text** widget in our column to be `RedTextWidget`:

```
RedTextWidget (
    text: 'You have pushed the button this many times:',
),
```

You will see that a **Text** widget has a required positional constructor parameter for the text, but our widget has a required named constructor parameter called `text`. If a parameter is fundamental to the widget, then having it as a positional parameter makes sense. However, many of the built-in widgets were created before the required named constructor parameters were an available feature in Dart. In general, named parameters are preferable because they help with readability and maintainability, and definitely reduce the chance of introducing bugs due to incorrect parameter ordering.

Let's run our app and check that it all works correctly. The app should appear and look like this:

Figure 8.4 – RedTextWidget incorporating the AutoSizeText plugin

We can see the text is now red as we hoped. Congratulations, you just used your first plugin!

You should now be starting to see the power of Flutter plugins and how they can boost the awesomeness of your app. In this section, we explored the `pubspec.yaml` file and learned about its purpose, we learned how to add plugins and ensure they are up to date, and we then experimented with adding a plugin to our app code. Using this same process, you can add whichever plugins you want to your app – the plugin world is your oyster.

The `AutoSizeText` plugin has no platform-specific code; it is purely presentational in its purpose. However, some plugins have deeper dependencies on the platform they run on. Let's explore that now.

How do plugins work on iOS and Android?

Many plugins will work with the different underlying platforms to use operating system functionality. This dependency changes the way your project is built and run because there is native code within your project that interfaces with the underlying platform. Let's look at how that interfacing works.

MethodChannel

Flutter communication between the client (Flutter) and the host (native) application occurs through platform channels. The `MethodChannel` class is responsible for sending messages (method invocations) to the platform side. On the platform side, `MethodChannel` on Android (API) and `FlutterMethodChannel` on iOS (API) enable receiving method calls and sending a result back. The structure of this relationship is shown in the following diagram.

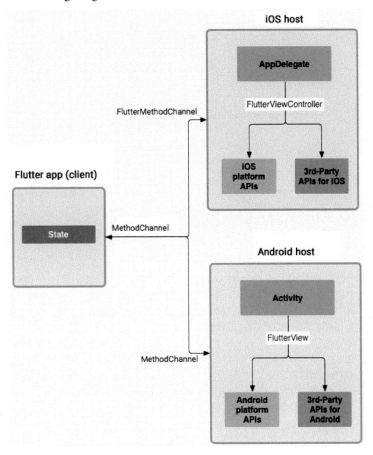

Figure 8.5 – Interface between Flutter and native

The platform channel technique allows for the decoupling of the UI code from the platform-specific native code. The host listens on the platform channel and receives a message request. It can use platform APIs to enact the request and then sends back a response to the client, the Flutter portion of the app.

In this way, the Flutter part of the app is agnostic to the host allowing you to write code that will work across all platforms.

Having this base understanding of plugins will allow you to better diagnose issues and assess plugin suitability for your app.

Let's explore a little further by adding a plugin to our project that uses native code. An example of such a plugin is the `device_info_plus` plugin. It retrieves information about your device from the underlying platform, such as the model and device name.

So, add the latest `device_info` to your `pubspec.yaml` file using the following command:

```
flutter pub add device_info_plus
```

If you want further information on the plugin, then head over to the `pub.dev` site and search for `device_info_plus`.

Take a look at the `pubspec.yaml` file and you will see that the `device_info_plus` plugin has been added within the `dependencies` section. Also, the `flutter pub get` has automatically been run to pull the Flutter code into your project. However, you do not yet have the native code available.

If you run (or build) the project, Flutter will automatically retrieve the native code dependencies. These are managed by **CocoaPods** in iOS and **Gradle** in Android.

CocoaPods

For iOS native code libraries, Flutter uses the **CocoaPods** dependency manager. Flutter plugins that need iOS native code will specify a dependency on a **CocoaPods** library and the **CocoaPods** dependency manager will download the relevant library at the correct version and include it in your iOS build.

After you have run your project on an iOS emulator or device, you may notice that there is a file that has appeared within the iOS folder within your project files. This is called `PodFile` and manages your **CocoaPods** dependencies.

When you run or build your project, the **CocoaPods** dependency manager is invoked by calling the `pod install` command within the `ios` folder. All the dependencies are retrieved at the correct versions for your project.

Sometimes plugins will ask you to manage your app permissions. This can be done in the `ios/Runner/Info.plist` file.

This part of the build process can often cause issues when you are changing your dependencies, so in the *Common issues* section of this chapter, we explore some solutions.

Gradle

Building and running Flutter apps on Android uses the **Gradle** build automation tool. You can explore some of the files in the `android` folder, but the ones that you will occasionally need to change to configure plugins will be the following:

- `android/build.gradle`
- `android/app/build.gradle`

These files manage the build process and dependencies that your project needs, and occasionally some manipulation of versions or build flow is needed for a plugin to work correctly.

Additionally, like iOS, some plugins will require updates to app permissions. This can be done in the `android/app/src/main/AndroidManifest.xml` file.

Now you have a basic idea of the plugin process, let's see some common issues you may encounter and how to solve them in the next section.

Common issues

Sometimes your Flutter run or build will fail, and often this is related to plugin issues. In this section, we will look at some of the common issues and give some hints for how to resolve them.

Plugin breaking change

When a plugin changes its major or minor version number, it can mean that there has been a breaking change and that you will need to make some changes to keep the plugin working correctly.

There are generally two reasons for breaking changes:

- A change in the way you use the plugin at a programming level. For example, the constructor parameters for a widget have changed, or the flow of method calls to the plugin needs to be modified. These are often simply notified via compilation errors and deprecation warnings.

- A required change in the configuration of your project. These can be less obvious and checking the plugin readme on pub.dev is often the best way to assess whether you need to change your project configuration.

On the pub.dev page, there is a section specifically dedicated to explaining why version changes have happened called **Changelog**:

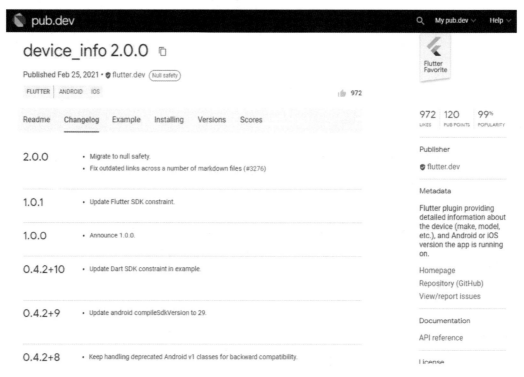

Figure 8.6 – Changelog section of the device_info plugin

In this section, plugin developers will often display the different types of updates that have happened during each version increment, including breaking changes, so that app developers can easily see what changes they need to make.

Additionally, plugin developers will make a mistake and release a breaking change without the correct version change. Plugin developers often give their time voluntarily to plugin development, so may make a mistake due to a lack of time or experience. Again, it is worth checking the readme and changelog at pub.dev if you are having any issues, just to check no sneaky breaking changes made their way into an update.

Plugin not working

There will be times when you believe that a plugin is not working in the way you expect it to. There is an easy way to report issues via the **View/report issues** link on the pub. dev page for the plugin. Generally, this link will take you to the **Issues** tab of the plugin's GitHub repository where you can check if the issue has already been raised and whether a fix is in progress:

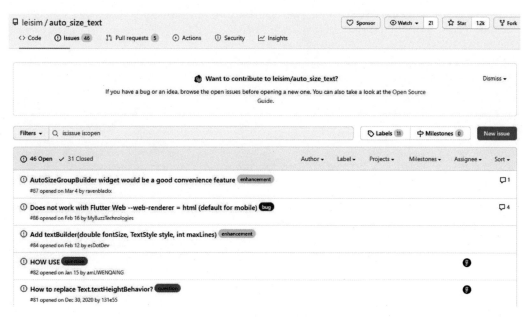

Figure 8.7 – Issues tab of the GitHub repository

It is worth noting that because plugins are generally community-created, there are often other developers that will attempt fixes for the plugin and share the **pull request** (**PR**) with the plugin developers to help them. When you are confident with Flutter, feel free to try to help the plugin developers if you identify an issue and think you know the solution.

PR not merged

Sometimes you will notice an issue with a plugin that someone in the community has fixed and they have issued a PR that has not yet been merged into the plugin's master code branch. This can happen often with less popular plugins where the number of contributors is low, and the main contributors have perhaps moved on from the plugin.

However, even without the PR being merged, you can still use it in your project as a dependency. This can be very useful if you need a fix, and a developer has already fixed it but it hasn't been merged. Sometimes, you can't wait for that merge to happen because the issue is blocking your next app release.

Therefore, to take advantage of the PR before it is merged, add a new section to your pubspec.yaml called dependency_overrides and add a link to the git entry. Here is an example for the device_calendar plugin that was required when Flutter moved to null safety and the device_calendar plugin PR for null safety had not yet been merged into the plugin's master branch:

```
dependency_overrides:
  device_calendar:
    git:
      url: https://github.com/thomassth/device_calendar_null.
      git
```

As you can see, you specify the plugin name and then the location of the override repository.

Inconsistent dependencies

As with any dependency management system, there are times when one plugin depends on a specific dependency that clashes with the version another plugin depends on.

Often the resolution is to make sure that all of your plugins are at the latest version. However, if this does not resolve the problem, then you may need to raise an issue with the plugin developer, and then move back to older plugin versions where the dependencies play more nicely together.

You may also have this issue when you are running a build on iOS. The **CocoaPods** dependencies sometimes clash unexpectedly. You can often resolve this by manually tidying up your **CocoaPods** repository.

If you open a terminal in the `ios` folder of your project, there are a few commands you can try to clean up the data. The first is to manually run the `pod install` and see what error messages you get:

```
pod install
```

You can try removing the `ios/Pods` directory (all the downloaded dependencies) and the `Podfile.lock` file and then rerun `pod install` on a fresh directory.

Additionally, you will sometimes need to update the **CocoaPods** repository. This lists all of the pods and versions of libraries that are available to **CocoaPods** and can become stale. To do this, run the following command:

```
pod repo update
```

If none of these resolve the problem, then a trip to the **Issues** section on GitHub is probably your answer.

MissingPluginException

There are many other issues, including the infamous `MissingPluginException`, that are often solved with a little cleanup of the Flutter folders.

Cleaning up is pretty easy. Firstly, run the following command:

```
flutter clean
```

This will clean up dependencies and build folders.

Then run the following command:

```
flutter pub get
```

This will retrieve all the dependencies again.

There are many other errors that you can get, most of which people have encountered many times and an internet search will often find you the answer, with **StackOverflow** being a great resource for identifying solutions.

Summary

In this chapter, we have explored the concept of plugins and what they are. We have explored the benefits of using plugins, and also some of the drawbacks that you need to be aware of.

We have investigated how you can find plugins and what to look for when choosing a plugin from the many that may be available. Specifically, we looked at `pub.dev` and all the information available on there to make using plugins easy.

We looked at how to add a plugin to your project, how to manage versions within the `pubspec.yaml` file, and how to use the plugin within your code.

Finally, we saw some of the common issues that can be encountered when using plugins and some suggestions for how to resolve them.

In the next chapter, we will look at some of the common plugins that are used in projects. This will give you an idea of the different areas of your project where plugins can be useful and highlight the most popular plugins with Flutter.

9
Popular Third-Party Plugins

In the previous chapter, we learned about what a plugin is and how it is used, and we experimented with our first plugin.

Flutter has a rich set of Flutter plugins, and sometimes it can be hard to know where to start from; you don't know what you don't know! This chapter will highlight some of the most popular plugins and give an overview of their uses.

We will start this chapter by looking into the Firebase plugins. Firebase is a set of services available on Google Cloud that you can use to create apps with advanced features. This includes authenticating users, storing data, sending push notifications, and analyzing app usage, among many other features.

We will then look at how to use Google Places for map and location information. Many apps have address lookups or show locations on a map, and the Google Places plugins really help here.

Next, we will look at plugins that exercise the capabilities of the device the app is being used on, including the camera and the photo store.

Finally, we will look at plugins that allow you to create more mature and supportable apps, including the app version plugin that surfaces the app version so that users can report their current version when asking for support.

This chapter will cover the following topics:

- Exploring Firebase plugins
- Understanding Google Maps and Google Places
- Exploring mobile device features
- Plugins to help with your app support

By the end of this chapter, you will have a wide knowledge of the plugins available to you, and some good ideas about how you can use those plugins to make your app awesome.

Technical requirements

You will need your development environment set up for this chapter as we will add a plugin to the Hello World project. Look back at *Chapter 1, An Introduction to Flutter*, if you need to set up your **integrated development environment** (**IDE**) or refresh your knowledge of the development environment requirements.

You can find the source code for this chapter on GitHub at `https://github.com/ PacktPublishing/Flutter-for-Beginners-Second-Edition/tree/ main/hello_world/lib/chapter_09`.

Exploring Firebase plugins

In this section, we will look at one of the most common sets of plugins that are used by Flutter app developers and explain how they can be used within your apps. Firebase is a Google product that provides multiple technologies for multiple platforms. If you are a mobile or web developer, you may be familiar with this amazing platform.

Among its offered technologies, the important ones are listed here:

- **Realtime Database**: A NoSQL (non-relational) database on the cloud. With this, you can store and access data in real time.
- **Cloud Firestore**: A NoSQL database, with a focus on big and scalable applications that provide advanced query support compared to a real-time database.
- **Cloud Functions**: Functions triggered by many Firebase products, such as the previous ones, and also by the user (using the **software development kit** (**SDK**)). We can develop scripts to react to changes in a database, user authentication, and more.
- **Performance Monitoring**: Collect and analyze information about the applications from the user's perspective.

- **Authentication**: Facilitates the development of the authentication layer of an application, improving **user experience** (**UX**) and security.
- **Firebase Cloud Messaging (FCM)**: Cloud messaging to exchange messages between applications and the server, available on Android, iOS, and the web.
- **AdMob**: Displays advertisements to monetize applications.
- **Machine Learning Kit (ML Kit)**: Tools to implant advanced **machine learning** (**ML**) resources in any application.

One of the main benefits of using Firebase is that all the services work tightly together. For example, the databases use Firebase Authentication to manage access, the cloud functions are triggered by Firestore or Realtime Database updates, and callable cloud functions use Firebase Authentication to identify users.

Flutter contains a variety of plugins to work with Firebase. We will be using some of them in the next sections to make some updates to the Hello World application. However, your first step is to register for the Firebase services.

Firebase registration

All of the Firebase services are managed from one dashboard or console, and you will need to set up your Firebase access and then register your app before you can use the services.

Firstly, head over to Firebase to set up your login and project: `https://console.firebase.google.com/`.

Immutable Firebase project settings

It is worth noting that some Firebase settings are immutable, such as the project **Uniform Resource Locator** (**URL**) and Realtime Database hosting location. Therefore, take your time to really understand what the settings will be, or assume in your planning that at some point down the line you may need to create a new project once you know which settings you will need.

Once you have a project created, you will then be able to register apps to the project.

Connecting the Flutter app to Firebase

It is possible to configure multiple applications from multiple platforms to connect with a Firebase project. On the Firebase project page, we have an option to add apps for iOS, Android, and the web.

Let's go ahead and register the Hello World app for both Android and iOS, in preparation for some of the Firebase service tinkering we will be doing later.

Note that full documentation on Firebase configuration is available here: `https://firebase.flutter.dev/docs/overview/`

In the following sections, we will look at the Android- and iOS-specific configurations.

Android

Here, the important setting is the package name that is checked in the Firebase SDK. The signing certificate is also important for authorization; we will cover that shortly.

You can find the package name of your Android app in the `android/app/build.gradle` file, within the `applicationId` property.

After completing registration, a `google-services.json` file is generated that has all the information your app will need to be able to access your project on Firebase. This should be added to your application project in the `android/app` directory.

There will be additional configuration settings needed. These are changing all the time, so view the preceding documentation link to understand the additional configuration changes you will need to make.

iOS

For the iOS version, the process looks very similar, starting with the configuration in the Firebase console, where we set the package name, as we did for Android.

After that, we can download the generated `GoogleService-Info.plist` file (the iOS equivalent of the `google-services.json` file) and add it to the project's `ios/Runner` directory. Note that it is very important to do this in **Xcode** by opening the iOS project on it and dragging the file into **Xcode** so that it gets registered for inclusion during builds.

Again, there will be additional configuration settings needed. These are changing all the time, so view the preceding documentation link to understand the additional configuration changes you will need to make.

Now you have registered your app and added the configuration to connect to your Firebase project, the addition of Firebase services simply follows the Flutter plugin model we saw in the previous chapter.

FlutterFire plugins

Note that, given the community-driven and open nature of Flutter, developers who are not directly involved in the creation of a service may choose to develop plugins that connect to a service such as Firebase. This may be because the "official" developers of a service have not yet chosen to engage with Flutter, there are limitations to the current "official" plugins (this can lead to a fork in the code base with new developers improving the existing code), or it may be that the design choices made on the "official" plugins are not to everybody's taste. Regardless, if you use the **pub.dev** scores, check the last published date, and view any plugin issues, you should be able to decide which plugin is suitable.

For Firebase, the official developers of the service have fully engaged with Flutter, and the plugins are excellent, both in quality, design, and documentation. Given that Flutter and Firebase are both Google products, you would expect that the Flutter and Firebase development teams would work closely together to create a good set of plugins. The plugins all support iOS and Android, and in most cases also support the web. The main plugin that does not support the web is the Realtime Database, and, although this may change, there are no obvious signs that web support will be coming to the Realtime Database. This is something to bear in mind if you plan to make your app available as a website, and you should consider using Firestore (which does have web support) instead.

Before we add any plugins, we need to add the `firebase_core` plugin, which all the other Firebase plugins depend on. As the name suggests, this plugin does all the core work, such as connecting to your project on Firebase. Here's the code you'll need to add this plugin:

```
dependencies:
  flutter:
    sdk: flutter
  firebase_core: ^1.2.0 #Check for the latest version
```

Once you have this, you are free to add the plugins that you need for your app. However, the key next step is to initialize Firebase within your app.

Firebase initialization

For any of the Firebase plugins to work, you first need to initialize the Firebase instance. This is effectively the work that Firebase Core will do to set up your connection to your Firebase project that you configured on the website.

There is just one step to this process, which aims to trigger the initialization and wait for this to complete.

There are a few ways to achieve this, but probably the easiest way is to modify your `main` method so that it is asynchronous, and then add a wait for Firebase initialization to complete. The code to do this is illustrated in the following snippet:

```
void main() async {
    WidgetsFlutterBinding.ensureInitialized();
    await Firebase.initializeApp();
    runApp(App());
}
```

As you can see, we have marked the `main` method as asynchronous using the `async` keyword and then added a line of code, as follows:

```
await Firebase.initializeApp();
```

The `Firebase.initializeApp()` method returns `Future` (that is, it is asynchronous, and you have to wait for the outcome of the method). We don't really care about any value returned, but what we do care about is that it has completed processing. Therefore, we have to use the `await` keyword to ensure our code execution waits here until the initialization has been completed. If we didn't include the `await` keyword, then code execution would continue immediately by running our app code. If we reached some Firebase service code before the initialization had been completed, then we could get some pretty nasty errors.

Note that there are more elegant ways to wait for initialization to complete (such as using the `init` method of a stateless widget), but for ease of understanding, this way seems as good as any other. Check out the online documentation for examples of other options.

Now you have Firebase initialized, let's look at the popular Firebase options available to you.

Authentication

Firebase Authentication allows you to secure access to your application and other Firebase services through a login/register process. To make this as easy as possible for your users, Firebase Authentication enables the use of multiple authentication options, such as email/password, phone authentication, and federated **identity providers** (**IdPs**) such as Google, Apple, Twitter, and Facebook.

The Flutter plugin that is supported by the Firebase team is `firebase_auth`. You can see the author in `pub.dev` by viewing the publisher details. In this case, it is the `firebase.google.com` team.

Setup

To set up the plugin, you would add the dependency to `pubspec.yaml`, as follows:

```
dependencies:
  flutter:
    sdk: flutter
  firebase_core: ^1.2.0
  firebase_auth: ^1.2.0
```

Voilà—you have authentication set up on your app. OK—it's not quite that easy, but you have managed to pull in the dependency, so next, you need to add code to your app to use the dependency in the correct way. Throughout this chapter, we will show snippets of the key pieces of code to give an idea of how you would use it. Additionally, we will include code samples in our GitHub source code so that you can see the plugins in action.

The first piece of code required is to initialize the `FirebaseAuth` instance (you'll notice a bit of a pattern forming for Firebase plugins), as follows:

```
FirebaseAuth auth = FirebaseAuth.instance;
```

Next, we need our code to listen on a stream that will let our code know of any changes in the authentication status of our app user.

If you need to refresh your knowledge of streams, refer back to *Chapter 5, Widgets –Building Layouts with Flutter*, where the concept of streams was first introduced.

Throughout the Firebase plugins and other plugins, you will see the regular use of streams so that the plugins can effectively be called back into your code to tell you that something has changed. They are very similar in concept to a callback method you supply that can be called regularly by the source of the stream.

authStateChanges stream

The specific stream we want to listen on is the `authStateChanges` stream, as illustrated in the following code snippet:

```
FirebaseAuth.instance
  .authStateChanges()
  .listen((User user) {
    if (user == null) {
      // User signed-out
```

```
    } else {
        // User signed-in
    }
});
```

In the preceding example, we get the instance (that we have already initialized), ask for the `authStateChanges` stream, and then specify what should happen when there is an update to the stream by supplying a callback function as an argument to the `listen` function. Whenever new data is added to the stream, our callback function will be called so that we can take action such as showing the login page (if the user is signed out) or accessing and displaying user-specific data (if the user is signed in).

Sign-in

Finally, we need to give the user an option to sign in to our app. To do this, you would either show email/password input fields or add a plugin for a federated IdP and receive their credentials that way. Ultimately, you will need to pass their credentials to Firebase, and in the email/password option, it would look something like this:

```
try {
    UserCredential = await
    FirebaseAuth.instance.signInWithEmailAndPassword(
        email: "tom.bailey@example.com",
        password: "WeLoveFlutter!"
    );
} on FirebaseAuthException catch (e) {
    if (e.code == 'user-not-found') {
        // User not found by Firebase
    } else if (e.code == 'wrong-password') {
        // Incorrect password
    }
}
```

In this example code, we try to sign in the user with their supplied credentials. In this case, we have hardcoded them, but you would use a couple of `TextFormField` instances and access their data, as described previously. The `signInWithEmailAndPassword` method will, unsurprisingly, sign in the user with their email and password.

Two obvious possible failures are that the email or the password might be incorrect, so adding a `catch` statement that deals with those failures completes the example.

Firebase Authentication can also deal with email validation, phone number registration, and password reset to give you a fully featured authentication solution. For example, after a user has signed in, you can do something like this:

```
User = FirebaseAuth.instance.currentUser;
if (!user.emailVerified) {
    await user.sendEmailVerification();
}
```

This will first get the current user's details as a `User` instance, upon which you can get information such as whether their email is verified. If it isn't, then you can send them another verification email so that they can verify their account.

As you can see, in very little code you can trigger the authentication flows and let the Firebase service take care of all the complications, which is why Firebase is so popular among Flutter developers.

Another key area of Firebase is the cloud databases. Let's take a look at those next.

Realtime Database

The Firebase Realtime Database started life as the database for a chat client. It is probably the oldest part of Firebase and, although it has some unique features, you often get the feeling that the Firebase team would prefer new developers to use Firestore (which we look at next) in preference to the Realtime Database. This view is highlighted by a lack of web support for the plugin and was also evident in the delayed move to null safety, long after the other Firebase plugin updates had been completed.

At its core, the Realtime Database is effectively an online store of a massive **JavaScript Object Notation (JSON)** data structure, and it is through JSON that you interact with the database, by adding, updating, and deleting data. It is also through JSON paths that you identify the area of the database you want to manipulate. Note that this is very different from a traditional relational database and is part of the NoSQL style of databases that are now becoming prevalent since massive scalability and cloud-based redundancy have become more important factors than the normality of data.

NoSQL versus SQL databases

There are two types of databases: **Structured Query Language (SQL)**-based relational databases and NoSQL databases. In relational databases, it is important that data is not duplicated, but instead normalized.

A big advantage is that there is no chance of data inconsistency if the data is only stored in one place. A big disadvantage in a cloud world is that ensuring data consistency across multiple servers running the same database instances can cause bottlenecks. This was fine when there was only one server running an instance of the database or multiple servers co-located with fast network connections, but when cloud computing came along, the requirement to copy every update to many other instances of a database over long distances became a huge burden.

NoSQL databases aim to resolve this problem by allowing data duplication and eventual consistency. Retrieving and updating data becomes very quick and scalable. On the flip side, there is a risk that the duplicated data in the database becomes inconsistent.

This is a huge topic and worth exploring more about before you decide on your database solution.

One of the biggest advantages of the Realtime Database is, as the name would suggest, the ability to interact with it in real time. This includes setting up listeners on specific paths within the database so that your code is notified if anything changes at that path's location. This can be incredibly useful, giving your app a very dynamic and responsive feel.

It is also very useful to be able to manage very specific parts of the JSON tree through the use of paths. This allows you to manipulate very precise pieces of the JSON structure, reducing exposure to bugs and also reducing costs. The costing model is important to consider, and for the Realtime Database it is based on egress, and— specifically—how much data you retrieve from the database.

A big drawback of the Realtime Database is a lack of good transaction support. There is a limited ability to transact on a path within the JSON tree, but you cannot make changes to two places in the JSON tree within the same transaction, which leads to complex timestamping solutions to ensure consistency.

Another drawback is the querying support of the Realtime Database. You can only query on a single field (yes—one field) when retrieving data. This can be hugely restrictive to your data structure design, pushing you to create some kind of amalgamated field for querying on.

Also, it is worth noting that the Realtime Database has a limitation of 100,000 concurrent users, whereas Firestore has unlimited scalability. You can work around this by having multiple Realtime Database instances set up, but this does add complexity to your setup.

Setup

As with authentication before, the plugin works alongside `firebase_core` as another dependency, as illustrated in the following code snippet:

```
dependencies:
  flutter:
    sdk: flutter
  firebase_core: ^1.2.0
  firebase_database: ^7.0.0-dev.3
```

Once you have the dependency, you will want to get a reference to the database. You can do this with the following code:

```
final _reference = FirebaseDatabase.instance.reference();
```

This `_reference` variable is what you will use to access and update the database data.

Data manipulation

As mentioned previously, the data stored is in a massive JSON structure. For example, suppose our data store looked like this:

```
messages: {
  a3bdj2: {
    text: "Hello friends",
    viewedBy: [
      "tim@example.com",
      "jane@example.com"
    ],
    sentAt: 1621835683907,
    sentBy: "tom@example.com"
  },
  4bajfasdf: {…}
}
```

In the preceding JSON structure, we have a top-level map named `messages` that holds mappings from message **identifiers** (**IDs**) to message objects. Within the message object is the text of the message, a list of who has viewed it, when it was sent as a timestamp, and who sent it.

Suppose we wanted to mark that message as deleted. There are many ways to do that, depending on how you want to structure your client and your queries, but one way is to add a deleted flag to the object data. An example of doing that is shown here:

```
_reference.child('messages/a3bdj2/deleted').set(true);
```

In the preceding code snippet, we are asking the database to follow the path to the messages map, and then to the message with reference a3bdj2, and finally to the deleted entry. At this point, we set the value to true. Even though there isn't currently a path that includes deleted because the property doesn't exist yet, the Realtime Database is clever enough to fill in the gap and complete the set operation, giving a structure like this:

```
messages: {
   a3bdj2: {
      text: "Hello friends",
      deleted: true,

      ...
   },
   4bajfasdf: {…}
}
```

You can similarly make updates (where only parts of the data are changed rather than replaced) or removals in the same way.

Security

The Realtime Database has a security model based around the authentication we used earlier. This is a real strength of the database because security becomes easy to set up and understand. When you set up a database, you are given access to a security configuration file that you can manage.

This security configuration file is also based on paths within the JSON. So, for example, suppose I only want the author of a message to be able to mark it as deleted. In that case, I could add a security rule that looks something like this:

```
"messages": {
   "$messageId": {
      "deleted": {
         ".write": "auth.token.email_verified == true &&
         auth.token.email == root.child("messages/" +
```

```
                    $messageId + "/sentBy").val() "
        }
    }
}
```

In this example, we have defined a path (through nested map entries) of `messages/$messageId/deleted`. The `messageId` property has a $ (dollar) sign in front to show that this is a dynamic part of the path that will change depending on the `messageId` property.

We have then specified that we have a rule for any changes to data, using the `".write"` entry. Within that, we have said changes are only allowed if the user has a verified email address and if their email address matches the email address specified in the database at the path location of `messages/$messageId/sentBy`.

If they match, then the change is allowed. If there is no match (that is, the user updating the `deleted` flag is not the one who wrote the message), then the change is rejected and an exception is thrown in your application.

As you can see, it is relatively easy to get up and running with the Realtime Database. Let's now look at Firestore and compare the features and functionalities of the two services.

Firestore

The Firestore database is also a NoSQL database but takes a very different approach to the storage and retrieval of data. Unlike the Realtime Database, Firestore stores data in files, much like the filesystem on your computer. So instead of a big JSON object, Firestore follows something like a folder and file structure.

However, there are many similarities between the two databases, outlined as follows:

- Both databases store data in JSON. The files in Firestore contain JSON, so the same object data can be stored in either database.

- Both databases use paths to identify changes. In Firestore, the path is split into two parts—the file path, and then the data path within the file.

- Both databases use similar access control. Firestore access control has more capabilities but can also be more limited in how it uses data from other files to control access.

The costing model is different from the Realtime Database, where costs are based on the numbers of files read, written, and deleted. This model can really impact applications that use small pieces of data. A prime example of this is a chat app where not only does a small snippet of data get placed in each file, but also every other member of the chat group will need to read that file. In this situation, the Realtime Database is a much better fit.

Additionally, Firestore does not respond as quickly to updates, so for anything real-time, such as live multiplayer games, the Realtime Database is a better fit. It's definitely not shabby in its update speed, though, but you are talking seconds rather than sub-seconds to get updates.

Unlike the Realtime Database, Firestore has much better querying capabilities, allowing you to query across many fields. There are a couple of gotchas, though, that are worth being aware of. These are described here:

- You can only query on fields that are present in all the files, so in the example for Realtime where we added the `deleted` field, in Firestore you should already have the `deleted` field set with either a `null` or a `false` value.

- If you query for more than one field, then Firestore needs to prepare an index for every combination of fields. For example, if you want to search for messages that were a) sent after midnight and b) haven't been read by the user, then you need to create an index for those two fields. If you then decide to update that query to include a third restriction that the message wasn't sent by the user, then you will need to create a new index on the three fields. Generally, this isn't an issue but does mean you need to check every combination of your queries if they are dynamic.

Finally, Firestore is infinitely scalable—there is no restriction on the number of concurrent users like there is on the Realtime Database.

Setup

Again, the plugin works alongside `firebase_core` as another dependency, as illustrated here:

```
dependencies:
  flutter:
    sdk: flutter
  firebase_core: ^1.2.0
  cloud_firestore: ^2.2.0
```

Once you have the dependency, you will want to get a reference to the database, as follows:

```
FirebaseFirestore _firestore = FirebaseFirestore.instance;
```

This `_firestore` variable is what you will use to access and update the database data.

Data manipulation

As mentioned previously, the data stored is in a folder and file structure. Recreating the Realtime Database example, suppose you have a single message in a file, like this:

```
text: "Hello friends",
viewedBy: [
   "tim@example.com",
   "jane@example.com"
],
deleted: null,
sentAt: 1621835683907,
sentBy: "tom@example.com"
```

Again, the message object contains the text of the message, a list of who has viewed it, when it was sent as a timestamp, and who sent it. However, note that we don't have a `messages` map holding references to each message. This is now held in the folder—or collection, as it is named in Firestore. Also, note that we added the `deleted` flag with a `null` value to allow us to query for messages that are not deleted.

To make the same update to set the `deleted` flag, we would do something like this:

```
DocumentReference messageRef = FirebaseFirestore.instance
   .doc('messages/a3bdj2')
   .update({deleted: true});
```

As you can see, the process is very similar to that for the Realtime Database; find the file—or document, as it is known in Firestore—using a path, and then update the contents of the file.

Security

The security configuration is slightly different from the Realtime Database setup, but is conceptually the same.

To restrict the ability to delete messages to the sender of the message, your configuration would look something like this:

```
match /messages/{document=**} {
   allow update: if request.auth.token.email ==
                        resource.data.sentBy
                  && request.auth.token.email ==
                        request.resource.data.sentBy;
}
```

In this example, we are specifying that this rule applies to all documents that are in the messages collection. It is specifically a rule that governs updates to the document that restricts all updates to the user who sent the message. Note that because we are controlling access to the whole file rather than one specific field, as we did with the Realtime Database, we have also decided to ensure that the update doesn't change the sentBy property, effectively making it read-only.

Analytics and Crashlytics

Understanding how your app is being used is crucial in deciding where to focus new development to improve your app. Google Analytics allows you to see how users move around your app, and Google Crashlytics allows you to receive stack traces when they are thrown within your app.

Add them using standard dependency entries, as follows:

```
dependencies:
  flutter:
    sdk: flutter
  firebase_core: "^1.2.0"
  firebase_crashlytics: "^2.0.4"
  firebase_analytics: "^8.1.0"
```

Ensure that you check the latest versions of the plugins on **pub.dev**.

Crashes

To record a crash using Crashlytics, you would insert code like this:

```
await FirebaseCrashlytics.instance.recordError(
  error,
  stackTrace,
```

```
    reason: 'bad times',
    fatal: true // or false for non-fatal crashes
);
```

In the preceding code snippet, we have called the `recordError` method on the `Crashlytics` instance to send crash information back to the Firebase server so that it can be reviewed there.

The Crashlytics dashboard is shown in the following screenshot:

Figure 9.1 – Crashlytics dashboard

Unfortunately, more extreme crashes can occur that we might not be able to catch within our code. To report these crashes, simply add an entry in the app's `main` method, as follows:

```
FlutterError.onError = FirebaseCrashlytics.instance.
recordFlutterError;
```

This, unfortunately, still does not catch all errors, but there are options to use **Zones** (an advanced Flutter topic) to catch errors. Check the Crashlytics documentation for further information, at `https://firebase.flutter.dev/docs/crashlytics/overview/`.

Analytics

Much as with reporting crashes, as just discussed, analytics is the reporting of all the other events that happen in the app. For example, to log that someone has opened the app, you would run the following code:

```
Analytics.observer.analytics.logAppOpen();
```

This would then be sent to the Firebase server so that you can analyze how many times your app has been opened.

Additionally, for general navigation around the app, this can be added to the Navigator so that the analytics are automatically uploaded.

In the widget where you create `MaterialApp`, simply define a new observer, as follows:

```
static FirebaseAnalytics analytics = FirebaseAnalytics();
static FirebaseAnalyticsObserver observer =
      FirebaseAnalyticsObserver(analytics: analytics);
```

Then, attach the observer to the `MaterialApp` through the `navigatorObservers` constructor parameter, as illustrated in the following code snippet:

```
@override
Widget build(BuildContext context) {
  return MaterialApp(
    title: 'Flutter Demo',
    navigatorObservers: <NavigatorObserver>[observer],
    ...
  );
}
```

Every time the user moves pages through the use of the Navigator, the move will be logged on Google Analytics.

Cloud Storage

As you have seen, the Realtime and Firestore databases are designed around storing JSON data. What if you need to store something else, such as a text document or an image? This is where Cloud Storage comes into play. Files are stored in a folder structure, and some basic security controls are available that are similar to Firestore and Realtime Database access control. Additionally, some metadata can be attached to the file to assist with access control.

The plugin to add to your dependencies is `firebase_storage`.

AdMob

When you play apps and see adverts on part of the screen, or sometimes have to watch a fullscreen video advert, then you are interacting with something such as Google AdMob. App developers need a way to monetize their apps, and one of the options is to add advertising.

There are several types of adverts available, outlined as follows:

- **Banner**: This is a rectangular advert that appears on part of the screen and refreshes after a set period of time.

- **Interstitial**: A full-page advert that appears at a natural break in the game, perhaps on completion of a level.

- **Rewarded**: An advert that a user chooses to view in exchange for benefits within the app such as additional coins, points, or lives.

The Flutter AdMob plugin supports all of these types. The plugin to add to your dependencies is `google_mobile_ads`. You will need to register for an `adUnitId` variable from Google AdMob so that you can request adverts. You can get this via the Firebase console.

Showing an advert requires several steps. The first step is requesting an advert from Google in preparation of showing it. Here's the code you'll need to do this:

```
RewardedAd.load(
    adUnitId: _adUnitId,
    request: AdRequest(),
    rewardedAdLoadCallback: RewardedAdLoadCallback(
        onAdFailedToLoad: (LoadAdError error) async {
            print("Failed to load ad ${error.message}");
        },
```

```
onAdLoaded: (RewardedAd ad) {
    myRewarded = ad;
  },
 ),
);
```

In this example, we request a rewarded advert using our `adUnitId` variable and specify a callback when the advert is loaded. We store the loaded advert in a variable named `myRewarded`.

Next, we set up callbacks in preparation of a user interacting with the advert, as follows:

```
myRewarded!.fullScreenContentCallback =
FullScreenContentCallback(
  onAdShowedFullScreenContent: (RewardedAd ad) {
    print('$ad onAdShowedFullScreenContent');
  },
  onAdDismissedFullScreenContent: (RewardedAd ad) async {
    print('$ad onAdDismissedFullScreenContent');
    await ad.dispose();
  },
  onAdFailedToShowFullScreenContent: (RewardedAd ad,
  AdError error) async {
    print('$ad onAdFailedToShowFullScreenContent: $error');
    await ad.dispose();
  },
);
```

In the preceding code snippet, we set up callbacks for when the advert is shown, dismissed, or failed to show. These are important so that your app can take the necessary steps to move on to the UX after the advert flow has been completed.

Finally, we actually show the advert to the user, as follows:

```
myRewarded.show(
  onUserEarnedReward: (RewardedAd ad, RewardItem
  rewardItem) {
    print('$ad onUserEarnedReward $rewardItem');
  },
);
```

In the preceding code, we request that the rewarded advert is shown, and specify a callback when the user has earned their reward.

It is worth noting that there is risk in issuing any rewards to the user from your app code because someone malicious can write code to emulate your app and issue themselves lots of rewards. Therefore, Google also supports a server-to-server approach for rewards. The Google AdMob server will contact your server and tell you that the user has received a reward, removing the risk of an attack.

Cloud Functions

Throughout this book, we have looked at client technologies, the technology that will run on the client device: a phone, tablet, web page, or computer. However, most apps also need to run some code on a server. There are many reasons for this, including the following ones:

- **Trusted integration code**: Code that runs on a server can include security secrets such as integration with payment providers or email servers. These secrets cannot be included in an app because malicious users could decompile your app code and take the secrets, allowing them to impersonate your company.

- **Elevated privileges**: There may be something that needs to run with elevated privileges—for example, accessing parts of your database that you do not want to give general access to.

- **Batch processing**: Perhaps you need to do some intense work to update your database (for example, hourly leaderboards) that would not make sense on a per-user basis.

And there are many other reasons, especially around security and performance, that mean you will need to have a server for many app designs.

If you are using Firebase services, then the Firebase Cloud Functions framework makes a lot of sense to use for executing your server code. These functions directly link to your databases, including allowing you to trigger server code when certain database updates happen. They also work directly with Firebase Authentication, allowing you to control who has access to the functions.

Cloud Functions are currently written in JavaScript (or TypeScript), so we will not look at examples here. There appear to be options to use Dart for Cloud Functions, but it is not a supported route to take yet.

You can directly call Cloud Functions from your Flutter app and would use the `cloud_functions` plugin to do this.

Let's look at an example of making a call to a cloud function to record the reward from our rewarded advert, as follows:

```
final HttpsCallable callable = FirebaseFunctions.
instance.httpsCallable('storeReward', options:
HttpsCallableOptions(timeout: Duration(seconds: 30)));
try {
  await callable.call({
    "email": email,
    "reward": 30,
  });
} catch (errorMessage) {
  print(errorMessage);
}
```

In the preceding example, the first line defines the name of the cloud function we wish to call, and the timeout we will allow for the call (30 seconds).

Then, within a `try/catch` block, we attempt the call to the cloud function with our parameters—in this case, an email address and the reward value. If the call fails, then we can mitigate the issue in the `catch` block.

ML with Firebase ML Kit

Firebase ML Kit helps to add ML features to our app without the need for an ML experience. There's no need to have deep knowledge of neural networks or model optimization to get started.

Firebase ML Kit provides multiple tools, which are outlined as follows:

- **Text recognition/optical character recognition (OCR)**: Recognize text in photos. Available as an on-device and cloud-based functionality.

- **Face detection**: Detect faces in an image, identify key facial features, and get the contours of detected faces. Available as an on-device functionality.

- **Barcode scanning**: Scan multiple types of barcodes. Available as an on-device functionality.

- **Image labeling**: Recognize entities in an image. Available as an on-device and cloud-based functionality.

- **Landmark recognition**: Recognize well-known landmarks in an image. Available as a cloud-based functionality.

- **Language identification**: Determine the language of a string of text. Available as an on-device functionality.

- **Custom model inference**: Use a custom TensorFlow Lite (`https://www.tensorflow.org/lite`) model with ML Kit. Available as an on-device functionality.

The on-device tools are **application programming interfaces** (**APIs**) that run offline and process data quickly. Cloud-based APIs, on the other hand, rely on **Google Cloud Platform** (**GCP**) to provide results with high accuracy. To do this on a device, you would use the `firebase_ml_vision` plugin.

Messaging

Firebase also has the ability to manage push notifications. You would use a server or the Firebase dashboard to push out push notifications, but you may want to allow your app to take certain actions when they receive a push notification or if they are opened through an action on a notification.

Push notifications can be hard to get right, mainly because a lot of the configuration is server side, and if a message fails to be received, it is often a configuration issue with the failure being hidden in the Firebase or App/Play Store servers. You will see lots of documentation on the web where other developers have had issues and resolved them. The best answer is to be really diligent when configuring this section. Ultimately, you will be able to get push notifications to work, but only if you really pay attention to the details. Again, the documentation from the Firebase team is excellent.

If you want to take actions in your app based on push notifications, then the plugin you will need is `firebase_messaging`.

Let's take a look at an example of responding to a push notification, as follows:

```
FirebaseMessaging.onMessage.listen((RemoteMessage msg) {
  print('on message $msg');
});
```

In the preceding code example, you register to receive updates from the `onMessage` stream. Whenever there is an update placed on the stream, the callback code in the argument is called—in this case, a simple function that prints the message.

This section on Firebase will hopefully give you a taste of both the power of Firebase and the way it seamlessly integrates with Flutter. We have explored the two databases, authentication, analytics, storage, advertising, cloud functions, messaging, and have seen a glimpse of the power of ML Kit.

Let's continue our exploration of plugins by moving to some more popular plugins, starting with everyone's favorite, Google Maps.

Understanding Google Maps and Places

You will have likely used Google Maps for navigation, but the use of Google Places is not so obvious. This is generally used when you enter an address into a textbox, and while you are entering it, there are suggestions for the full address.

Simply put, Google Places is where you find an address, and Google Maps is where you display that address. There are many plugins that support Google Maps and Places, so when choosing, make sure you look at the pub.dev scores.

A very good Google Maps plugin is google_maps_flutter, which is created by the Flutter development team. In pub.dev, you can click on the author—in this case, flutter.dev—and view all the plugins that the development team has created. Looking through the flutter.dev team's plugins is a great way to get a feel for all the different plugins available.

There are plugins for Google Places, but an alternative is the google_maps_webservice plugin, which is a wrapper on the Google Maps web services and allows access to the Places API and many other APIs such as Directions, Time Zone, and Distance Matrix.

Note that when using Google Maps in any of its forms, you will need to request an API key. Unfortunately, Google Places is a paid-for service, so your API key will link to how much you are charged for the service.

To register for an API key, follow this link: https://developers.google.com/maps/documentation/places/web-service/get-api-key.

Once you have an API key, you will need to include that in any calls you make to the APIs so that Google can identify who you are.

Let's look at an example of displaying a map from a place ID, as follows:

```
final places = GoogleMapsPlaces(apiKey: "__API_KEY__");
PlacesDetailsResponse placeDetailsResponse = await places.
getDetailsByPlaceId(_placeId);
Widget mapWidget = GoogleMap(
  mapType: MapType.hybrid,
  markers: Set.from([
    Marker(
```

```
        position: LatLng(
                        _placeDetails.geometry?
                        .location.lat ?? 0,
                        _placeDetails.geometry?
                        .location.lng ?? 0,
        ),
        markerId: MarkerId(_placeDetails.placeId))
    ]),
    initialCameraPosition: CameraPosition(
      zoom: 15,
      target: LatLng(
        placeDetails.geometry?.location.lat ?? 0,
        placeDetails.geometry?.location.lng ?? 0,
      ),
    )
  );
```

In this example, we use a `placeId` property to retrieve information about the place. We then use a `GoogleMap` widget to display the place marked on the map, using the geometry details about the place.

Additionally, we are able to specify information about a map such as the type—in this case, `hybrid`, meaning it has satellite images and a road overlay—and the zoom level. This means we can really tailor the map so that it fits the needs of our app.

Let's next look at some plugins that give us access to the features and functionality of the device the user is viewing our app on.

Exploring mobile device features

There are a lot of features in devices, especially mobile phones or tablets, that your app can use to make the UX better. Normally, you would need to write device-specific code to access these features, but in Flutter, access to the features is generally available within a plugin. In this section, we will take a whistle-stop tour of some of these features, including the camera, web browser, local storage, and video playback, so that you can enhance the usability of the apps you create using the plugins that are already available to you.

Camera and QR codes

A key feature that mobile phones and tablets have is the camera. This can obviously be used for photos, but it can also be used for other functionality such as **Quick Response (QR)** scanning.

A couple of plugins to check out are `camera` (built by the `Flutter.dev` team) and `qr_code_scanner`.

The `qr_code_scanner` plugin contains the following two key things:

1. A `QRView` widget that you place in your widget tree and will show the view from the camera

2. A `QRViewController` controller that you attach to the `QRView` widget and that supplies a stream of `ScanData` you can listen on to receive details of any QR codes that are identified

Note that if you are using the QR code scanner or the camera plugin, you will need to specify the reason why your app will need access to the camera. You do this by updating `info.plist` and adding the entry, as follows:

```
<key>NSCameraUsageDescription</key>
<string>Why my app needs to use the camera</string>
```

This will pop up for the user when the app tries to access the camera so that the user can make an informed decision on whether they will give the app access to their camera.

Let's see an example of the `QRView` widget and the `QRViewController` controller in action, as follows:

```
// Widget fields
final GlobalKey _qrKey = GlobalKey(debugLabel: 'QR');
QRViewController? _qrController;
// Widget tree in build method
...
  QRView(
    key: _qrKey,
    onQRViewCreated: _onQRViewCreated,
  )

...
// Widget method
  void _onQRViewCreated(QRViewController controller) {
```

```
      this._qrController = controller;
      controller.scannedDataStream.listen((scanData) {
        setState(() {
          _controller.text = scanData.code;
          _showingScanner = false;
        });
      });
    }
// Widget dispose
  @override
  void dispose() {
    _qrController?.dispose();
    super.dispose();
  }
```

There are a few parts to this example, so let's explore each part in turn, as follows:

- Two fields are defined—the first to hold a global key so that on a rebuild of the widget a new QRView widget is not created, and the second to hold a reference to the QRViewController controller when it is created.

- A QRView widget is created in the widget tree. When it is first created, it will call the method specified in the onQRViewCreated parameter.

- A method is defined to be called when the QRView widget is created. This method, onQRViewCreated, receives a controller, which it stores in the qrController field, and then sets up a stream listener to receive updates on scanned data.

- Finally, in the dispose section, we clean up the _qrController variable so that we are not still scanning for QR codes after we have left this screen.

If you are scanning QR codes, then you probably also need a way to generate them. The qr_flutter plugin does an excellent job at this. Simply give it the data you want to embed in the QR code as part of the QrImage widget construction and your app will show a QR code, as illustrated in the following code snippet:

```
QrImage(
  data: "Whitby",
  version: QrVersions.auto,
  size: 200.0,
)
```

In this example, the `"Whitby"` data will be embedded in the QR code displayed.

Opening web pages

Sometimes, you need to open a web page from within your app. This might be for license agreements, further information, advertising links, and many other possible reasons. Devices will generally have a web browser available, so all that is required is to pop open the web browser at a specified URL.

A plugin that allows you to do this very easily is the `url_launcher` plugin. To pop open the web browser, create a method that's something like this:

```
void _launchURL(url) async =>
    await canLaunch(url) ? await launch(url) :
    print('Failed to launch $_url');
```

This method will take any URL, check whether the device can launch the URL, and if it can, it launches it.

You would then call this method from any button or `InkWell` within the `onPressed` or `onTap` methods, and the browser will be popped open. Note that the app will not be closed, just moved to the background while the user browses the website.

Local storage

Sometimes, you don't want to—or cannot—use online storage such as the Firebase databases. Another option is to use local storage on the device, and there are many plugins that will facilitate that, including the `shared_preferences` plugin.

Generally, these plugins will allow you to save data to the local device storage in a map structure. For example, storing a name to a device using the `shared_preferences` plugin would look something like this:

```
SharedPreferences prefs = await
                        SharedPreferences.getInstance();
await prefs.setString('name', name);
```

If you want to store more data on the local device, then you may want to use a database to allow you to structure the data. One plugin that is very popular is `sqflite`. This plugin uses the SQLite database and has full support for insert, query, update, and delete operations. It also has powerful features such as transaction and batch support.

Video

Devices generally have the ability to play back video, and embedding videos in your app can increase engagement. The `video_player` plugin is simple to set up and allows you to play videos that you have included in your `assets` folder or that are stored as a file on the network.

If you want to stream videos, especially from YouTube, then you will need to use a dedicated YouTube plugin. The most popular is `youtube_player_flutter`, which allows you to manage which controls are shown to the users, whether the video auto-plays, the colors of the controls, and many other things.

Payment providers

If you want to take payments in your app, then you will need to use one of the payment providers that have support for Flutter. The two most prominent of these are Stripe and Square. Both will need you to set up server processing for payments, so it is a non-trivial setup process.

Both providers support integration with Apple and Google Pay, allowing you to create a very smooth customer payment flow.

In-app purchases

If you are planning to have in-app purchases in your app, then you have a couple of options. You can go for the `in_app_purchases` plugin, which is well suited to one-off purchases where renewal and cancellation of subscriptions are not an issue. If you were to do subscriptions, you would need some server-side coding to cope with the renewal and cancellation flows from Apple and Google.

Alternatively, if you want to have a more complex purchase process, perhaps including subscriptions, and purchases outside of the App or Play Stores (which helps you avoid the 15% or 30% in-app payment charges), then you may want to look at RevenueCat. This service takes care of all the management of your purchases, including subscription renewal and cancellation, and has Stripe integration, giving you the option to sell your purchases on the web. Their plugin is `purchases_flutter` and requires that you have registered for the RevenueCat service in advance.

Opening files

Unlike on the web, where file opening is generally done on computers that have great support for a range of file types, on an app users are generally on more restricted devices and need a way to open files. The `open_file` plugin can manage this flow for you. Add a button or `InkWell` that a user can tap to open the file, and then in the `onPressed` or `onTap` methods, add the following code:

```
OpenFile.open("fileLocation");
```

Check out the `open_file` plugin page on `pub.dev` to see all the different file types that are supported.

Plugins to help with your app support

Finally, in this chapter, I wanted to make a special mention of plugins that help you support your app once it is in the wild. We saw the Crashlytics plugin earlier, and it cannot be said strongly enough that any live app must have a way to report crashes. On Android, there are so many different devices by so many different manufacturers that it is impossible to test across all of them.

Let's look at some other plugins that will make your life easier.

App version

Although most people have auto-update set on their device's settings, some people choose to manually install updates. If someone has an issue and sends you details, you really want an easy way to see which version of the app they are running.

The `package_info_plus` plugin is perfect for this. It will read the information from your `pubspec.yaml` file and make it available for you to surface in a widget. Adding this information to your app's settings page is a must, but it is also worth showing this information before any login screens in case the user is unable to log in to the app.

The `PackageInfo` class needs to be initialized first, so you will probably want to create a version string asynchronously and then refresh the display using `setState` to display the version string. The code to do this is illustrated in the following snippet:

```
_initialiseVersionInfo() async {
    PackageInfo info = await PackageInfo.fromPlatform();
    String version = "${_packageInfo.version}-
    ${_packageInfo.buildNumber}";
    setState(() {
        _version = version;
    });
}
```

In this example, we build a version string from the app version and build number.

Device information

Another piece of key information when trying to diagnose issues is to know about the device they are on. Often, users will know their device's make and model but not the software version that is running.

The `device_info_plus` plugin is able to get that information for your app so that you can again surface that information in a place that will help you diagnose any issues. If you can get a user to send you a screenshot of a page that holds the app and device information on it, then you will be in a much better place to start diagnosing any issues.

Suppose we want to print the name of the device to show on screen. As with the app version just before, we need to get the data asynchronously using code like this:

```
_initialiseDeviceInfo() async {
    DeviceInfoPlugin deviceInfo = DeviceInfoPlugin();
    if (defaultTargetPlatform == TargetPlatform.windows) {
        WindowsDeviceInfo info = await deviceInfo.windowsInfo;
        print("Computer name ${info.computerName}");
    } // and other platforms...
}
```

For each platform, you choose the information you want to surface.

Summary

In this chapter, we have explored a wealth of Flutter plugins and have hopefully given you a taste of all the options available to you as you develop your Flutter apps.

We started by looking at the Firebase service and all the plugins available within that. Firebase is certainly an easy way to get up and running with features that can often take months to develop, and if created bespoke will probably cost more and be less secure. These plugins included all the core capabilities that are needed within an app, including authentication, data and document storage, push notifications, analytics, and server-side functions. Additionally, we looked at how we can monetize our app through the AdMob plugin.

Next, we looked at some plugins that exercise the features of the device they are running on. This is certainly an area that could be explored a lot further via the **pub.dev** site. These plugins allow you to create a great UX, from using media such as videos, cameras, documents, and the web browser, to simplifying the user's interactions with the app via QR code scanners, local storage, payments, and in-app purchases.

Finally, we saw a couple of plugins that will help with supporting your app once you have released it. If there are issues, you are able to respond quickly using crash reports, often before users even report the problem, using analytics to identify areas of the app that receive higher or lower usage.

In the next chapter, we will move back into coding mode and look at adding some animations to our Hello World application.

10
Using Widget Manipulations and Animations

The built-in widgets and those available via plugins will allow you to create a great-looking app, but Flutter allows you to manipulate these widgets with layout transformations, such as opacity, rotations, and decorations, allowing you to further improve the **user experience** (**UX**) of your app. In this chapter, you will learn how to add these transformations to widgets.

Taking this widget manipulation a step further, Flutter has great support for animations that can be combined and extended to bring the **user interface** (**UI**) to life. You will learn about animations, including the use of `Tween` animations to manage an animation timeline and curve and using `AnimatedBuilder` to add and combine beautiful animations.

Finally, we will look at some widgets that have animation built directly into them, allowing you to skip the added complication of animation setup and management. They don't fit every situation, but when just a touch of animation is required, they can be perfect.

The following topics will be covered in this chapter:

- Transforming widgets with the `Transform` class
- Introducing animations
- Using animations
- Using `AnimatedBuilder`
- Implicitly animated widgets

Technical requirements

You will need your development environment again for this chapter as we will explore animations for the `Hello World` project. Look back at *Chapter 1, An Introduction to Flutter*, if you need to set up your **integrated development environment** (**IDE**) or refresh your knowledge of the development environment requirements.

You can find the source code for this chapter on GitHub at `https://github.com/PacktPublishing/Flutter-for-Beginners-Second-Edition/tree/main/hello_world/lib/chapter_10`.

Transforming widgets with the Transform class

We have looked at lots of widgets throughout the previous chapters, but sometimes we may need to change a widget's appearance to improve the UX. In response to user input or to make cool effects in the layout, we may need to move the widget around the screen, change its size, or even distort it a little bit.

If you've ever tried to achieve this in native programming languages, you may have found it difficult. Flutter, as mentioned previously, is highly focused on UI design and aims to make the developer's life easier by simplifying what could easily have been a complicated area.

In this section, we will first look at the `Transform` widget because it is an incredibly useful widget when you look at widget manipulation. We will then delve deeper into the widget to see the kinds of manipulations it allows us to do.

The Transform widget

The `Transform` widget is one of the best examples of the Flutter framework's power and consistency. It's a single-purpose widget that simply applies a graphic transformation to its child, and nothing more. Having widgets focused on one single purpose is fundamental to a better layout structure, and Flutter does this very well.

The `Transform` widget, as its name suggests, does a single task—it transforms its underlying child. Although its task is very complex, it hides most of this complexity from the developer. Let's have a look at its constructor, as follows:

```
const Transform({
    Key,
    required Matrix4 transform,
    Offset origin, AlignmentGeometry alignment,
    bool transformHitTests: true,
    Widget child
})
```

As you can see, besides the typical `key` property, this widget does not need many arguments to do its job. Let's see these arguments, as follows:

- `transform`: This is the only required property and is used to describe the transformation that will be applied to the `child` widget. The type is a `Matrix4` instance, a **four-dimensional** (**4D**) matrix that describes the transformation in a mathematical way. We will look in more detail at this in the next section, *Understanding the Matrix4 class*.

- `origin`: This is the origin of the coordinate system at which to apply the `transform` matrix. The `origin` property is specified by the `Offset` type, representing, in this case, a point (x,y) in the Cartesian system that is relative to the upper-left corner of the `render` widget.

- `alignment`: As with `origin`, it can be used to manipulate the position of the applied `transform` matrix. We can use this to specify `origin` in a more flexible way, as `origin` requires us to use real positional values. Nothing prevents you from using both `origin` and `alignment` at the same time.

- `transformHitTests`: This specifies whether hit tests (that is, taps) are evaluated in the transformed version of the widget.

- `child`: This is the child widget to which the transformation will be applied.

The `Matrix4` transform is critical to the `Transform` class, so let's look at that in more detail.

Understanding the Matrix4 class

In Flutter, transformations are represented by a 4D matrix. Although it sounds very intimidating, a 4D matrix is simply a matrix that has four rows and four columns, as shown here:

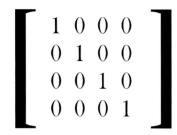

Figure 10.1 – 4D identity matrix

The value of the matrix shown is the **identity** matrix. This is a special value because it effectively says to make no changes in the transformation. As the values in the matrix are changed, then the widget is transformed in different ways.

Often, we don't need to know the specific values of the matrix to make a transformation. Besides methods such as matrix addition or multiplication, the `Matrix4` class contains methods that help with the construction and manipulation of geometric transformations. Some of them are listed here:

- Rotation: `rotateX()`, `rotateY()`, and `rotateZ()` are some examples of methods that rotate the matrix through a specific axis.

- Scale: `scale()`, with some variants, is used to apply a scale on the matrix using double values of the corresponding axes (x, y, and z) or through vector representations with the `Vector3` and `Vector4` classes.

- Translation: Just as before, we can translate the matrix using the `translate()` method with specific x, y, or z values and `Vector3` and `Vector4` instances.

- Skew: This is used to skew the matrix around the *x* axis with `skewX()` or *y* axis with `skewY()`.

Let's see how we can use the `Matrix4` class to enact different types of transformations.

Exploring the types of transformations

The `Transform` class provides facilities to the developer through its factory constructors. There are many of them for each of the possible transformations, making it extremely easy to apply a transformation to a widget without any deeper knowledge of geometric calculations. They are listed here:

- `Transform.rotate()`: Constructs a `Transform` widget that rotates its child around its center.

- `Transform.scale()`: Constructs a `Transform` widget that scales its child uniformly.

- `Transform.translate()`: Constructs a `Transform` widget that translates its child by an x,y offset.

Let's look at each of the transformation types in more detail.

Rotate transformation

The rotate transformation appears in situations where we want to simply make our widget rotate. By using the `Transform.rotate()` constructor, we can get a rotated widget. It does not differ too much from the default `Transform` constructor. The differences are listed here:

- Absence of the `transform` property: We are using the `rotate()` variant because we want to apply a rotation, so we do not need to specify the whole matrix for this. We simply use the `angle` property instead.

- Angle: This specifies the desired rotation in clockwise radians.

- Origin: By default, the rotation is applied relative to the center of the child. However, we can use the `origin` property to manipulate the origin of the rotation, as if we were translating the center of the widget by the `origin` offset, causing the rotation to be relative to another point if we want to.

We can use something like this:

```
Transform.rotate(
  angle: -45 * (math.pi / 180.0),
  child: ElevatedButton(
    child: Text("Rotated button"),
    onPressed: () {},
  ),
);
```

In this example, we have specified the angle in radians (315° clockwise is the same as -45° anti-clockwise), and the `child` widget that will be rotated—in this case, an `ElevatedButton` widget.

The exact same result is achieved using the `Transform` widget's default constructor and a `Matrix4` transformation instead, as illustrated in the following code snippet:

```
Transform(
    transform: Matrix4.rotationZ(-45 * (pi / 180.0)),
    alignment: Alignment.center,
    child: ElevatedButton (
        child: Text("Rotated button"),
        onPressed: () {},
    ),
);
```

The arguments that we need to provide in order to get the same result are a `transform` property with the rotation through the *z* axis, and an `alignment` property of the transformation specifying the center of the `child` widget.

Scale transformation

The scale transformation appears in situations where we want to simply cause our widget to change its size, either by increasing or decreasing its scale. Just as with the `rotate()` factory constructor, this variant does not differ too much from the default one. Here are some further details regarding this:

- Absence of the `transform` property: Here, again, we use the `scale` property instead of the whole transformation matrix.

- Scale: This is what we use to specify the desired scale in double format, `1.0` being the widget's original size. It represents the scalar to be applied to each *x* and *y* axis.

- Alignment: By default, the scale is applied relative to the center of the child. Here, we can use the `alignment` property to change the origin of the scale. Again, we can combine the `alignment` and `origin` properties to get the desired result.

For example, to scale up a widget, we can run the following code:

```
Transform.scale(
    scale: 2.0,
    child: ElevatedButton(
        child: Text("scaled up"),
```

```
        onPressed: () {},
    ),
);
```

Here, we have specified a `scale` property of `2.0`, which doubles the size of the `child` widget, and again specified that the `child` widget is `ElevatedButton`. Obviously, you could just set the size of `ElevatedButton` to avoid having a transformation.

And to get the same result using the default `Transform` constructor, we use the following code:

```
Transform(
    transform: Matrix4.identity()..scale(2.0, 2.0),
    alignment: Alignment.center,
    child: ElevatedButton(
        child: Text("scaled up"),
        onPressed: () {},
    ),
);
```

In a very similar way to the rotation, we must specify both the origin of the transformation with the `alignment` property and the `Matrix4` instance describing the `scale` transformation.

Translate transformation

The translate transformation is likely to appear in animations, as described later in the chapter in the *Using animations* section.

Here, we have even fewer properties compared to previous transformations. The differences are listed as follows:

- The absence of the `transform` and `alignment` properties: The transformation will be applied by the `offset` value, so we do not need the transform matrix.

- Offset: This time, `offset` simply specifies the translation to be applied on the `child` widget; this is different from the previous transformations, where it affects the origin point of the applied transformation.

By using the `Transform.translate()` constructor, we move the widget around the screen, by adding a `Transform` widget as a parent of the widget we want to move around, as illustrated in the following code snippet:

```
Transform.translate(
    offset: Offset(100, 300),
    child: ElevatedButton(
        child: Text("translated to bottom"),
        onPressed: () {},
    ),
);
```

The default constructor can also be used with `Matrix4` specifying the translation, as follows:

```
Transform(
    transform: Matrix4.translationValues(100, 300, 0),
    child: ElevatedButton(
        child: Text("translated to bottom"),
        onPressed: () {},
    ),
);
```

We only need to specify the `transform` property with the `Matrix4` instance describing the translation.

Composed transformations

We can—and most probably will—combine a number of the previously seen transformations to achieve unique effects, such as rotating at the same time as we move and scale a widget.

Composing transformations can be done in two ways, as follows:

- Using the default `Transform` widget constructor and generating our desired transformation using the `Matrix4`-provided methods to compose it.

- Using multiple `Transform` widgets in a nested way with the `rotate()`, `scale()`, and `translate()` factory constructors, achieving the same effect.

For clarity, let's look at how we would nest multiple `Transform` widgets, as follows:

```
Transform.translate(
  offset: Offset(70, 200),
  child: Transform.rotate(
    angle: -45 * (math.pi / 180.0),
    child: Transform.scale(
      scale: 2.0,
      child: ElevatedButton(
        child: Text("multiple transformations"),
        onPressed: () {},
      ),
    ),
  ),
);
```

As you can see, we add a `Transform` widget as a child to another `Transform` widget, composing the transformation. Although simpler to read, this method has a drawback: we add more widgets than needed to the widget tree.

When we add multiple transformations to a widget at the same time, we have to pay attention to the order of transformations. Experiment by yourself: exchanging the `Transform` widgets' positions will cause different results.

As an alternative, we can use the default `Transform` constructor with the composed transformation with the `Matrix4` object instead, as follows:

```
Transform(
  alignment: Alignment.center,
  transform: Matrix4.translationValues(70, 200, 0)
    ..rotateZ(-45 * (math.pi / 180.0))
    ..scale(2.0, 2.0),
  child: ElevatedButton(
    child: Text("multiple transformations"),
    onPressed: () {},
  ),
);
```

Just as before, we specify the alignment of the transformation as the center of the `child` widget and then the `Matrix4` instance to describe it. As you can see, it is very similar to the multiple `Transform` widgets version but without nested widgets, causing a deeper widget tree.

Now we have explored how to manipulate widgets in a static way, let's look at making an animation to allow a widget to move from one state to another in a smooth way.

Introducing animations

In Flutter, animations are widely supported, and the framework provides multiple ways of animating widgets. Additionally, there are built-in ready-to-use animations that we only need to plug into widgets to make them animate. Though Flutter abstracts many of the complexities that animations involve, there are some important concepts we need to understand before diving into the subject of animations.

The Animation<T> class

In Flutter, animations consist of a status and a value of type `T`, where the `T` type is defined on the creation of the `Animation` classes. The animation status corresponds to the animation state (that is, whether it's running or completed); its value changes while the animation runs, and it is this value that is intended to drive any widget changes during the animation execution.

Besides holding the information about the animation, this class also exposes callbacks, so other classes can know the animation's current status and value.

An `Animation<T>` class instance is only responsible for holding and exposing the status and value properties. It does not know anything about visual feedback, what is drawn on screen, or how to draw it (that is, the `build()` functions).

One of the most common kinds of animation you will see is the `Animation<double>` type representation, as a double value can easily be used to manipulate any kind of value in a sense of proportional space.

The `Animation` class generates a sequence (not necessarily linear) of values between determined minimum and maximum values. This process is also known as interpolation and is not only linear—it can be defined as a step function or a curve. Flutter provides multiple functions and facilities for operating animations. These are listed as follows:

- `AnimationController`: Despite what its name suggests, it is not used to control the `animation` objects. Instead, it inherits from `Animation<T>` and allows control over the generation of animation values.

- CurvedAnimation: This is an animation that applies a **curve** to another animation. There is a whole range of built-in curves available that will manipulate the animation values generated to fit different needs.

- Tween: This helps to create a linear interpolation between a beginning and ending value.

The Animation class exposes ways of accessing its state and value during a running cycle. Through status listeners, we can know when an animation begins, ends, or goes in the reverse direction. By using its addStatusListener() method, we can, for example, manipulate our widgets in response to animation start or end events. In the same way, we can add value listeners with the addListener() method, so we are notified every time the animation value changes, and we can rebuild our widgets by using the setState method.

AnimationController

AnimationController is one of the most used Flutter animation classes. It is derived from the Animation<double> class and adds some fundamental methods for manipulating animations. The Animation class is the basis of animation in Flutter; as mentioned in the previous section, it does not have any animation control-related methods. AnimationController adds these controls to the animation concept, such as the following:

- Play and stop controls: AnimationController adds the ability to play an animation forward or backward or to stop it.

- Duration: Real animations have a finite time to play—that is, they play for a while and finish, or repeat.

- Allows setting of the animation's current value: This causes the animation to stop and notifies the status and value listeners.

- Allows definition of the upper and lower bound of the animation: This is done so that we can know the deemed values before and after playing the animation.

Let's check the AnimationController constructor and analyze its main properties, as follows:

```
AnimationController({
    Double? value,
    Duration? duration,
    String? debugLabel,
    double lowerBound: 0.0,
```

```
    double upperBound: 1.0,
  AnimationBehavior animationBehaviour:
    AnimationBehavior.normal,
  required TickerProvider vsync,
})
```

As you can see, some properties are self-explanatory, but let's review them, as follows:

- value: This is the initial value of the animation, and it defaults to lowerBound if not specified.

- duration: This is the duration of the animation.

- debugLabel: This is a string to help during debugging. It identifies the controller in debug output.

- lowerBound: This cannot be null, so it will default to 0.0 if not supplied. It is the smallest value of the animation in which it is deemed to be dismissed—typically, the start value when running.

- upperBound: Also, this cannot be null, so it will default to 1.0 if not supplied. It is the largest value of the animation at which it is deemed to be complete— typically, the end value when running.

- animationBehavior: This configures how AnimationController behaves when animations are disabled, possibly due to accessibility requirements. If it's value is set to AnimationBehavior.normal, the animation duration will be reduced to match the request to disable animations. If it's set to AnimationBehavior. preserve, AnimationController, it will preserve its behavior, perhaps because the functionality of the app will be impacted by disabling the animation.

- vsync: This is a TickerProvider instance that the controller will use to obtain a signal whenever a frame triggers.

You may be wondering what TickerProvider is, so let's take a deeper look at that concept.

TickerProvider and Ticker

The TickerProvider interface describes objects capable of providing Ticker objects.

Tickers are used by any class that needs to know when the next frame is going to be built. They are commonly used indirectly via AnimationController instances. When using the State class, we can extend it with TickerProviderStateMixin or SingleTickerProviderStateMixin to have TickerProvider and use it with AnimationController objects.

CurvedAnimation

The `CurvedAnimation` class is used to define the progression of an `Animation` class as a non-linear curve. We can use this to modify an existing animation by changing its interpolation method. It is also useful when we want to use a different curve when playing an animation forward in reverse mode, by using its `curve` and `reverseCurve` properties respectively.

The `Curves` class defines many curves ready to use in our animation rather than the `Curves.linear` one. Let's look at some of the options as listed on the Flutter documentation web pages, as follows:

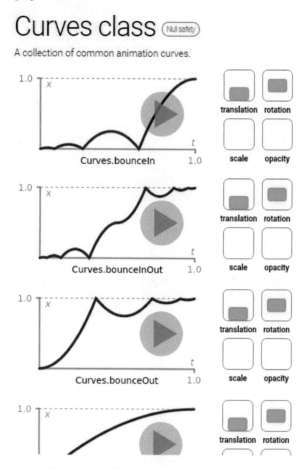

Figure 10.2 – Flutter Curves documentation

Check out the `Curves` documentation page to see, in detail, how each of the curves behaves: `https://api.flutter.dev/flutter/animation/Curves-class.html`.

Tween

Besides all of these classes, we have one that can help in specific tasks regarding the range of the animation. As we have seen, by default, the simple start and end values of animation are `0.0` and `1.0` respectively. We can, by using a `Tween` class, change the range or type of `AnimationController` without modifying it. `Tween` classes can be of any type, and we can also create our custom `Tween` class if we want. The point is, a `Tween` class returns values at periods between the beginning and the end, which you can pass as props to whatever you're animating, so it's always getting updated. For example, we can change the size of a widget, position, opacity, color, and so on by using specific `Tween` classes for each one.

We also have other `Tween` descendant classes such as the `CurveTween` class available so that we can modify an animation curve, or `ColorTween`, which creates interpolation between colors.

Now you have a base knowledge of animations, let's actually see them in action in the next section.

Using animations

When working with animations, we are not going to always be creating exactly the same `animation` objects, but we can find some similarities in use cases. `Tween` objects are useful for changing the type and range of an animation. We will, most of the time, be composing animations with `AnimationController`, `CurvedAnimation`, and `Tween` instances.

Before we use a custom `Tween` implementation, let's revisit our widget transformations from the earlier *Transforming widgets with the Transform class* section by applying the transformation in an animated way. We will get the same final effect but in a smooth and dynamic way.

Rotate animation

Instead of changing the button rotation directly, we can instead make it progressive by using the `AnimationController` class. An example of this kind of animation is shown in the following screenshot:

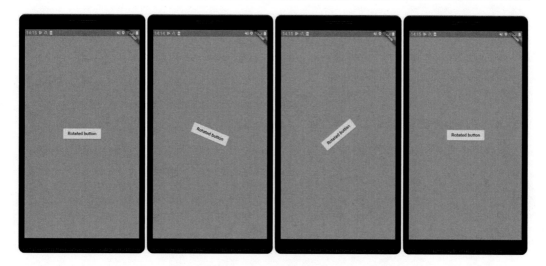

Figure 10.3 – Using animation to rotate a button

In the following example, we are creating our widget in a very similar way to the earlier *Rotate transformation* section:

```
_rotationAnimationButton() {
  return Transform.rotate(
    angle: _angle,
    child: ElevatedButton(
      child: Text("Rotated button"),
      onPressed: () {
        if (_animation.status == AnimationStatus.completed) {
          _animation.reset();
          _animation.forward();
        }
      },
    ),
  );
}
```

As you can see, there are two important things to notice, as follows:

- The `angle` value is now defined with an `_angle` property instead of directly assigning a literal.

- In the `onPressed` property, we check whether `_animation` is completed, and if it is, we restart it from the beginning.

Now, let's see how the animation part is done. We need to know how to create our `AnimationController` object and make it run. Let's take a look at our example class first, as follows:

```
class _RotationAnimationsState extends
    State<RotationAnimations> with
    SingleTickerProviderStateMixin {
  double _angle = 0.0;
  AnimationController? _animation;
  ...
}
```

A few things are important to notice in this class, as follows:

- We have created a `StatefulWidget` object called `RotationAnimations`, to make use of the `SingleTickerProviderStateMixin` class and provide the required `Ticker` object for our controller to run.

- Besides that, we have the `_angle` property, used to define our button's current angle. We can use the `setState()` method to cause it to be built with a new angle.

- And finally, we have our `_animation` object, to hold an animation and allow us to manage it.

The `initState()` function from our `State` class is the perfect place to set up the animation and start it. This function is illustrated in the following code snippet:

```
@override
void initState() {
  super.initState();
  _animation = createRotationAnimation();
  _animation.forward();
}
```

As you can see, we define our animation through the `createRotationAnimation()` method and make it run by calling its `forward()` function. Now, let's see how the animation is defined, as follows:

```
createRotationAnimation() {
  var animation = AnimationController(
    vsync: this,
    debugLabel: "animations demo",
```

```
    duration: Duration(seconds: 3),
);

animation.addListener(() {
    setState(() {
        _angle = (animation.value * 360.0) * (pi / 180);
    });
});

    return animation;
}
```

We can break up the creation of the animation into two important parts, as follows:

- There's the animation definition itself, where we set the animation debugLabel property for debugging purposes; the vsync property, so that it can have Ticker and know when to produce a new animation value; and finally, the animation duration.

- A second important step is to listen for the animation value changes. Here, whenever the animation has a new value, we get it, multiply it by 360°, and then convert it to radians so that we get a proportional rotation value.

As you can see, we can generate our desired values based on double animation values, so, most of the time, Animation<double> will be enough to play with animations.

If we wanted to, we could add a different curve to the animation by using CurveTween, for example, as you can see in the createBounceInRotationAnimation() method shown here:

```
createBounceInRotationAnimation() {
    var controller = AnimationController(
        vsync: this,
        debugLabel: "animations demo",
        duration: Duration(seconds: 3),
    );

    var animation = controller.drive(
        CurveTween(
            curve: Curves.bounceIn,
```

```
    )
  );

  animation.addListener(() {
    setState(() {
      _angle = (animation.value * 360.0) * _toRadians;
    });
  });

  return controller;
}
```

Here, we create another `animation` instance by using the controller's `drive()` method and passing the desired curve with a `CurveTween` object. Notice that we have added listeners to the new `animation` object instead of the controller, as we want values relative to the curve.

An important point to notice is that we have to dispose of our `AnimationController` class instance at the end of the lifetime of our `State` class to prevent memory leaks, as illustrated in the following code snippet:

```
@override
void dispose() {
  _animation.dispose();
  super.dispose();
}
```

This must be done for every kind of animation we do, as we will always be working with `AnimationController`.

Now, let's see how to create scale animations.

Scale animation

To create a scale animation and have a more fluid UI than changing the `scale` attribute directly, we again can use the `AnimationController` class to achieve a result similar to this:

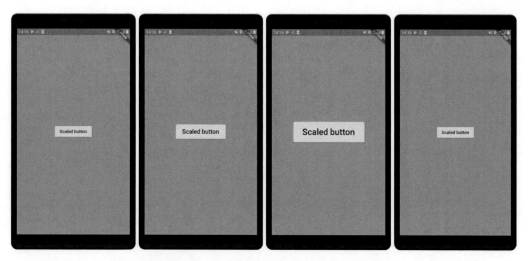

Figure 10.4 – Using animation to scale a button

This time, to build our ElevatedButton widget with a scale, we define a Transform widget with the well-known Transform.scale constructor, as follows:

```
_scaleAnimationButton() {
  return Transform.scale(
    scale: _scale,
    child: ElevatedButton(
      child: Text("Scaled button"),
      onPressed: () {
        if (_animation.status == AnimationStatus.completed) {
          _animation.reverse();
        } else if (_animation.status ==
        AnimationStatus.dismissed) {
          _animation.forward();
        }
      },
    ),
  );
}
```

Notice that we now use a _scale property and take a look at the change in the onPressed method. Here, we play the animation in reverse mode by using the reverse() function of AnimationController if it is completed, and play forward if it is at its initial state (that is, after reversing it).

The creation of an `animation` object occurs in a very similar way to rotation animation, but there are slight modifications to the controller construction, as illustrated in the following code snippet:

```
createScaleAnimation() {
  var animation = AnimationController(
    vsync: this,
    lowerBound: 1.0,
    upperBound: 2.0,
    debugLabel: "animations demo",
    duration: Duration(seconds: 2),
  );

  animation.addListener(() {
    setState(() {
      _scale = animation.value;
    });
  });

  return animation;
}
```

As you can see, we now change the controller's `lowerBound` and `upperBound` values to make more sense in our case, as we want the button to grow until its size is twice as big, and we do not want it to be smaller than its initial size (scale = `1.0`). Besides that, we change our animation value listener just to get the value from the animation without any calculations.

Translate animation

Just as we have done with the rotate and scale animations, we can accomplish a better look in our translation transformation and make it smoother by using `AnimationController`, as illustrated in the following screenshot:

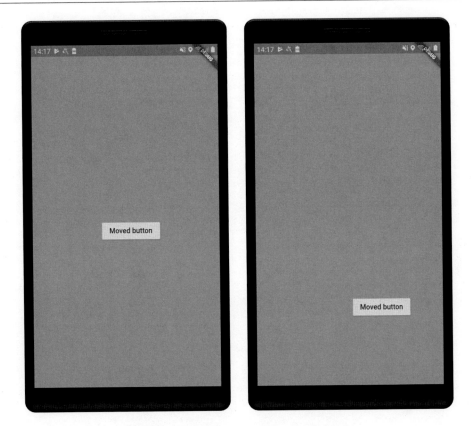

Figure 10.5 – Using animation to move a button

The construction of our widget is similar to the rotate and scale animations; the only exception is the usage of the `Transform.translate()` construction. Now, we have a different value type than `double`. Let's see what we need to change to make an `Offset` animation. Here's the code you'll need:

```
createTranslateAnimation() {
  var controller = AnimationController(
    vsync: this,
    debugLabel: "animations demo",
    duration: Duration(seconds: 2),
  );
```

```
var animation = controller.drive(
  Tween<Offset>(
    begin: Offset.zero,
    end: Offset(70, 200),
  ),
);

animation.addListener(() {
  setState(() {
    _offset = animation.value;
  });
});

return controller;
}
```

As you can see, here, we used a different approach to modify our `Offset` widget. We used a `Tween<Offset>` instance and passed it down to the `AnimationController` object through the `drive()` method, just like we did with `CurveTween` before. This works because the `Offset` class overrides mathematical operators such as subtraction and addition. The code is illustrated in the following snippet:

```
// part of geometry.dart file from dart:ui package
class Offset extends OffsetBase {
  ...
  Offset operator -(Offset other) => new Offset(dx -
  other.dx, dy - other.dy);
  Offset operator +(Offset other) => new Offset(dx +
  other.dx, dy + other.dy);
  ...
}
```

This makes the calculation of intermediate offsets (animation values) possible, and then the interpolation between two `Offset` values can be achieved.

Now we have explored animations, let's look at how we can use the `AnimatedBuilder` class to improve the quality of our code.

Using AnimatedBuilder

Looking at the code that we wrote in the last section, there is nothing wrong with it— it's neither too complex nor too big. However, looking closely, we can see a small problem with it—our button animation is mixed up with other widgets. As long as our code does not scale and get more complex, this is fine, but we know this is not the case most of the time, so we might have a real problem.

The `AnimatedBuilder` class can help us with the task of separating responsibilities. Our widget, whether it is `ElevatedButton` or anything else, does not need to know it is rendered in animation, and breaking down the `build` method to widgets that each have a single responsibility can be seen as one of the fundamental concepts in the Flutter framework. Let's look at the `AnimatedBuilder` class and then revisit our animation with our new knowledge.

The AnimatedBuilder class

The `AnimatedBuilder` widget exists so that we can build complex widgets that wish to include animation as part of a larger build function. Just as with any other widget, it is included in the widget tree and has a `child` property. Let's check its constructor, as follows:

```
const AnimatedBuilder({
  Key,
  required Listenable animation,
  required TransitionBuilder builder,
  Widget child
})
```

As you can see, we have a few important properties here, besides the well-known `key` property. Let's have a look at these in more detail, as follows:

- `animation`: This is the proper animation as a `Listenable` object. `Listenable` is a type that holds a list of listeners and notifies them whenever the object changes. As you may already be thinking, `AnimatedBuilder` will listen for animation updates, so we do not need to do it manually with the `addListener()` method anymore.

- `builder`: This is where we modify the `child` widget based on the `animation` values.

- `child`: This is the widget that exists regardless of the `animation` object. So, we construct this widget as we would do without `animation`.

Revisiting our animation

To break down our code, modify our animation, and make it more maintainable, we start separating what we need for each responsibility. Typically, the following three things are needed:

- The animation itself: Here, we do not need to change anything. Our `AnimationController` class will still be the same.

- Adding the `AnimatedBuilder` widget to our `build()` method: We will be extracting much of the code related to the animation of the button to make it clearer.

- The `child` widget: In our case, it is just `ElevatedButton` that changes according to the progress of the animation.

Now, let's update the translation animation code we created in the *Rotate animation* section to use the `AnimatedBuilder` concept. The first section that changes is the `_createTranslateAnimation` method, as illustrated in the following code snippet:

```
createBounceInRotationAnimation() {
  _controller = AnimationController(
    vsync: this,
    debugLabel: "animations demo",
    duration: Duration(seconds: 3),
  );

  _animation = _controller.drive(CurveTween(
    curve: Curves.bounceIn,
  ));
}
```

This method now creates a controller and animation but does not define a `setState` action. This is no longer the responsibility of the surrounding widget.

We still need the `dispose` method to clear up the animation when the parent widget is disposed, as illustrated in the following code snippet:

```
@override
void dispose() {
  _controller.dispose();
  super.dispose();
}
```

There is no change here, but it is worth noting that disposal is still required.

We still trigger the creation of an animation and its controller from the `initState` property and store the variables in two fields of our widget, as follows:

```
class _RotationAnimationsState extends
State<RotationAnimations> with SingleTickerProviderStateMixin {
  late AnimationController _controller;
  late Animation _animation;

  @override
  void initState() {
    super.initState();
    createBounceInRotationAnimation();
  }
```

Again, this is very similar to the previous examples. The key change occurs in the `build` method, as illustrated in the following code snippet:

```
  @override
  Widget build(BuildContext context) {
    return AnimatedBuilder(
      animation: _animation,
      child: ElevatedButton(
        child: Text("Rotated button"),
        onPressed: () {
          print("Rotating");
          print("${_animation.status}");
          if (_animation.isCompleted ||
          _animation.isDismissed) {
            _controller.reset();
            _controller.forward();
          }
        },
      ),
      builder: (context, child) {
        print("Building");
        return Transform.rotate(
          angle: _animation.value * 2.0 * pi,
```

```
            child: child,
          );
        },
      );
    }
```

As mentioned previously, the `setState` property is no longer in the parent widget—the `AnimatedBuilder` class takes care of that and constrains the redraw to just the children of the `AnimatedBuilder` class.

Two key things to notice in the code are outlined here:

- The `_animation` variable is now passed to the `AnimatedBuilder` class so that the `setState` property can be triggered within the widget's scope.

- The child widget is defined within the `child` parameter of the `AnimatedBuilder` class and the same child is returned as an argument to the `builder` method, allowing you to manipulate the same widget in both the `child` and `builder` methods.

Now, the redraw on the `setState` property is more efficient because potentially far fewer widgets are being re-evaluated on an animation update.

Now you've looked at the fundamentals of animation, let's briefly look at some widgets that hide all the complexity away and give you an easy way to set up animations that fit many situations.

Implicitly animated widgets

Flutter has a whole set of widgets that have animation built directly into them. This is great, but these animated widgets also mirror lots of widgets we have already seen, allowing a very easy drop replacement in your widget tree to get some great animations.

These widgets work by animating any changes to their internal state. For example, if a widget has been drawn to the screen in one color, and then a `setState` property changes the widget's color, then the change in color is animated rather than a single frame color switch. Let's first take a look at the `AnimatedContainer` widget, and then we will explore the other implicitly animated widgets available.

AnimatedContainer

The first widget to look at, and probably the most powerful, is the `AnimatedContainer` widget. This is very similar to the `Container` widget we first saw in *Chapter 5, Widgets – Building Layouts in Flutter*, but adds some key properties that allow it to animate changes.

Suppose in our widget tree we have an entry like this:

```
Container(
    width: _winner ? 50 : 400,
    child: Image.asset('assets/trophy.png'),
),
```

As you can imagine, if the `_winner` variable is initially set to `false` and then a `setState` call changes it to `true`, the `trophy` image will suddenly jump from `50px` wide to `400px` wide.

This would potentially be quite jarring to a user, and would not look like the action of a high-quality app. To solve this, adding an animation would make this image enlargement look much more professional.

We could animate the size change, as we saw in the previous *Scale animation* section, where we could use a controller, curved animation, and tween. However, this time, let's use `AnimatedContainer` to do the same thing, as follows:

```
AnimatedContainer(
    width: _winner ? 50 : 400,
    child: Image.asset('assets/trophy.png'),
    duration: Duration(seconds: 2),
),
```

Firstly, you'll see how similar the creation and constructor parameters are. The notable difference is the `duration` parameter. This parameter denotes how long any animations should take.

Now, when the `setState` property is called and `_winner` is changed from `false` to `true`, the `trophy` image will grow smoothly from `50px` to `400px` in `width` value over the course of 2 seconds. All interpolation (transitioning between the old and new `width` values) will be done by the widget itself.

However, it gets even better, because the `AnimatedContainer` widget can also take a `curve` parameter, allowing us to change the animation from a simple linear growth in `width` value to something much more interesting such as a `bounceOut` curve, which feels like the `trophy` image is dropping onto the screen and bouncing until it settles.

Once we add the curve to the code, it now looks like this:

```
AnimatedContainer(
  width: _winner ? 50 : 400,
  child: Image.asset('assets/trophy.png'),
  duration: Duration(seconds: 2),
  curve: Curves.bounceOut,
),
```

Adding the `curve` parameter allows you to set the animation curve to any of the curves supported by Flutter.

AnimatedFoo

The implicitly animated widgets that come with Flutter are often referred to as `AnimatedFoo`, where `Foo` is the name of the non-animated version of the widget.

There are a vast number of them, but some key ones to use are listed here:

- `AnimatedAlign`: Animates changes in alignment, such as changing `alignment` of the widget from one position on the screen (for example, `topRight`) to another part of the screen (for example, `bottomLeft`).

- `AnimatedOpacity`: Animates the opacity of the widget. Great for fading in or out a `child` widget.

- `AnimatedPadding`: Animates how a widget sits within a parent widget.

- `AnimatedPositioned`: Can only be used within a stack, and allows a widget to be moved around and for the size of the widget to change.

- `AnimatedSize`: Animates the change in the size of a widget.

These widgets can be great fun to play around with, so try plugging some of them into the `HelloWorld` app and see how you can animate them. They are also a great way to prototype any designs that require animations. Ultimately, you may need to use more complex animation management, but you will at least be able to see whether a design will work without investing lots of time in its development.

Summary

In this chapter, we got to know how to change our widgets' look by using the `Transform` class and its available transformations, such as scaling, translating, and rotating. We also saw how we can compound transformations by using the `Matrix4` class directly.

We learned the fundamental concepts of animation and how to apply them to child widgets to make changes smooth and dynamic.

We saw the important `AnimationController`, `CurvedAnimation`, and `Tween` `framework classes`. We also revisited our `Transformation` examples and added animations to them by using the concepts learned in this chapter. Finally, we saw how to create our own custom `Tween` objects, and we looked at how to clean up our code through the use of the `AnimatedBuilder` widget.

Lastly, we saw the `AnimatedFoo` classes that have animation embedded inside them, allowing you to develop slick animations without complicated code.

In the next chapter, we will look at the app as a whole, complete program and at how we can test and debug it in preparation for user trials and finally release it to the world!

Section 4:
Testing and App Release

Complex and unique apps involve features that the developer needs to know how to use, such as writing platform-native code and customizing framework resources to their needs. In this section, you will learn about all of this.

This section comprises the following chapters:

- *Chapter 11, Testing and Debugging*
- *Chapter 12, Releasing Your App to the World*

11
Testing and Debugging

Flutter provides great tools to help the developer manage their app development and ensure that it is ready for production – from a test API to IDE tools and plugins. This is especially crucial in app development where, unlike in some scenarios such as web pages, a bug fix can take several days to be reviewed by the relevant store, and then be updated on user devices.

In this chapter, you will learn how to add tests to identify bugs within your app, use debugging tools to identify where an issue is within your code, profile your app performance to find bottlenecks, and inspect the UI widgets.

We will start the chapter with an exploration of how you can unit test your Dart code. This can be useful if you create a reusable library of functions that you are using across many apps and want to ensure that any changes to the library code continue to function as intended.

The following topics will be covered in this chapter:

- Unit testing
- Widget testing
- Debugging your app
- DevTools

Technical requirements

You will need your development environment again for this chapter if you want to practice testing and debugging the `Hello World` project. Look back at *Chapter 1, An Introduction to Flutter*, if you need to set up your IDE or refresh your knowledge of the development environment requirements.

You can find the source code for this chapter on GitHub at the following links:

- `https://github.com/PacktPublishing/Flutter-for-Beginners-Second-Edition/tree/main/hello_world/lib/chapter_11`.

- `https://github.com/PacktPublishing/Flutter-for-Beginners-Second-Edition/tree/main/hello_world/test/chapter_11`

Unit testing

It is generally agreed that writing bug-free software is impossible, especially when your code runs on third-party hardware, such as a mobile phone, and has to interact with users, who can (and will) do all kinds of unexpected things.

However, for some situations, such as reusable function libraries, the requirements can be well defined, and the data inputs known in advance. In these situations, not only is a strong set of tests a great way to ensure the library is as bug-free as possible, but it also allows you to make changes to the code (for example, performance improvements, memory optimizations), knowing that your changes have not affected the expected behavior of the library.

Unit tests are one of the things that can help us to write modular, efficient, and bug-free code. The unit test is not the only way of testing code, of course, but it's a crucial part of testing small pieces of software in a manner that isolates it from other parts, helping us to focus on specific things.

Covering all of the application code with unit tests does not guarantee that it's 100% bug-free; however, it helps us to achieve mature code progressively, and this is one of the steps to ensuring a good development cycle, with stable releases from time to time.

Dart also provides some useful tools to work with tests. Let's take a look at the starting point of unit testing Dart code: the Dart `test` package.

The Dart test package

The Dart test package is not part of the **Software Development Kit** (**SDK**) so it has to be added as a dependency using the `pubspec.yaml` file as we saw done often in *Chapter 8, Plugins – What Are They and How Do I Use Them?*.

Unlike with the previous plugins that we depended on, this is a dependency that is required only during development and not at runtime. Therefore, it is added to another part of the pubspec.yaml file, specifically the area in dev_dependencies:

```
dev_dependencies:
  test: ^1.17.5
```

Just like the standard dependencies, these plugins are listed on the pub.dev site, and the installation section will advise you how to add the plugin to the correct part of the pubspec.yaml file.

Including this dependency enables us to use the test package's provided libraries to write unit tests.

Writing unit tests

Now, let's suppose that we want to create a function that sums two numbers:

```
class Calculator {
  num sumTwoNumbers (num a, num b) {
    return 0; // TODO
  }
}
```

We would probably choose to put the file holding this function in a sub-folder, allowing us to manage our code structure. Let's say we put it in the location lib/maths/calculator.dart.

We can now write a unit test to evaluate this method implementation by using the test package:

```
import 'package:test/test.dart';
import 'package:hello_world/maths/calculator.dart';

void main() {
  late Calculator _calculator;

  setUp(() {
    _calculator = Calculator();
  });
```

```
test(
    'calculator.sumTwoNumbers() sum both numbers',
    () => expect(_calculator.sumTwoNumbers(1, 2), 3),
    );
}
```

In the preceding example, we started by importing the test package's main library that exposes functions, for example, setUp(), test(), and expect(). Each of the functions has specific roles, as follows:

- setUp() will execute the callback we pass to it before each of the tests in the test suite.

- test() is the test itself; it receives a description and a callback with the test implementation.

- expect() is used to make assertions about the test. In the preceding example, we are just asserting a sum of 1 + 2, which should result in the number 3.

Tests should be stored in their own test folder, separate from the lib folder. Let's say we put this file in test/calculator_test.dart.

To execute a test, we use the following command:

```
flutter pub run test <test_file>
```

In the preceding example, the command would be (from the root of the project) as follows:

```
flutter pub run test test/calculator_test.dart
```

Before we correctly implement the sumTwoNumbers() method, let's run the test to see what output we get:

```
PS C:\Flutter\hello_world> flutter pub run test test/
calculator_tests.dart
00:00 +0: calculator.sumTwoNumbers() sum both numbers
00:00 +0 -1: calculator.sumTwoNumbers() sum both numbers [E]
  Expected: <3>
    Actual: <0>
```

```
package:test_api                        expect
test\calculator_tests.dart 11:61   main.<fn>


00:00 +0 -1: Some tests failed.
pub finished with exit code 1
```

A little intimidating, but there are four key pieces of information here:

- `00:00 +0 -1: Some tests failed`: This is stating that the tests took 0 seconds to run, that 0 tests passed (`+0`), and that 1 test failed (`-1`). At this point, you know you have some investigating to do!

- The test that failed had the title `calculator.sumTwoNumbers() sum both numbers` because it has a `-1` before its name.

- The test failed because the `expect()` statement was expecting a result of 3 but received a result of 0.

- The failure occurred in the `calculator_tests.dart` file on line `11`, character `61`. This is exactly where the `expect()` statement is defined.

With this information, you should be able to identify where your test is failing, and start to diagnose what bug you have uncovered (which could potentially be a bug in your test code rather than the code it is testing).

Let's change the implementation of the `sumTwoNumbers()` method, and then rerun the test to check it is all correct:

```
class Calculator {
  num sumTwoNumbers(num a, num b) {
    return a + b;
  }
}
```

Now we return the two numbers added together, and a rerun of the test gives the following:

```
PS C:\Flutter\hello_world> flutter pub run test test/
calculator_tests.dart
00:00 +0: calculator.sumTwoNumbers() sum both numbers
00:00 +1: All tests passed!
```

The test name is shown, and this time there is no error, just an `All tests passed!` message.

Note that we could have made this test pass by simply returning 3 from the sumTwoNumbers() method, which shows that the creation of a range of tests is necessary to be confident of the quality of your function.

You can also create groups of tests so that it is easy to manage and report on specific parts of the code being tested. Let's suppose that we create a new file to hold a test suite with a group of tests, as follows:

```
import 'package:test/test.dart';
import 'package:hello_world/maths/calculator.dart';

void main() {
  late Calculator _calculator;

  setUp(() {
    _calculator = Calculator();
  });

  group("calculator tests", () {
    test(
      'sumTwoNumbers() sum both numbers',
      () => expect(_calculator.sumTwoNumbers(1, 2), 3),
    );
    test(
      'sumTwoNumbers() sum negative number',
      () => expect(_calculator.sumTwoNumbers(1, -1), 1),
    );
  });
}
```

The preceding code should look very similar to the single test example, with a main method containing a setup method. However, instead of also containing a test method, the main method contains a group method that itself will contain the tests.

In this example, we call the group method with two parameters: the name of the group of tests, and an anonymous function that will run the tests. The anonymous function simply calls the test() method twice with two tests.

Notice the output for the preceding tests:

```
PS C:\Flutter\hello_world> flutter pub run test test/
calculator_group_tests.dart
00:00 +0: sum tests calculator.sumTwoNumbers() sum both numbers
00:00 +1: sum tests calculator.sumTwoNumbers() sum negative
number
00:00 +1 -1: sum tests calculator.sumTwoNumbers() sum negative
number [E]
  Expected: <1>
    Actual: <0>


  package:test_api                            expect
    test\calculator_group_tests.dart 15:7   main.<fn>.<fn>


00:00 +1 -1: Some tests failed.
pub finished with exit code 1
```

There was one successful test (+1) and one failure (-1) – with the details of the failure noted as an incorrect expectation. With this in mind, we can investigate the location of the failure and realize that our expect() statement is incorrect. We were expecting 1 + -1 = 1, which is clearly incorrect. Modifying the test to expect 0 and then rerunning the test group gives the following output:

```
PS C:\Flutter\hello_world> flutter pub run test test/
calculator_group_tests.dart
00:00 +0: sum tests sumTwoNumbers() sum both numbers
00:00 +1: sum tests sumTwoNumbers() sum negative number
00:00 +2: All tests passed!
```

In this output, we can see +1 as the first test passes, then +2 as the second test passes.

Unit tests can help us prevent logical errors in our functional libraries from occurring in production. Of course, tests generally can't be exhaustive, but using techniques such as boundary value analysis and equivalence partitioning can allow us to test most of the possible scenarios, which our library function will have to deal with. These topics are outside of the scope of the book, but a search on the internet for these terms will give further explanation and help you to write a strong set of tests for a function.

Unit test mocking

Sometimes our unit tests may rely on accessing a service or reading live data from a database. This can be troublesome in a unit test because the service may not be available from the test environment, you don't want to be manipulating live data from a test, and the test may not be repeatable if the service or database returns unexpected results.

To solve this problem, unit testing generally replaces, or mocks, these services or databases so the dependency is removed. You can either choose to write these mocks yourself, by replacing a live service class with your custom mock class, or you can use a framework such as Mockito.

Mockito is available as a plugin, so adding it to your project is as easy as updating your `pubspec.yaml` file to include the `dev` dependency. Exploring the use of mocks is beyond the scope of this book, but a great place to start your investigation is on the **pub. dev** page at `https://pub.dev/packages/mockito`.

As mentioned at the start of this section, unit testing is great for testing a library function that has well-defined inputs, outputs, and requirements. As we start to involve outside actors such as users, networks, and devices, we need to look at other testing options. Let's start that exploration with a look at testing widgets.

Widget testing

Getting the right mix of tests is important so that you can test your app optimally without reducing iteration and development velocity. Writing unit tests for well-defined library functions makes sense, but when it comes to user interactions, you often want to iterate and understand user interactions before settling on a design, which then may change as fashion or best practices change. Therefore, your test itself should be more high-level, looking at components rather than specific functions. One example of this is widget tests, and Flutter helps us to write widget tests to test that widgets work as expected.

Widget tests are used to validate widgets in an isolated way. They look very similar to unit tests but focus on widgets. The main goal is to check widget interactions and whether widgets visually match expectations. As widgets live in the widget tree inside the Flutter context, widget tests require the framework environment to be executed. That is why Flutter provides tools for writing widget tests through the `flutter_test` package.

The flutter_test package

The flutter_test package is shipped with the Flutter SDK. It is built on top of the test package, and provides a set of tools for helping us to write and run widget tests.

As said in the previous section, widget tests need to be executed in the widget environment and Flutter helps with this task with the WidgetTester class. This class encapsulates the logic for us to build and interact with the widget being tested and the Flutter environment.

We do not need to instantiate this class by ourselves as the framework provides the testWidgets() function. The testWidgets() function is similar to the Dart test() function that we saw in the *Unit testing* section. The difference is the Flutter context – this function sets up a WidgetTester instance to interact with the environment.

The testWidgets function

The testWidgets() function is the entry point of any widget test in Flutter:

```
void testWidgets(
  String description,
  WidgetTesterCallback callback,
  { bool skip: false, Timeout? timeout },
)
```

The method takes two required and two optional parameters:

- description: This required parameter helps to document the test; that is, it describes what widget features are being tested.

- callback: This required parameter is WidgetTesterCallback. This callback receives a WidgetTester instance so that we can interact with the widget and make our validations. This is the body of the test, where we write our test logic.

- skip: We can skip the test when running multiple tests by setting this optional flag. The default value is false.

- timeout: This optional parameter is the maximum time the test callback can run. The default value is to have no limitation.

Let's look at an example of how we could use this method.

Widget test example

When we generate a Flutter project, we have the `flutter_test` package dependency added for us automatically and a sample test is generated in the `test/` directory.

First, in the `pubspec.yaml` file, we can see the `flutter_test` package dependency was added to our `HelloWorld` project when it was created:

```
dev_dependencies:
  flutter_test:
    sdk: flutter
```

Note that the package version is not specified. This is because the origin is configured as the Flutter SDK, so it matches whatever version of Flutter we have installed on our system.

Next, let's take a look at the basic widget test in the `test/widget_test.dart` file:

```
import 'package:flutter/material.dart';
import 'package:flutter_test/flutter_test.dart';
import 'package:hello_world/main.dart';


void main() {
  testWidgets(
    'Counter increments smoke test',
    (WidgetTester tester) async {
      // Build our app and trigger a frame.
      await tester.pumpWidget(MyApp());
      // Verify that our counter starts at 0.
      expect(find.text('0'), findsOneWidget);
      expect(find.text('1'), findsNothing);
      // Tap the '+' icon and trigger a frame.
      await tester.tap(find.byIcon(Icons.add));
      await tester.pump();
      // Verify that our counter has incremented.
      expect(find.text('0'), findsNothing);
      expect(find.text('1'), findsOneWidget);
  });
}
```

This sample widget test validates the behavior of the famous Flutter counter app. The test goes as follows:

1. The test is defined with a description and the `WidgetTesterCallback` property as we saw in the *The flutter_test package* section earlier. Also, note the callback has the `async` modifier, as it returns a `Future` type.

2. We want to test a widget, so the test fires up the widget we want – in this case, `MyApp` – by running `await tester.pumpWidget(MyApp());`. This renders the widget ready for us to test it.

3. If we need to rebuild the widget at any point, we can use the `tester.pump()` method. This is needed because, although the code may initiate `setState()`, Flutter will not automatically rebuild the widget in a test environment.

4. In widget tests, three additional pieces are important and very common: `expect()`, `find`, and `Matcher`.

    The `expect()` method is used in conjunction with `finder` and `Matcher` to make assertions on widgets found – just like the `expect()` function that we looked at in the *Unit testing* section.

    The `Finder` class is what allows us to search specific widgets in the tree. The `find` constant provides `Finders` that search the widget tree for specific widgets.

    The `Matcher` class helps to validate the found widget characteristic with an expected value.

> **Important note**
> Check all available `Finders` provided by `find`: `https://api.flutter.dev/flutter/flutter_driver/CommonFinders-class.html`.

Let's step through the test code that is run, after the widget is pumped via `WidgetTester`, so that we can better understand the test.

The first assertions check for the presence of a single widget with the text `'0'` and none with the text `'1'`. This is done by using the `find` function `find.text()`, to find a widget with specific text, and then using the two Matchers, `findsOneWidget` and `findsNothing`, to specify the expectation of how many widgets should be found, as shown here:

```
expect(find.text('0'), findsOneWidget);
expect(find.text('1'), findsNothing);
```

Then, `tap()` is executed on `WidgetTester`, followed by a `pump()` request to refresh the widget. The tap occurs on a widget that contains the `Icons.add` icon by using the `find.byIcon()` function to find the correct widget:

```
await tester.tap(find.byIcon(Icons.add));
await tester.pump()
```

The final step is to verify the correct text is shown again. But this time, the `findsOneWidget` constant is used to verify that only the text, `'1'`, is visible and that there are no widgets that now have the text `'0'`:

```
expect(find.text('0'), findsNothing);
expect(find.text('1'), findsOneWidget);
```

Like the `find` constant, which has multiple `find` functions, there are multiple Matchers in addition to `findsNothing` and `findsOneWidget`. Check all available Matchers in the `flutter_test` library documentation:

https://api.flutter.dev/flutter/flutter_test/flutter_test-library.html

Running a widget test

To run a widget test, use this command:

```
flutter test <testFile>
```

So, in our example, we would run this command:

```
flutter test test/widget_test.dart
```

Let's just change the test so that it will fail. In this case, we will change the final assertion to see if the widget has the text "2" instead of "1". If we run the test, the output is the following:

```
PS C:\Flutter\hello_world> flutter test test/widget_test.dart
00:05 +0: Counter increments smoke test
====| EXCEPTION CAUGHT BY FLUTTER TEST FRAMEWORK |====
The following TestFailure object was thrown running a test:
   Expected: exactly one matching node in the widget tree
   Actual: _TextFinder:<zero widgets with text "2" (ignoring
offstage widgets)>
   Which: means none were found but one was expected

When the exception was thrown, this was the stack:
<Stack trace here>
...


This was caught by the test expectation on the following line:
   file:///C:/Users/geeky/Documents/Apps/Flutter/hello_world/
test/widget_test.dart line 28
The test description was:
   Counter increments smoke test


====================================================
00:05 +0 -1: Counter increments smoke test [E]
   Test failed. See exception logs above.
   The test description was: Counter increments smoke test


00:05 +0 -1: Some tests failed.
```

As you can see from the output, the test runner wasn't very happy. Although there is a lot of information, the format is very similar to what we saw in the *Unit testing* section. We can see the difference in expectation from what actually happened, the name of the test, and the line that the test failed on.

Let's run the test again with the correct expectation:

```
PS C:\Flutter\hello_world> flutter test test/widget_test.dart
00:11 +1: All tests passed!
```

When the tests passed, the output was very minimal, just reporting that `All tests passed!`.

Even with lots of testing, apps will fail or exhibit incorrect behavior. In these cases, you will need to inspect the execution of the app code to find the issues. This activity, known as debugging, is our next topic.

Debugging your app

Debugging is an important part of software development. Small mistakes, strange behaviors, and complex bugs can be solved with the help of debugging. With this, we can do the following:

- Make logic assertions
- Determine required improvements
- Find memory leaks
- Perform flow analysis

Flutter provides multiple tools to help you debug your app. Specifically, Flutter IDEscan assists with debugging. However, the Dart tooling also allows debugging without the IDE, which we will see in the following sections.

Observatory

Flutter debugging is based on the Dart Observatory tool. Dart Observatory is present in the Dart SDK and helps with profiling and debugging Dart applications such as Flutter apps.

You can explore the Observatory by running Dart specific code using the dart
run --observe command where you will receive an address:port part of the
output. This address is the Observatory UI address; you can access it through standard
web browsers:

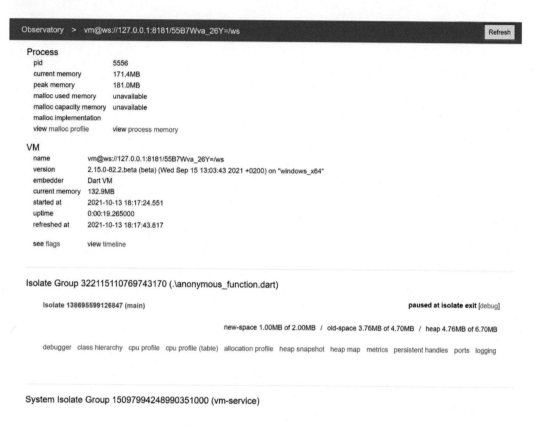

Figure 11.1 – The Dart Observatory

The Observatory shares information about the app that's running, such as the current and peak memory, class hierarchy, and logs. Also, amongst the many sections of the Observatory is an important additional tool, the debug tool:

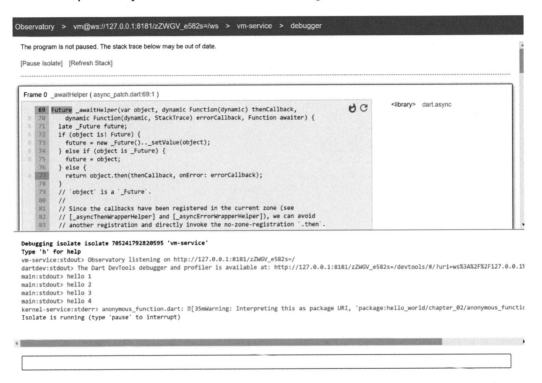

Figure 11.2 – Debug tool

On this page, as you can see, we have access to all of the debugging functionalities, such as the following:

- Adding and removing breakpoints
- Running step by step and line by line
- Switching and managing isolates

Check all available Observatory UI functionalities and a full usage tutorial at the following link:

```
https://dart.dev/tools/dart-devtools
```

When you use an IDE such as Visual Studio Code or Android Studio/IntelliJ, you will not be using tools such as the Observatory UI directly. IDEs use Dart Observatory under the hood to expose its functionalities through the IDE interface.

Additional debugging features

Dart provides additional features to help with advanced debugging through variants of the common tools that can make the debugging process even more useful. These are as follows:

- The debugger() statement: Also called programmatic breakpoints, this is where we can add a breakpoint only if an expected condition is true:

```
void login(String username, String password) {
    debugger(when: password == null);

    ...
}
```

  In this example, a breakpoint will occur only if the condition specified in the when parameter is true, that is, only if the password argument is null. Let's say this is an unexpected value: pausing the execution at this point may help to see why it occurs and how to react to it. This is very useful for tracing unexpected states and logic fails.

- debugPrint() and print(): print() is a method to log information into the Flutter log console. When we use the flutter run command, its log output is redirected to the console and we can see anything that comes from print() and debugPrint() calls. The only difference between these calls is that the debugPrint() version throttles the rate of message creation to avoid data loss on Android.

- Asserts: assert() is used to break app execution when some condition is not satisfied. It is similar to the debugger() method, but instead of pausing execution, it interrupts the execution by throwing an AssertionError. If you look at plugin or built-in widget code, you will often see assert statements on the constructors to ensure the widgets are being constructed correctly.

It's worth noting that debugger() and assert() function calls are ignored in production code.

The tools you have seen so far are pretty raw. You generally wouldn't debug your code by adding debugging statements or accessing the Observatory, but it serves as a useful baseline for your knowledge. Let's look at how you can do debugging directly within the IDE.

Debugging in the IDE

To be able to debug within your IDE, you first need to run your app from within your IDE. If you are running Visual Studio Code, then you will see a **RUN AND DEBUG** button on the left side of the IDE. Click this, and then at the top of the section, you will see a **Run debugging** button beside the name of the Flutter project **hello_world**:

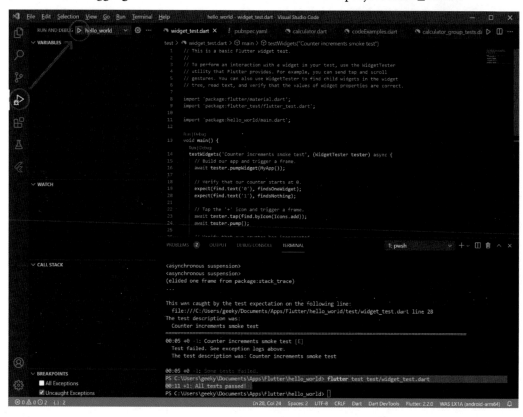

Figure 11.3 – Running Flutter from Visual Studio Code

If you are using Android Studio/IntelliJ, then make sure you run in debug mode so that you have access to all the tooling.

Once you have the app running in the IDE, you can add breakpoints. Try adding a breakpoint in the _MyHomePageState class within the main.dart file. Specifically, add a breakpoint within an onPressed function of a button. To do this in Visual Studio code, simply click to the left of the line number of the line you want as the breakpoint. A red dot will then appear to show that a breakpoint is set, and on the left pane at the bottom, you will see the list of breakpoints that are set.

When you are running your app and press the button that has a breakpoint set on it, your IDE will pause execution of the code and show something like this:

Figure 11.4 – Visual Studio Code pausing execution at a breakpoint

There is a lot going on here, so let's take it a piece at a time:

- The main pane highlights the line in yellow where the code execution is paused.

- The top-left pane shows the **VARIABLES** that are currently set.

- The **CALL STACK** pane shows the current call stack (that is, all the method calls that allowed the code to reach this point).

- The bottom-right pane shows the **DEBUG CONSOLE** and any log statements that have come from the app.

The next step is to use the debug controls (top left) to either step the execution to the next line, step into a method/function call, step out of a method/function, or continue the execution of the code.

As you can imagine, this gives you a great ability to see exactly what is happening within the code and understand where there may be issues.

One warning is that when you reach an asynchronous section of code, you may need to set another breakpoint to allow you to catch the execution again after the asynchronous work is done. Also, asynchronous sections can lead to an incomplete call stack, potentially making it difficult to understand how a piece of code was reached. However, generally, the debugger is a lifesaver and should be used as much as possible!

Debugging your app is incredibly important, so ensure you revisit this section whenever you have issues with your app code so that you can get adept at the use of the debugger. However, there are also other tools available that will help you investigate how your app is running from both a layout and performance perspective, so let's look at those next.

DevTools

Dart **DevTools** is defined in the documentation as follows:

> *"A suite of performance tools for Dart and Flutter."*

DevTools can also be accessed via the web browser. You may have seen the URL alongside the Observatory URL when you did a `flutter run`. However, most people will use DevTools from within their IDE, so let's explore that option further.

If you still have the Hello World app running, then you will see a magnifying glass on the debug controls. Click this button to open up the wonderful world of DevTools.

The widget inspector

We are currently in debug mode, so the widget inspector will be opened for us, allowing us to inspect the layout of our app. The widget inspector allows us to check whether our widget tree is taking more space than needed, whether it has more widgets than needed, or whether a widget is being created at the right time/level.

Open up the widget inspector and you will have a view similar to this:

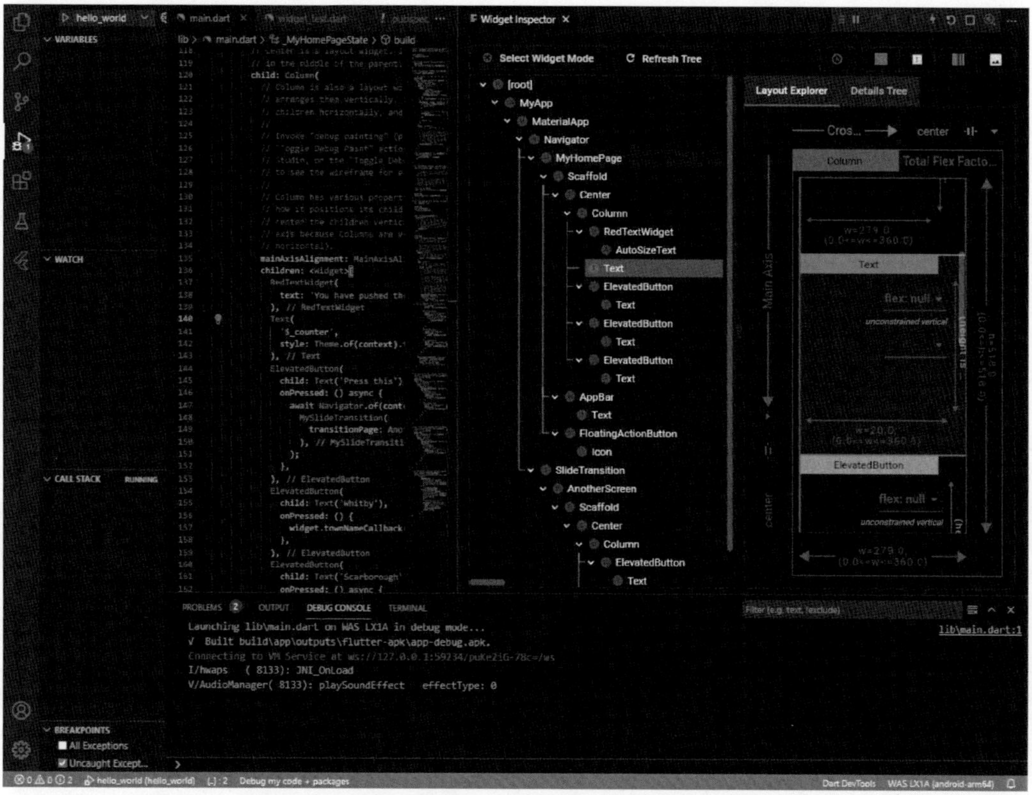

Figure 11.5 – Widget inspector in Visual Studio Code

As you can see, the widget tree is presented and we can access all details about each widget. For web developers, this will look very similar to element explorers in web developer tools, such as the one in Chrome, for instance.

You can also manipulate the widgets by changing properties such as `flex` and `fit` to experiment with layout changes. Whenever you click on a widget in the tree, Visual Studio Code will show you the relevant code that created the widget in the `code` pane, allowing quick identification of why the tree is structured as it is.

Two amazing features are the **Show debug paint** and **Select widget mode** buttons.

The **Show debug paint** button will draw all of the layout rules directly onto the screen so that you can see why a widget is positioned the way it is:

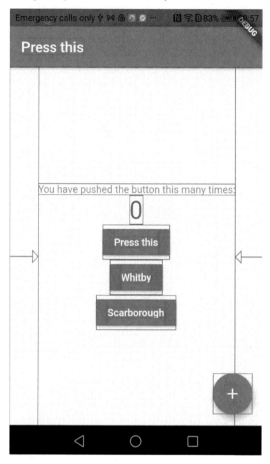

Figure 11.6 – Hello World app with Show debug paint enabled

As you can see, **Show debug paint** shows arrows explaining how the layout is defined, and boxes to show the boundaries of the widgets. In this example, the `buttons` column has been centered, as shown by the two arrows on the side pushing in the column. You can also see that the textbox is the widest widget in the column and is the width it is, therefore the column width is defined by the width of the `text` widget because the `column` widget resizes to match the size of its children.

The **Select Widget Mode** button allows you to tap a widget on your app and instantly see where that widget is in the widget tree. And vice versa, you can click a widget in the widget tree and instantly see the widget highlighted on the app.

Profile mode

When we execute our Flutter application in default debug mode, we cannot expect the same performance as the release mode. As we already know, Flutter executes in debug mode using the JIT Dart compiler as the app runs, unlike the release and profile modes, where the app code is pre-compiled using the AOT Dart compiler.

To make performance evaluations, we need to make sure the app is running at its maximum capability; that's why Flutter provides different execution methods: debug, profile, and release.

In profile mode, the application is compiled in a very similar way to release mode, and this is clearly understandable, as we need to know how the app will perform in real scenarios. The only overhead added to the app is the required ones to make the profiling enabled (that is, the Observatory can connect to the application process).

Another important aspect of profiling is the necessity of a physical device. Simulators and emulators do not reflect the real performance of real devices. As the hardware is different, app metrics can be influenced, and the analysis might be correct.

To run an app in profile mode, we should add the `--profile` flag to the `run` command (remember, it's only available on real devices):

```
flutter run --profile
```

Running in this mode, we have all of the required information to inspect the app performance in general. Another useful tool the profile mode enables is the performance overlay.

To achieve this in Visual Studio Code, click the settings cog to the right of where you would run the app in debug mode, to open the `launch.json` file. Alternatively, find the `launch.json` file in the `explorer` pane, within the `.vscode` folder.

You will see `configurations` like this:

```
    "configurations": [
        {
            "name": "hello_world",
            "request": "launch",
            "type": "dart"
        }
    ]
```

This will run `flutterMode`, which is debug. To add another option, update the `configurations` list to include a `profile` option like this:

```
"configurations": [
    {
        "name": "hello_world",
        "request": "launch",
        "type": "dart"
    },
    {
        "name": "hello_world_profile",
        "request": "launch",
        "type": "dart",
        "flutterMode": "profile"
    }
]
```

Once you save this file, you will see an additional option in the dropdown of run targets. This time, run the profile version, `hello_world_profile`.

When the app is running, you will notice that the magnifying glass for DevTools is now a wave. Click on this to open the **Performance** page. Flutter aims to provide high-performance apps with a high frame rate and smoothness. Like debugging can help to find bugs, profiling is a useful tool that helps developers to find performance bottlenecks in their application, prevent memory leaks, or improve app performance.

When you open the performance page, you will see a display similar to this:

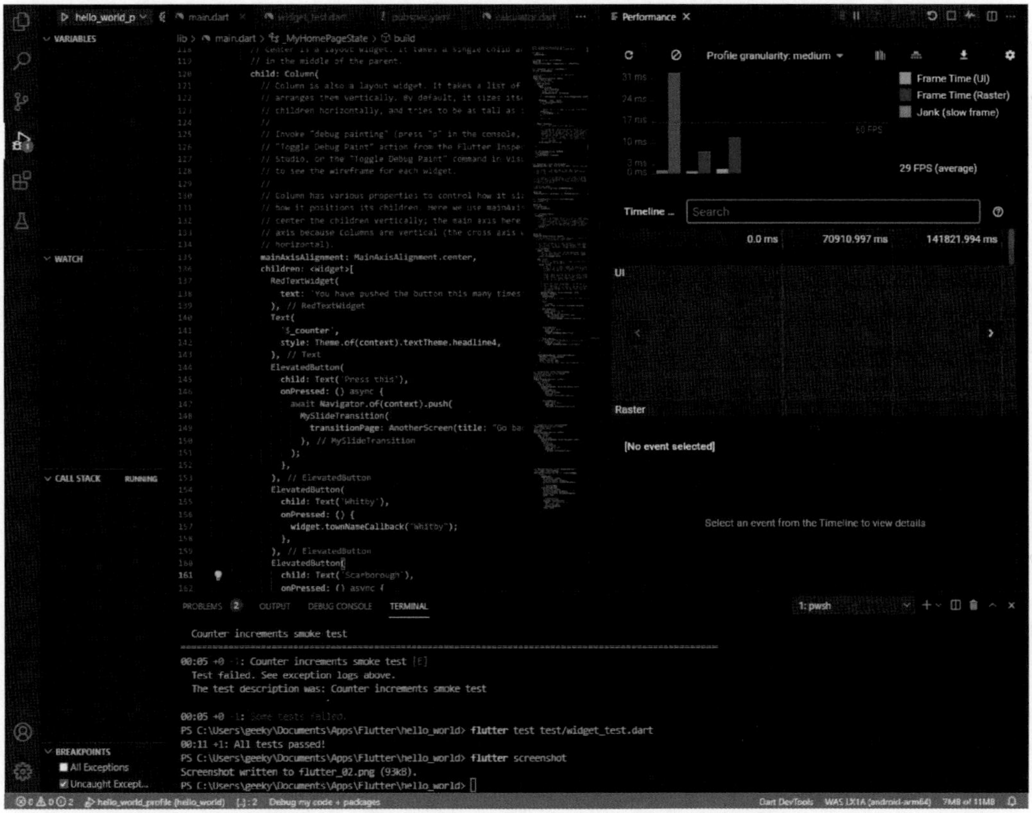

Figure 11.7 – Performance page in Visual Studio Code

Memory, CPU usage, and other information are available through the monitor so that we can evaluate different aspects of the application.

One very useful button is the **Show performance overlay** button.

Performance overlay

When you use the **Show performance overlay** button, the performance overlay is shown on the app. The visual feedback displayed provides multiple helpful performance statistics. Specifically, it displays information about rendering time. Here is an example of performance overlay being displayed:

Figure 11.8 – HelloWorld app with performance overlay

Two graphs are displayed representing the time to render frames taken by the two threads, UI and Raster. The current frame is displayed by a full-height vertical green bar, seen on the image about a quarter of the width of the screen from the left overlaying the two performance graphs. Additionally, we can see the last 300 frames and have an idea about critical rendering stages.

Flutter uses multiple threads to do its job. UI and Raster contain the display work of the framework, and that's why both are shown in the performance overlay.

UI thread

The UI thread is where your Dart code is executed, and any Flutter framework code required to execute on behalf of your app. Any user interface requirements you specify in your code are converted into a layer tree, a set of painting commands, which are sent to the raster thread.

The raster thread

This thread is where the graphics are brought to life. It does this by taking the layer tree and working with the **Graphics Processing Unit** (**GPU**) to draw the painting commands on the screen. The thread also includes a graphics library named Skia. You will never directly interact with this thread, but if it is running slowly, then it will be because of something that is happening in the UI thread.

Other threads

In addition to those threads, Flutter also contains the platform thread, where the plugin code runs, and the I/O thread, where expensive I/O tasks are run. Neither of these threads appear on the platform overlay.

Summary

In this chapter, we learned about unit testing Dart so that we can be confident that our library functions are following the requirements under a range of data inputs.

We saw an introduction to Flutter widget tests and how they can be used to test widgets individually. We looked at how they are structured with the `WidgetTester` class in the `testWidgets` function.

We also saw how to debug our app, first by looking at the Dart Observatory and the method calls of debugging and assertions, and then by using the debugging facilities of the IDE.

Finally, we investigated how we can use Flutter DevTools to explore the widget tree in debug mode and application performance in profile mode.

In the next chapter, we will finish the journey of our app by looking at how we can release it into the world for everyone to use!

12
Releasing Your App to the World

You've written the code, run some tests, debugged some issues, and you've reached a point where your app is ready for the big time! Ultimately, you want to release your app to the world – that's why you embarked on your **Flutter** journey in the first place.

This chapter explores how you will achieve that within the **Apple App Store**, **Google Play Store**, and the **web**. Each route to market brings its own challenges, so this chapter will act as a guide by pointing out the key steps in your release process and identifying any pain points you may need to overcome.

In *Chapter 9*, *Popular Third-Party Plugins*, we touched on how you can track the usage and issues users are seeing within your app. In this chapter, you will build on that knowledge with a deeper look at the **Firebase** tools for usage analysis and crash reporting.

The following topics will be covered in this chapter:

- Preparing your app for deployment
- Releasing your app on **Android**
- Releasing your app on **iOS**
- Releasing your app on the web
- Tracking app usage and crashes

Technical requirements

You will need your development environment again for this chapter as we will add a plugin to the Hello World project. Look back at *Chapter 1, An Introduction to Flutter*, if you need to set up your **Integrated Development Environment** (**IDE**) or refresh your knowledge of the development environment requirements.

Preparing your app for deployment

At this point, you may be thinking that you've been successfully running your app on devices, so the job is done! From a Flutter point of view, you are virtually ready for production – but there is one piece we need to revisit as a refresher.

Let's remind ourselves of a couple of the Flutter aims. One key aim is to ensure that app development is optimized for developers as far as possible to ensure the following:

- Reduce the feedback loop so that developers can see how their changes have changed the app without a lengthy compile time. Hot reload is an example of this.

- Have great debugging tools allowing the developer to really understand what is going on within the app. The widget tree in **DevTools** is an example of this, allowing you to manipulate the widget tree in real-time and see exactly how it aligns with your code.

An app framework that can allow these features is likely to have very slow running apps because the code must be compiled **just-in-time** (**JIT**) to allow for code changes, and must be sharing lots of information with the outside world to allow the debugging and manipulation of widgets to take place.

On the flip side, Flutter has a key aim to be incredibly performant, rivaling the speed and responsiveness of native apps. You may remember from *Chapter 2, An Introduction to Dart*, that **Dart** has a killer feature that allows these two contradictory aims to make sense, and that is because Dart has two different ways in which it builds code.

When preparing an app for release, things such as on-the-fly compiling provided by Dart **JIT** do not make sense – instead, the best thing is to have a smaller, optimized, and performant app provided by the Dart **ahead-of-time** (**AOT**) compiler. In release mode, debugging information is stripped out from the app and the compilation is realized with performance in mind. Remember, in release mode, like in profile mode, the application can only be run on physical devices (for the same reasons too).

Interestingly, it is possible to run the app in release mode. We just need to add the `--release` flag to the `flutter run` command and have a physical device connected. Although we can do so, we typically do not use the `flutter run` command with the `--release` flag. Instead, we use this flag with the `flutter build` command to have a built app file in the target Android/iOS/web formats for distribution.

However, Flutter has optimized this step for each platform you are releasing to, so we will take a look through how to create a release build for the three platforms (iOS, Android, and web) in detail later in the chapter.

It's worth noting that it wasn't until this point that we had to start getting platform-specific. Flutter has done an incredible job of ensuring that 99% of what you work on is platform-agnostic, and even during the next step, there has been lots of work to minimize the amount of platform-specific work needed.

Preparing the stores

Before you can release your app you may have to do a little bit of admin to ensure you are able to use each of the platforms.

The first step is to ensure you are a registered developer on the mobile app stores, as releasing an app on the Google Play Store and Apple App Store requires valid publisher accounts. Refer to the documentation of both platforms to learn how to publish to their stores after creating a release version of your app.

It's worth noting at this point that there are other Android stores available, but only the Play Store has the Google client services that your app may depend on (such as Google Maps). Also, many of the plugins, such as in-app purchases, do not support other stores (such as the **Amazon Appstore**). Therefore, this guide focuses on the Google Play Store as most releases will follow that route.

Registering as a developer

To register with the Play Store as a developer, and therefore be able to upload your app, Google requests a one-off $25 registration fee. You can register at the following link: `https://play.google.com/apps/publish/signup`.

Similarly, the Apple App Store requests a $99 membership fee per year, which you also need to pay before you can upload an app. You can find details and register at the following link: `https://developer.apple.com/programs/enroll/`.

There are generally no other direct costs associated with releasing your app on the two stores. Hosting your app in the stores is free because the stores make their money from sales fees.

A business model

It is worth highlighting at this point that there are sales fees that both platforms impose. If you are building a business plan around the sales of your app, then it is important that you know up-front the kind of sales fees you will encounter on the two mobile platforms. These tend to fall into three areas:

- **App purchase**: If you require a one-off charge from the users of your app for them to either use the app or continue using it after a free trial period, then both stores will charge you a fee of 30% on the sale. So, if you sell your app for $1 on the store and make a sale, Apple or Google will take 30¢ of that sale as a sales fee, leaving you with 70¢.

- **Subscriptions**: Some apps follow a subscription model to take regular payments from users to use their app. This is generally for apps that constantly add new content (for example, a wellness app that regularly adds new meditation videos) or have an ongoing service that users can access (for example, a workout app with regular live workouts). Again, the stores will take 30% of a new subscription for the first year, and then 15% if you keep that customer for more than 12 months.

- **In-app purchases**: An in-app purchase is a sale made within the app that is designed around unlocking new content or new parts of the app. All in-app purchases are charged at 30%. You may think that you would just push the user to another purchase channel (for example, link to a website to make the in-app purchase), however, both app stores are very strict and will not allow alternative purchase routes to be advertised within the app. Any attempt to do so will lead to rejection at the app review stage.

There are some interesting changes developing in this space, as some commentators are suggesting monopolistic practices may be at play. Apple has already dropped its 30% sales fee to 15% for companies making less than $1 million revenue per year, and other changes may be likely in the future.

As a cautionary note, there are very strict guidelines around what your app can contain, especially on the app stores, and the documentation is long and difficult to read. The best advice is to try and look at the documentation as much as possible when your business model relies on a certain fundamental feature, but to also try and release prototypes as soon as possible so that you can go through the review process and identify issues early.

> **A cautionary tale**
>
> A feature of one of our apps is to allow parents to donate to a fundraising cause that a school has set up. We spent lots of time developing the feature by integrating a payment provider and making an intuitive and gamified flow for the parents. Proud of our work, we submitted it to the two stores for review and were mortified when it was rejected by Apple due to a hidden-away requirement that only apps from charities can allow fundraising within their apps. If we had made a quick prototype we would have encountered this issue in an early review, but we didn't even know it could be a reason for rejection, so didn't follow this advice!

Preparing for web

Releasing your app to the web has quite different preparation requirements. There is no ubiquitous store that all web users will visit first, there is no overarching company that you register with, and there are no strict payment models or development guidelines to follow. Therefore, the guidance here will have to be more general, but some of the key things to think about are as follows:

- **Hosting**: Your app will need to live somewhere on the web, and generally this will require getting a third-party company to host your code in a way that other web users can access. One easy option is to use Firebase hosting, especially if you are using other Firebase services.

- **Domain**: For users to be able to find your app, you will need a web address, or domain, that users type into their web browser to access your site. There are plenty of companies willing to sell you a domain. Once you have one, link it up to your hosting supplier using **DNS** magic.

- **Payments**: In the mobile stores you have the simplicity of taking payments using the store services, such as in-app payments and subscriptions. These services are not so easily available on the web, but on the flip side, when you do find a payment solution, you are unlikely to incur such high sales fees. Options here include the large payment providers of **Stripe** and **Square**, which have plugins for Flutter.

So, let's assume you are registered for the stores (or have a web hosting solution ready), and you have a viable business plan to make some money – it's now time to release your app.

Releasing your app on Android

In Android, **appbundle** is the format expected to be published in the Google Play Store. When we run the `flutter build appbundle` command, we generate the file ready for deployment.

You may have previously seen the Android **APK** (short for **Android application package**) option instead of the appbundle. Releasing your app as an APK has been deprecated by Google as an option on the Play Store, and will be fully withdrawn soon. Under the covers, an appbundle effectively generates APKs for devices but hides that complexity away.

Before we generate the file for deployment and publishing in any store, we need to make sure all of the information is correct (that is, the name and package), all needed assets are provided, and all platform-specific adjustments are made.

Let's start by preparing our HelloWorld app for release on Google Play so that we can review all of the final steps of publishing a Flutter app.

AndroidManifest and build.gradle

For each platform, Flutter has a folder that holds all of the files needed to configure the build processes for that platform. You will see `ios`, `android`, and `web` folders in your project. Generally, you should ignore these folders unless you need to make configuration changes required for plugins.

In Android, the meta-information about the app is provided in the `android` folder in both the `app/src/main/AndroidManifest.xml` and `app/build.gradle` files, so we may need to review and make some adjustments in these ready for the app release build.

Permissions

One important step we need to do is review the permissions requested in the `app/src/main/AndroidManifest.xml` file. Asking only for the permissions that your app will actually need is a good and recommended practice, as your app may be analyzed and your publication may be revoked if you request more than the required permissions.

In our HelloWorld app, our initial `app/src/main/AndroidManifest.xml` file didn't have any permissions required. If you have added plugins to it then you may have needed to add permissions. Here is an example file with some permissions requested:

```xml
<manifest xmlns:android="http://schemas.android.com/apk/res/
android" package="com.example.hello_world">


    <uses-permission
        android:name="android.permission.INTERNET"/>
    <uses-permission
        android:name="android.permission.READ_CONTACTS" />
    <uses-permission
        android:name="android.permission.WRITE_CONTACTS"/>
    <uses-permission
        android:name="android.permission.CAMERA" />
    <uses-feature
        android:name="android.hardware.camera"
        android:required="false" />

    ...
</manifest>
```

The permissions your app is requesting are listed within the `uses-permission` tags. The names of the permissions are defined by Android, and plugins will guide you to add the correct permissions as required.

Besides permissions, there is also the `uses-feature` tag, which can limit installation on devices with a specific feature available. The use of `android:required` here is critical if the camera is not required, allowing devices that do not have a camera to still install and use the app. When you go through the publishing process on the Play Store, there are warnings if one of your permissions is likely to restrict the devices the app can be installed on. You should review this because a slight change to your `AndroidManifest.xml` may make a huge change to your available market.

Some of the permissions are *normal permissions*, which means they are granted on the installation of the app, and some permissions are requested at runtime, so the user needs to choose to grant the permission to your app. You may have seen other apps requesting permission to view your photo album or access your camera. Your app will need to cope with users choosing not to enable that permission.

Meta tags

Another very important step is to review the meta tags added to the app for working with services such as **AdMob** or **Google Maps**. You may have set up the app to use test configurations, so now is the time to review your settings and make sure they are set up for production use. Here is an example of the setting for AdMob:

```
<manifest xmlns:android="http://schemas.android.com/apk/res/
android" package="com.example.handson">
  ...
  <application>
    ...
    <meta-data
        android:name="com.google.android.gms.ads.APP_ID"
        android:value="ADMOB-KEY"/>
  </application>
</manifest>
```

Again, the plugin documentation will guide you to add the correct metadata tag within the `AndroidManifest.xml` file.

Application icon and name

Until now, when we launch the application in our tests we've the app icon as a Flutter logo. For release, you need to create a unique icon to make sure your users can distinguish your app among the millions of other apps available. Also, you need to come up with an awesome name for your app. Now is the time to do both.

For setting your icon, there are two options available to you – an easy automated way, and a harder manual way. For completeness, let's first look at the harder manual way while also setting the app name.

Manually setting the icon and name

The icon and name are defined in the `AndroidManifest.xml` `application` tag. By default, the icon refers to the default Flutter icon, as you can see:

```
<manifest ...>
    <application
        android:label="hello_world"
        android:icon="@mipmap/ic_launcher">
```

```
    ...
    </application>
</manifest>
```

So, we need to make two changes:

- Change the `label` value to the final name of our app – that is, the name by which our users will recognize our app.

- Update the icon that is pointed to by the `icon` value.

In Android, image resources such as the icon are located in the `android/app/src/main/res/` directory. Under this directory, there are many folders with variants of a resource, tailored for specific regions, screen sizes, system versions, and so on.

We need to replace the `ic_launcher.png` file in each of the `mipmap-xxxdpi` folders to make a full replacement of the app icon.

Check the **Material Design** guidelines on icons to make sure you create an awesome icon for your app: `https://material.io/design/iconography/`.

Setting the icon using a plugin

You have a lovely icon for your app and you don't want to spend ages resizing it for all the different device types and the two different platforms. This is where the awesome `flutter_launcher_icons` plugin comes in handy.

To use the plugin, first, modify your `pubspec.yaml` file to add the plugin to the `dev_dependencies` section:

```
dev_dependencies:
    flutter_launcher_icons: "^0.8.0"
```

And then further down add details of the icon you want to use in the app:

```
flutter_icons:
    android: true
    ios: true
    image_path: "assets/icon/icon.png"
```

The `true` value beside the `android` and `ios` properties specifies that the plugin can override the existing launcher icon for those platforms.

The `image_path` tells the plugin where the icon image file is. Note that this is placed in your `assets` folder within your app.

Make sure you get this dependency downloaded and ready to go by running the following command:

```
flutter pub get
```

Then run the plugin itself to generate all the icons:

```
flutter pub run flutter_launcher_icons:main
```

Magically, all of your icons are generated in the right sizes for each platform.

After changing the name and replacing the icon, we can review the `app/build.gradle` file to make the final adjustments for the deployment.

Application ID and versions

The `applicationID` value is what makes an app unique in Play Store and the Android system. A good practice is to use the organization domain as the package and have the app name following it:

```
com.companyname.appname
```

In our HelloWorld app we are using `com.example.hello_world` as the application ID. Make sure to review your application ID because it cannot be changed after you upload the app to the store.

You can find this code in the `app/build.gradle` file, inside the `defaultConfig` section:

```
defaultConfig {
    applicationId "com.example.hello_world"
    minSdkVersion 20
    targetSdkVersion 30
    versionCode flutterVersionCode.toInteger()
    versionName flutterVersionName
}
```

As you can see, we can change more settings than just `applicationId`.

The `minSdkVersion` setting denotes the minimum version of the Android API level that our app will be supported on. In Flutter, the `minSdkVersion` setting is typically changed in two cases:

- If the Flutter framework requirements change

- If we use a plugin that requires a higher minimum **Software Development Kit (SDK)** version

The `targetSdkVersion` setting denotes the Android API level that our app is designed to run on. This is used to manage what manifest elements and behaviors are available. Generally, this can simply be set to the latest Android API level.

The `versionCode` and `versionName` settings are automatically drawn from our `pubspec.yaml` file. So, suppose our `pubspec.yaml` file contains:

```
version: 1.0.0+1
```

This value will be split into a `versionCode` of 1 and a `versionName` of 1.0.0. The beauty of deriving this from the `pubspec.yaml` file is that it ensures our versioning is consistent across platforms.

Signing the app

The signing step is the final but most important step before releasing an app to the public, even if you do not want to publish it in the Google Play Store. It is the signing that confirms the ownership of the application – in short, whoever has the signature owns the app. You need this so you can publish updates to your app, for example.

Start by taking a look at the `buildTypes` section of the `app/build.gradle` file:

```
buildTypes {
    release {
        signingConfig signingConfigs.debug
    }
}
```

It contains the `signingConfig` property, pointing to a default signing configuration. We need to change this to our own signing configuration for the reasons mentioned before. We do this by performing the steps below.

1. Generate a keystore file

We generate our developer **keystore file** (you can use the same keystore for multiple apps). This is done with the following command:

```
keytool -genkey -v -keystore DESTINATION_FILEPATH -keyalg RSA -
keysize 2048 -validity 10000 -alias key
```

Follow the prompts and this will generate a keystore in the DESTINATION_FILEPATH path. You should reference this file in the app/build.gradle file now.

2. Create a key.properties file

Create a key.properties file in the android folder with the following content:

```
storePassword=<password used for generating key>
keyPassword=<password used for generating key>
keyAlias=key
storeFile=<key store file path>
```

3. Load the key.properties file

In app/build.gradle, we load this new key.properties file and create a new signingConfig class for it. Just before the android { line, add the configuration:

```
def keystoreProperties = new Properties()
def keystorePropertiesFile = rootProject.file('key.properties')
if (keystorePropertiesFile.exists()) {
    keystoreProperties.load(new
    FileInputStream(keystorePropertiesFile))
}

android{
    ...
```

This configuration defines a new keystoreProperties variable of type Properties, then defines a variable of type File that points to our new key.properties file, and finally, if the file exists, we load the contents of the file into our keystoreProperties variable.

4. Use keystoreProperties

We now need to use `keystoreProperties`, which we read in from the `key.properties` file, to create a new signing configuration named `release` that we can refer to later in the build process:

```
signingConfigs {
    release {
        keyAlias keystoreProperties['keyAlias']
        keyPassword keystoreProperties['keyPassword']
        storeFile keystoreProperties['storeFile'] ?
        file(keystoreProperties['storeFile']) : null
        storePassword keystoreProperties['storePassword']
    }
}
```

This configuration simply links the build variables of `keyAlias`, `keyPassword`, `storeFile`, and `storePassword` to the properties we read in from `key.properties`.

5. Use the new signing configuration

Finally, replace the `signingConfig` property in the release option in the previous `buildTypes` section with the new one:

```
buildTypes {
    release {
        signingConfig signingConfigs.release
    }
}
```

Now, when we build the release appbundle, the app will be signed with our own key.

Build and upload your appbundle

With all the configuration ready, it's time to build the appbundle. You do this by running the following command:

```
flutter build appbundle
```

This will generate an `appbundle` file at the following location:

```
<project location>/build/app/outputs/bundle/release/app.aab
```

In the **Google Play Console**, you will be able to create a new release and upload your `appbundle` as part of that.

There are several types of release available in the Google Play Console:

- **Internal testing**: The app is only available to a small subset of specified testers. New versions are made available to testers within a few minutes.

- **Closed testing**: Similar to internal testing, but with a slightly larger audience, and there may be a review delay for the release.

- **Open testing**: A wider audience again, and anyone can join an open test and then submit private feedback.

- **Production**: Your release to the world (or specific geographies if you so choose). This may have a lengthy review before being available on the Play Store.

As soon as you upload to the Play Store you should aim to do an internal test so that you can check there are no surprise gotchas before you share the app more widely. For all types of testing or production, testers simply need to go to the Play Store and the correct version of the app will be available for them to install.

You will also need to set up your store presence with images, screenshots, descriptions, links to your privacy and terms-of-service documents, and contact details, among other things like content ratings. It can take a long time to set up the store presence, so don't leave this to the last moment assuming it will only take a few minutes.

And there you have it – you are good to go on Android. Let's now look at the Apple iOS release process.

Releasing your app on iOS

Releasing on Apple iOS is more complex when compared to Android. Although you can test on your own device when developing, making an app public requires you to have a valid **Apple Developer** account with the ability to publish on the App Store, as it's the only supported app publishing channel.

Like Android and the configuration we had to make in `AndroidManifest.xml`, iOS has a similar configuration file that is used by the iOS build tool **Xcode**.

> **What is Xcode?**
>
> Xcode is an IDE that is only available on macOS and is used for the development of native iOS apps. You can download it from the Apple App Store for free. It is used by Flutter to package your app code ready for release on the App Store.

iOS apps can only be built on a Mac computer, so if you are a Windows or Linux user you will either need to invest in a Mac or get a virtual machine you can use.

App Store Connect

In Android, we did not need to configure anything in the Play Store Console before we created `appbundle` ready for publishing. In iOS, the process is different. The upload and publishing are managed inside Xcode, and to upload the app we first create a record on **App Store Connect**. Then, on Xcode, we build and upload our iOS app using the App Store Connect bundle identifier. To register the app, perform these steps:

1. Register the bundle ID

All iOS applications are associated with a **bundle ID**. This is a unique identifier that is registered with Apple.

To register your app bundle ID, head over to your developer account web page at `https://developer.apple.com/account/ios/identifier/bundle:`.

1. Select the **Identifiers** section.
2. Click the **+** and select **App Ids**.
3. Select the type as **App** (not **App clip**, which is like a very lightweight app).
4. Enter your new bundle ID as an **Explicit Bundle ID**. This ID can be (and for simplicity should be) the same as the one you set on your `applicationId` for the Android build – so something like:

   ```
   com.companyname.appname
   ```

5. To finish setting up your bundle ID, complete the registration, including adding any required capabilities.

2. Create your app entry

Next, create an app in the App Store Connect portal at `https://appstoreconnect.apple.com:`.

1. Open the **My Apps** section.
2. Click the **+** to create a new app.
3. Enter your app details, ensuring that the iOS platform is selected, and click **Create**.
4. Open the App Store tab for your app, and then the **App Information** option from the side menu.
5. Select the bundle ID we registered in the previous step.

After completing these steps in App Store Connect, let's look at configuring the app in Xcode.

Xcode

In Xcode, we need to make a few changes to get the app ready for release. We need to change the application icon, public name, and bundle ID. This is very similar to what we did in Android.

So, open Xcode on your Mac (or virtual machine), and you will get a popup asking for the project location. A workspace file has been created in your project, so point Xcode to the location:

```
<project location>/ios/Runner.xcworkspace
```

Note that there is also a file in that folder called `Runner.xcodeproj`. Do not use that file, as it will not set up Xcode correctly for your project.

Xcode will then pop open and show you your app details:

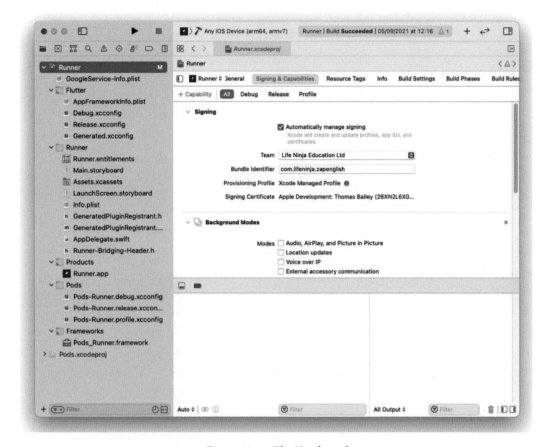

Figure 12.1 – The Xcode tool

Ensure you have the **Project Navigator** view open and the top-level `Runner` folder is selected.

Application details and bundle ID

In the *General* tab of the Runner project, you can edit the application's **Display Name**, which is the name of your app.

Set the **Bundle Identifier** to the same value as you specified in the *Application ID and versions* section earlier in this chapter. Keeping the application ID consistent across platforms will make it much easier to maintain your app in the future, and will reduce the chance of configuration issues as you add new plugins and services to your app.

In **Deployment Target**, you can set the minimum required iOS version, which is *8.0* by default (the minimum version Flutter supports). As discussed in the Android section, this minimum version will likely be modified based on the plugins that are being used by your app. For example, the **flutter_stripe** plugin requires a minimum iOS level of *11*.

If you do need to change the **Deployment Target** setting, then you will also need to update the ios/Flutter/AppframeworkInfo.plist file and set the MinimumOSVersion value to match the value you set in Xcode.

Note also the **Version** and **Build** values – they are similar to version name and version code in Android respectively. For each upload to the App Store, we need to ensure we have increased the version value in the pubspec.yaml file, otherwise the build will be rejected by App Store Connect.

App icon

We saw in the Android section how we can use a plugin to generate the app icon. I would strongly recommend following that approach, but for completeness here is the process for manually updating the iOS app icon.

Firstly, it is useful to review the iOS app icon guidelines to ensure your icon adheres to their constraints. One gotcha is that icons with any transparency are rejected, so ensure your icon is fully opaque. The guidelines can be viewed here: https://developer.apple.com/ios/human-interface-guidelines/icons-and-images/app-icon/.

Once you have an icon you are happy with, in Xcode, select **Assets.xcassets** in the Runner folder and add your icons in all the various sizes and resolutions.

Signing the app

Like on Android, we need a way to assert the ownership of the application. In this case, Xcode manages it for us, and we do not need to touch any file directly. When we register as an **Apple Developer** and enroll in the **Apple Developer Program**, we have all of this ready.

If you move to the **Signing & Capabilities** tab, you will see that **Automatically manage signing** is selected. If you decide to have complex functionality, like **Apple Pay**, then you will probably need to manage signing more closely. But generally, this setting is sufficient.

Ensure that your **Team** has correctly been set. If you cannot select it from the drop-down menu, then select **Add Account…** and update the values.

After these settings have been made, we can build an iOS version of the app.

Build and upload

Much like the Android process, there is a *build* step and then an *upload* step. To build the code, run the following command:

```
flutter build ipa
```

This will build an `ipa` file which, a bit like `appbundle`, contains the iOS app bundles within it, as well as some other configuration files.

The first step of this build process is where **CocoaPods** is installed, as discussed in *Chapter 8, Plugins – What Are They and How Do I Use Them?*, and you may want to review the *Common issues* section of that chapter if you have any issues at this stage.

When you have successfully built the `ipa` file, you will need to open Xcode and choose to open it at the following location:

```
build/ios/archive/MyApp.xcarchive
```

This will pop up a window showing all of your uploads of the app. Select **Distribute App** to start the upload. You will need to review some build settings before the upload commences, but the default selections should be fine.

Once the upload has been completed, there are some automated reviews that Apple runs on its servers to ensure the app is configured correctly. If there are any issues, then you will receive emails from their review system detailing the suggested corrections.

After about 30 minutes, the automated reviews should be complete, and you are free to use your app for testing or put it forward for production review. Testing on iOS is a little different from Android. There is only really one testing stage, but you can choose whether testing has an internal and/or external audience. In the case where you choose an external audience, then a short review is needed before the app is made available.

Testers have to install the **TestFlight** app to be able to install pre-release versions of your app. This is relatively painless, and in many ways preferable to the Android approach, because it is very easy to switch between test and production versions of an app.

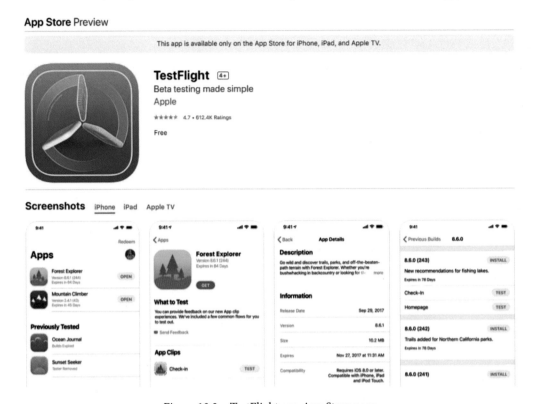

Figure 12.2 – TestFlight app App Store page

Again, like Android, before the production release, you will also need to set up your store presence with images, screenshots, descriptions, links to your privacy and terms-of-service documents, and contact details, among other things like content ratings. It can take a long time to set up the store presence, so don't leave this until last, assuming it will only take a few minutes.

Once you put an app version forward for production review, you will have to wait a couple of days for your app to be reviewed before it is released. There are some great controls on iOS to manage the release process after review completion. In addition to automatically releasing on review completion, you can choose to manually release or schedule the release at a specific date and time. On Android, the same control is not available, and you are not even alerted when the review and release are completed!

Make sure you install the **App Connect** app on your phone so that you can get push alerts as your app moves through the review stages. If you notice your app is stuck in the *In review* state for a long time, there are a few possible reasons for this which I've experienced during our app releases:

- The app is failing to install on the reviewer's device.
- The reviewer is having issues logging into your app, or following your specific guidance if you have supplied some.
- There is something that the reviewer thinks may contravene an app guideline, and has asked for assistance from another reviewer. This one sometimes happens if the review is happening outside of USA working hours and the reviewer wants guidance from a USA team member.

Ultimately, there are many reasons why your app may get stuck in the review state, but getting stuck there suggests something isn't quite right, and it is worth starting to investigate possible issues early so that you can diagnose the problem quickly and restart the review.

I'll be honest with you – releasing on iOS is definitely the hardest platform to release on. The App Store review process is infamously difficult to traverse. However, I've generally found that any review violations are clearly explained and, on the odd occasion we feel the need to appeal a decision, our appeal has been upheld. In contrast, the web release process has literally no review to go through. Let's now look at the web release process.

Releasing your app on the web

Compared to the configuration headaches of Android and iOS, the web release process can be much simpler. You only need to run the following command:

```
flutter build web
```

This will generate the app and all required assets and place them into the following folder:

```
/build/web
```

The trickiest part is to decide how to host your web app. As mentioned previously, Firebase hosting is a great choice for this. Not only is the setup very easy, but it's also cheap until you start to really scale up.

Firebase hosting

To set up Firebase hosting, set up a Firebase account (as discussed in *Chapter 8, Plugins – What Are They and How Do I Use Them?*). Then, on your local machine, install the **Firebase CLI** (explained at the following link): `https://firebase.google.com/docs/cli`.

This will give you the ability to run `firebase` commands from your command line.

Next, run the Firebase initialization command on your project:

```
firebase init
```

This will connect your Flutter project to your Firebase project.

Finally, deploy your app to the hosting by running the following command:

```
firebase deploy
```

And your web app will be uploaded and made available publicly.

However, as discussed in the Android and iOS instructions, it is useful to have a testing option before you go live. In Firebase hosting, there is also a way to run testing in advance of a production release. To do this, run the following command:

```
firebase hosting:channel:deploy <test_name>
```

This will create a temporary deployment channel with an obscure URL that you can share with testers and get feedback. If you use the same `test_name` value on future deployments when you act on the feedback from testers, then you will have to update the same test version at the same URL, and testers will automatically see your updates.

PWA support

Flutter web apps include support for the core features of an installable, offline-capable **progressive web app** (**PWA**). This is currently a work-in-progress, but quite well advanced, so if this is an area that is important to you then take a look and engage with the Flutter development team, who are keen for feedback.

Now your app is on its way to production, let's see how we can keep track of it out in the wild.

Tracking app usage and crashes

When your app is in production use, it can be very hard to know how the app is being used and whether your users are encountering issues. Knowing when there are issues with app usage or crashes at the earliest opportunity is especially important when your app is released on mobile stores because the update cycle can take days.

There are two Firebase tools that are great for tracking this information, such as **Crashlytics** and **Google Analytics**, and we looked at how to set them up in *Chapter 9, Popular Third-Party Plugins*. In this chapter, let's take a look at some of the output that is generated and how that can help us as we improve our app.

Crashlytics

Every time your app has an unexpected crash, or you specifically send a crash report from within your code, Crashlytics will receive that information and display it on the dashboard.

This can be especially useful if you have an asynchronous operation that doesn't directly impact the running of the app but stops some underlying service from functioning within your app. For example, a database listener may fail and Crashlytics would report this. The user of the app may not actually know that the failure has occurred, so wouldn't report it to you, but you can see from the dashboard that the issue has occurred and you are able to start investigating a fix.

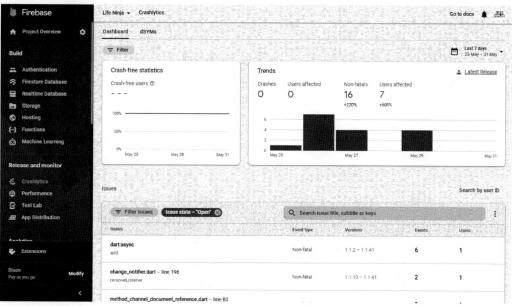

Figure 12.3 – Crashlytics dashboard

The Crashlytics dashboard is relatively easy to navigate. It shows the number of issues impacting users, the versions of the app the crash was on, whether the crash was fatal (that is, the app closed and had to be restarted), details about the device the crash was recorded on (such as operating system version and manufacturer/model), and, most usefully, the stack trace when the crash occurred.

When you build your app for release, if you have Crashlytics configured, then the Android mapping file or iOS debug symbol (dSYM) file is uploaded to the Crashlytics server. This means that when a stack trace is created by the app, this can be mapped to your code and specifically the files and line numbers, allowing you to find the failing code quickly and easily.

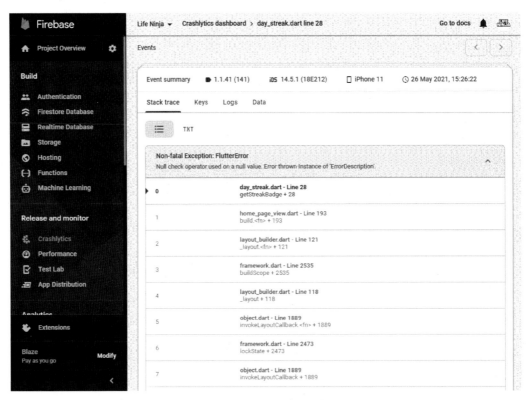

Figure 12.4 – Example of a crash report

Crashlytics will group issues when they are similar and allow you to manage whether an issue is resolved, and also alert you when a resolved issue reappears.

Google Analytics

If you want to track how your app is used, there are few tools as well known as Google Analytics. Initially used by many people for tracking traffic through a website, it is now also available for mobile apps.

Google Analytics is especially useful if you are trying to convert users. Perhaps there is a page to unlock features or to make an in-app purchase, and you want to see how many users you are converting.

To do this, within your app you will record *events* that denote either an action or a navigation by the user. These are reported back to Google Analytics, allowing you to get a view of how users are traversing your app.

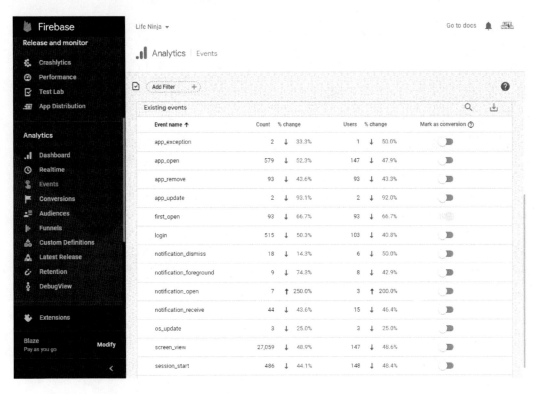

Figure 12.5 – Google Analytics events

Additionally, Google Analytics adds useful data such as demographics and user location, allowing you to see what your audience is like.

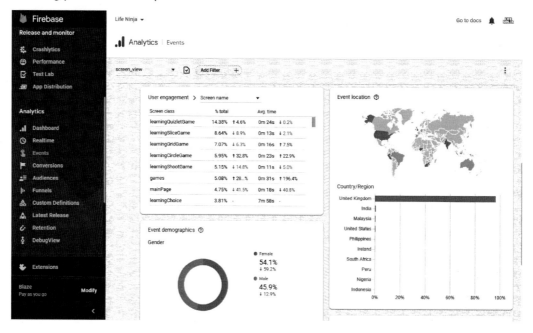

Figure 12.6 – Diving into further details on Google Analytics

In this example, we've dived into one event type, `screen_view`, and can see the breakdown of the pages within the app that users are accessing, where those users are located, and demographic data.

Summary

In this chapter, we explored the steps required to make our app ready for deployment.

Firstly, we looked at some admin to get the app ready for the production build, including registering for a developer account and preparing your hosting provider for the web.

We then looked at releasing an app on the Google Play Store, including configuring the `AndroidManifest.xml` and `build.gradle` files, looking at the build process, and exploring the testing options on Google Play.

Next, we did the same for the App Store, including registering our app bundle ID, using Xcode, looking at the build process, and exploring the different test processes.

We then dug into the release process of our app on the web, and finally covered how to use Crashlytics and Google Analytics for tracking app usage and crashes.

And that's all folks. In this book, I have tried to show you the basic but fundamental concepts of this incredible framework. I hope you enjoyed the book, learned something new, and are excited about using Flutter in the future!

`Packt.com`

Subscribe to our online digital library for full access to over 7,000 books and videos, as well as industry leading tools to help you plan your personal development and advance your career. For more information, please visit our website.

Why subscribe?

- Spend less time learning and more time coding with practical eBooks and Videos from over 4,000 industry professionals

- Improve your learning with Skill Plans built especially for you

- Get a free eBook or video every month

- Fully searchable for easy access to vital information

- Copy and paste, print, and bookmark content

Did you know that Packt offers eBook versions of every book published, with PDF and ePub files available? You can upgrade to the eBook version at `packt.com` and as a print book customer, you are entitled to a discount on the eBook copy. Get in touch with us at `customercare@packtpub.com` for more details.

At `www.packt.com`, you can also read a collection of free technical articles, sign up for a range of free newsletters, and receive exclusive discounts and offers on Packt books and eBooks.

Other Books You May Enjoy

If you enjoyed this book, you may be interested in these other books by Packt:

Flutter Projects

Simone Alessandria

ISBN: 978-1-83864-777-3

- Design reusable mobile architectures that can be applied to apps at any scale
- Get up to speed with error handling and debugging for mobile application development
- Apply the principle of 'composition over inheritance' to break down complex problems into many simple problems
- Update your code and see the results immediately using Flutter's hot reload

Flutter Cookbook

Simone Alessandria , Brian Kayfitz

ISBN: 978-1-83882-338-2

- Use Dart programming to customize your Flutter applications
- Discover how to develop and think like a Dart programmer
- Leverage Firebase Machine Learning capabilities to create intelligent apps
- Create reusable architecture that can be applied to any type of app
- Use web services and persist data locally
- Debug and solve problems before users can see them
- Use asynchronous programming with Future and Stream

Packt is searching for authors like you

If you're interested in becoming an author for Packt, please visit authors. packtpub.com and apply today. We have worked with thousands of developers and tech professionals, just like you, to help them share their insight with the global tech community. You can make a general application, apply for a specific hot topic that we are recruiting an author for, or submit your own idea.

Hi!

We are Tom Bailey and Alessandro Biessek, authors of *Flutter for Beginners Second Edition*. We really hope you enjoyed reading this book and found it useful for increasing your productivity and efficiency in Flutter.

It would really help us (and other potential readers!) if you could leave a review on Amazon sharing your thoughts on *Flutter for Beginners Second Edition*.

Go to the link below to leave your review:

```
https://packt.link/r/1800565992
```

Your review will help us to understand what's worked well in this book, and what could be improved upon for future editions, so it really is appreciated.

Best Wishes,

Tom Bailey   Alessandro Biessek

Index

Made in the USA
Columbia, SC
12 May 2022

60337872R00206